Tales of Ghosts

Ronald W. Hawker

Tales of Ghosts: First Nations Art in British Columbia, 1922-61

UBCPress · Vancouver · Toronto

For my Laila ... Asheghetam

09 08 07 06 05 04 03   5 4 3 2 1

Printed in Canada on acid-free paper ∞

National Library of Canada Cataloguing in Publication Data

Hawker, Ronald William, 1963-
Tales of ghosts: First Nations art in British Columbia, 1922-61 / Ronald William Hawker.

Includes bibliographical references and index.
ISBN 0-7748-0954-X (bound); ISBN 0-7748-0955-8 (pbk.)

1. Indian art – British Columbia – History. I. Title.
E78.B9H345 2002   704.03'970711   C2002-911080-7I

Canada

UBC Press gratefully acknowledges the financial support for our publishing program of the Government of Canada through the Book Publishing Industry Development Program (BPIDP), and of the Canada Council for the Arts, and the British Columbia Arts Council.

This book has been published with the help of grants from the Humanities and Social Sciences Federation of Canada, using funds provided by the Social Sciences and Humanities Research Council of Canada, from the International Council for Canadian Studies, through its Canadian Studies Publishing Fund, and with the help of the K.D. Srivastava Fund.

UBC Press
The University of British Columbia
2029 West Mall
Vancouver, BC V6T 1Z2
604-822-5959 / Fax: 604-822-6083
www.ubcpress.ca

Contents

Illustrations

Acknowledgments

There have been two people whose help has been absolutely essential to the completion of this project. The first is my wife Laila. Her aid has extended beyond moral (and financial) support to seven years of dinner-time (and every other time) conversations that have continually shaped and reshaped my approach not only to the material in this book, but also to the world at large. She has also contributed greatly by sharing her personal research.

The other is my friend Don Bains, whose generosity in sharing his ideas is only surpassed by his generosity in sharing archival sources. I thank him particularly for making available his personal research materials from the archives of the Canadian Museum of Civilization and the Museum of Anthropology at the University of British Columbia.

This book is a revised version of my doctoral dissertation, which was completed at the University of British Columbia in 1998. The dissertation developed critically from the teaching, writing, comments, criticism, and guidance of my supervisory committee, Drs. Marvin Cohodas, John O'Brian, and Marjorie Halpin. In addition to their professional expertise, their support has also extended to my family – support that was both unexpected and greatly appreciated.

Thanks as well to all my friends, family, and colleagues who have supported and inspired me.

Tales of Ghosts

1
Introduction

Totem poles are among the best known forms of Native American and First Nations[1] material expression. For many, the monumental weathered cedar carvings, now grey with years of winter rain, conjure up a romantic and sadly nostalgic image of the displacement of Aboriginal America by European colonization. Canadian history of art surveys thus may begin with the "totem" as a way of introducing the fall of an Aboriginal past and the rise of a modern present.[2] However, totem poles are still produced. Freshly carved and painted, they line the highways of the Pacific Northwest, are unveiled at international festivals and museums, and are dedicated at winter ceremonies in the remotest reaches of North America's cold Pacific edge. Furthermore, totem poles are but one of the many forms of visual culture widely created by the peoples grouped together under the European-coined term, Northwest Coast.[3]

These carvings generally remain mysterious. Supernatural and composite creatures wrap enigmatically around the shaft of these great poles or spread out across the surfaces of the plank house fronts in the museums. The images are also ubiquitous – T-shirts, greeting cards, calendars, posters, books. They are replicated en masse and in miniature. It is natural for a visitor, or someone unfamiliar with the objects and the people that produce them, to ask: what does Northwest Coast art mean? The answer differs, according to whom is addressed. And this gives rise to the question: why doesn't it mean the same thing to everyone?

For example, houseposts carved by Charlie James and erected in Stanley Park as touristic symbols of Vancouver (see Figure 1) once served as props in Edward Curtis's fictionalized Kwakwa̱ka̱'wakw romance *In the Land of the Headhunters*.[4] Before that, they stood in the house of Tsa-wee-nok of Kingcome Inlet,[5] powerful symbols inherited through the Kwakwa̱ka̱'wakw ceremonial cycle that referred to a mythical time when the boundaries between spirit and human realms were fluid – a time, not coincidentally, when the founding ancestors of lineage groups received gifts of access to resource sites and other forms of spiritual and terrestrial wealth.[6] At each moment, in each context, the meanings projected through these houseposts differed according to their respective audiences. There is not one over-arching narrative that satisfactorily explains and encapsulates the meanings of these Northwest Coast objects.

In this book I chart the conflicting and shifting assertions of meaning for Canadian Northwest Coast objects by looking at a series of representational projects implemented between 1922 and 1961. In January 1922 the Department of Indian Affairs (DIA) prosecuted participants in the Cranmer potlatch, which took place in late 1921. The Cranmer prosecutions represent the severest implementation of the federal government's potlatch ban and have

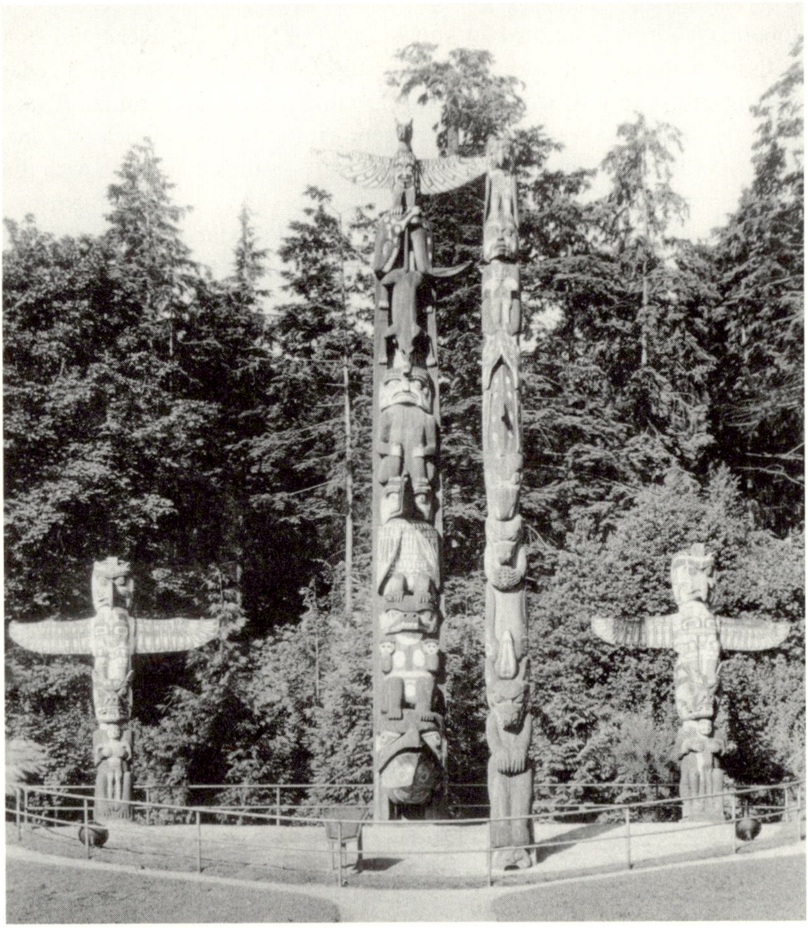

1 Two Charlie James houseposts flank the free-standing poles at Lumberman's Arch in Stanley Park, Vancouver. They have all since been removed and new replicas installed and rearranged.

become a symbol of the systematic attack on First Nations institutions carried out by Canadian government authorities. In 1961 Canada's Parliament approved the federal enfranchisement of First Nations people, thus signalling a theoretical end to the era of assimilation.

These events bookend a period perceived in most art history texts as the "Dark Ages of Northwest Coast art."[7] Prior to the Second World War, scholars of European descent argued that the passing of First Nations culture was an inevitable part of North America's march towards modernity. In the postwar period, outdated policies of assimilation, of which the potlatch ban was an integral part, were blamed for hastening the loss of Aboriginal traditions. In contrast, I argue that, during this era, Northwest Coast objects functioned in a complex and multifaceted manner, at once asserting the integrity and meaningfulness of First Nations identities and resisting the intent and effects of assimilation.

Neither simply vestiges of an irretrievable past nor symbolic markers of ancestral encounters with the spirit world, the objects produced and displayed between 1922 and 1961 operated through the projects I describe to affect the intertwined transformative processes of identity construction and boundary marking both among individual First Nations groups and with regard to Canada's national identity. Through these projects important steps were taken towards formulating two major characteristics of the post-1960 period: (1) a burgeoning market in "traditional" Northwest Coast objects and (2) First Nations activism with regard to land claims and self-determination – an activism premised upon notions of "tradition" and "art."

The history of Northwest Coast art is part of a larger history of attempted displacement through assimilation. Plainly said, industrialization, urbanization, and mass immigration engineered by government authorities resulted in Aboriginal and non-Aboriginal peoples being in conflict over land and marine resources. To understand how this affected the production and meaning of Northwest Coast art, it is important to recognize that, in 1900, these carvings and paintings played a different role in Northwest Coast societies than they did in European societies. Furthermore, the battle over land and resources was fought symbolically rather than openly. Government strategy was to replace Aboriginal meaning systems with those familiar to the immigrants and to replace Aboriginal modes of authority with European modes. They thus attacked the social phenomenon that they identified as the heart of Aboriginal identity and social structure: the potlatch (i.e., a series of ceremonial occasions during which ritual prerogatives were asserted through performance and display, and were validated through feasting and the distribution of wealth to invited guests).

As legal historian Tina Loo points out, the 1887 potlatch ban served an important function for Canada: "Laws express the rules that limit and shape behaviour and expectation, but they are also expressions of ethical norms," writes Loo. "Thus, not only are we ruled by law, but law also embodies and articulates the broad ideas around which we are constituted as a society."[8] While Loo seems to interpret the ethical norms promoted in public institutional spheres as reflections of already existing shared values, the point is that both law and public policy are strategically designed to shape these values. This strategy was particularly important to a people attempting to forge a nation based specifically on British norms but necessarily reliant upon non-British Aboriginal and immigrant labour.[9]

As the potlatch ban was enforced, Canadian museums expanded their collections of Aboriginal objects. The removal of masks and poles and other ceremonial paraphernalia to these institutions radically altered their meaning, and the replacement of their Aboriginal values with European values reinforced the new social order defined in Canadian law.[10] There is, therefore, an intersection between the law as it constructs a collective social identity and the reification of Northwest Coast objects as this constructs a collective social memory confirming that identity. As Paul Connerton suggests, "it is an implicit rule that participants in any social order must presuppose a shared memory ... [and] control of a society's memory largely conditions the hierarchy of power."[11]

While the justification for the potlatch ban ranged from disease prevention to halting what was perceived to be a regressive, "superstitious" ceremony that imprisoned First Nations peoples in a spiralling cycle of impoverishment, what may have been closer to the point was Marius Barbeau's suggestion that the potlatch was "in reality the old 'Indian chief' form of government and ... that it should not be tolerated by the white man's Government."[12]

Throughout the Coast, the potlatch system was essential to economic and social management. First Nations lineages had controlled both real and incorporeal property, including the rights to salmon-spawning streams, lakes, trapping sites, patches of edible plants, stands of cedar, rookeries, stretches of coastline, winter village sites, and, according to Niblack and Swanton (writing in 1890 and 1905, respectively), halibut banks.[13] In other words, the access to the land and resources essential to the colonial development of British Columbia were already vested in First Nations lineage systems. Although clan and lineage hierarchy, descent, and the rituals that validated the transfer of rights varied from group to group, individual ranking within the lineages was generally accomplished through the inherited rights to a repository of names, dances, songs, stories, and crest figures displayed and validated at potlatches and feasts.[14] The highest ranking members of the lineage were also lineage trustees, and they were responsible for the management of the lineage-owned resources – both corporeal and incorporeal.[15] The integral relationship between the kinship system, ceremonial objects, and resource utilization was succinctly summarized by Delgam Uukw (Ken Muldoe) in the 1987 filing of the Gitxsan-Wet'suwet'en suit in the Supreme Court of British Columbia (which also demonstrates the ongoing political currency of the potlatch system among certain First Nations leaders):

> My power is carried in my House's histories, songs, dances, and crests. It is recreated at the Feast when the histories are told, the songs and dances performed, and the crests displayed. With the wealth that comes from respectful use of the territory, the House feeds the name of the Chief in the Feast Hall. In this way, the law, the Chief, the territory, and the Feast become one. The unity of the Chief's authority and his House's are witnessed and thus affirmed by the other Chiefs at the Feast.[16]

On the central coast, Kwakwa̲ka̲'wakw social structure differs from that of the Gitxsan-Wet'suwet'en in that kinship is bilateral rather than strictly matrilineal. However, as in the North, rights to both corporeal and incorporeal resources resided in kin groups. Each of the thirty autonomous Kwakwa̲ka̲'wakw groups commonly called tribes consisted of several corporate kin groups termed *numayms,* and claims to resource areas were frequently based on *numaym* membership.[17] As the potlatch centres on First Nations ownership of the very resources that non-First Nations coveted, state officials attempted to circumvent resistance to their authority by prohibiting the potlatch.

In addition, the competitive destruction of property associated with the late nineteenth-century Kwakwa̲ka̲'wakw was exaggerated and constructed as a threat to the Christian/bourgeois system of private property. Anthropologist Helen Codere argues that population decline among the Kwakwa̲ka̲'wakw in the last quarter of the nineteenth century led to empty *numaym* positions. This coincided with changes in settlement patterns as tribes congregated around the new trading posts and cannery towns. Participation in the colonial economy in conjunction with these social changes resulted in the elaboration of the potlatch as a means of sorting out multiple claims to the *numaym* positions. This elaborated form of the potlatch was the focus of the intensified state hostility towards Northwest Coast ceremony around the time of the First World War.[18] At this time, according to Bill Holm, the production of art objects continued "unabated" and became "progressively more elaborate."[19]

First Nations in British Columbia mounted organized resistance to assimilation and Anglo-conformity, the allocation of reserve land, and the limited definition of Aboriginal rights. First Nations resistance organizations included the Nishga Land Committee, the Indian Rights Association, the Interior Tribes of British Columbia, and the Allied Tribes of British Columbia. All of these groups were formed between 1900 and 1916 and were active until the de facto ban on land claims instituted in a 1927 amendment to the Indian Act.[20]

The federal government demonstrated its disdain for First Nations interests through a series of patriarchal amendments to the Indian Act between 1913 and 1927 – amendments that gave Indian Agents more leverage in enforcing the potlatch ban and that stripped First Nations peoples not only of the rights to hire legal counsel and lobby for land claims, but also of the right to sell totem poles and other "heritage" objects without the consent of the DIA.[21] Canadian "cultural" agencies also undertook a number of important programs that reconfigured the meaning for Northwest Coast objects. Poles were turned towards the nation's rail lines and erected in civic parks. At the same time, masks and other painted and carved objects were exhibited at the National Gallery and written about as though they were part of an earlier heritage. These activities enclosed targeted First Nations peoples within a temporal construction that barred their participation in contemporary decision making. It followed that state paternalism was necessary to ensure that they "evolved" from their enclosure in the past to the point where they could obtain the rights and obligations of "modern" Canadian citizenship.[22]

As a result, a common academic perception is that the history of Northwest Coast art involves a nineteenth-century climax (often referred to, following European art history models, as the "classic" period), an early twentieth-century decline (instigated by the potlatch ban and the spectrum of assimilationist projects), and a mid-twentieth-century renaissance. Within this paradigm, the period following the First World War is deemed the lowest ebb of the peoples of the Coast: swamped by the influence of White assimilation; directionless, confused, and sick with newly introduced diseases; the communities and their modes of symbolic expression were, to all intents and purposes, dead. This was a time, according to Margaret Blackman, when a visitor on the Northwest Coast would have to go to a museum to see an example of *good* Northwest Coast Indian "art" (emphasis mine).[23] As recently as 1993 Peter Macnair, curator at the Royal British Columbia Museum, suggested that, among the arts of the Northwest Coast, "the classic forms either disappeared altogether or were replaced by substitute styles."[24] An artistic hierarchy was set up in which products outside the discursive poles of "tradition" and "authenticity" were categorized, in Macnair's words, as "consistently well-finished charming souvenirs" that "lack the vitality of the older school."[25] In the same recent anthology, Martine Reid concurs, suggesting that "post-classic" Northwest Coast art "has become a pseudo-language shared and produced by an elite because the created objects no longer signify potent cultural messages. They merely reproduce or imitate past objects and concepts that are not culturally relevant to the present society. Art has lost its sign value."[26]

In the "revival" view, projects aimed at communicating the value of First Nations art to a general non-First Nations Canadian audience were made possible in the 1950s and 1960s through a greater allocation of public funds. Within this context of institutional interest, the idea of a mid-century renaissance – what Marjorie Halpin refers to as an "enthusiastic revival"[27] – began to emerge. In 1967 a cross-country network of artists, ranging in style and geographic origin from George Clutesi on the west coast of Vancouver Island to Norval Morrisseau in Ontario, was formed through preparations for the Indian Pavilion at Expo '67 in Montreal.[28] Also in 1967 Bill Reid, Henry Hunt, and other contemporary Northwest Coast artists received recognition by having their work displayed next to that of Charles Edenshaw (who died in 1920)[29] and other, mostly anonymous, masters of the "classic" nineteenth- and early twentieth-century Northwest Coast formline style[30] at the *Arts of the Raven* exhibition at the Vancouver Art Gallery.[31] In 1968, with two-thirds of its funding coming from government grants and other donations, the 'Ksan Historic Indian Village Association proudly opened its museum, reconstructed village, and accompanying Kitanmaax School of Northwest Coast Indian Art.[32] According to the new "revival" myth, popular support of First Nations art all across Canada was fuelling the re-emergence of "traditional" Northwest Coast art.

As part of the centennial celebration, both Expo '67 and the *Arts of the Raven* shows received substantial amounts of government and corporate money.[33] One might, therefore, suggest that the expansion of Canada's cultural infrastructure in the 1960s and 1970s through a combination of increased public spending and public-/private-sector cooperation stimulated the "revival"; that "museum- and government-supported projects for the restoration or recreation of 'traditional' objects that the Indians had largely ceased producing"[34] were successful. 'Ksan and the Kitanmaax art school have been called "satellite museums,"[35] part of the federal government's cultural "democratization and decentralization" program announced in 1968,[36] itself an institutional premonition of Canada's symbolic shift to official state multiculturalism in 1971 and the acknowledgment of non-English and non-French contributions to Canadian national "culture."[37]

Exhibitions in public institutions appear to have encouraged the private acquisitions of contemporary First Nations art. In discussing the post-1967 impact of large exhibitions on a new audience, Tom Hill, in his history of Aboriginal Canadian art, commented: "Exhibitions of material culture and contemporary art further enhanced and popularized the ethnic identity for the consumer. Whether out of genuine appreciation, guilt over past sins, or a need to acquire something Canadian, the art-buying public chose to look at the new art emerging from Indian communities as a significant statement from a fellow Canadian."[38] An example of the principles of state capitalism applied to "cultural products,"[39] public funding bolstered a burgeoning private market. In this view, state sponsorship of First Nations production through displays in public cultural institutions allowed for widespread public exposure. The Cultural Affairs Division within the DIA was established in 1967 and was responsible for publishing articles, producing exhibitions, establishing a permanent collection, and undertaking a series of market evaluations on the work of several First Nations artists.[40]

But even the strongest proponents of the "renaissance" myth admit that certain groups never ceased producing ceremonial objects.[41] In addition, the question of why the state would first openly ban the raison d'être of ceremonial First Nations objects in British Columbia and then later invest public funds in the production of the same kinds of objects needs to be addressed. Both the pre-1950 narrative of "cultural death" and the post-1950 assertion of "decline and revival" have been openly contested by First Nations carvers and painters. In 1948 Kwakwaka'wakw Ellen Neel firmly stated:

> This point of mine which I shall endeavor to illustrate deals with an idea that the native art is a dead art and that efforts should be confined to preservation of the old work. To me, this idea is one of the great fallacies where the art of my people is concerned. For if our art is dead, then it is fit only to be mummified, packed into mortuary boxes and tucked away into museums. Whereas to me it is a living symbol ... And our art must *continue* to live, for not only is it part and parcel of us, but it can be a powerful factor in combining the best of the Indian culture into the fabric of a truly Canadian art form.
>
> ... if the art of my people is to take its rightful place alongside other Canadian art, it must be a living medium of expression. We, the Indian artists, must be allowed to create! We must be allowed to use new and modern techniques; new and modern tools; new and modern materials ... I do not mean that we should discard the old, only that we be allowed to use the new.[42]

In 1983 another Kwakwaka'wakw carver, Tony Hunt, pointing to the less than altruistic intentions of museum curators, also suggested that the revival narrative was false:

> It was in the seventies that museum curators recognized Northwest Coast art both as public relations and promotion for their own museums and as promotion of themselves. Before that, during the fifties and sixties, curators and ethnologists had a low profile. Mungo Martin who taught and raised me (and with whom I moved to Victoria in 1952) – to say to him there was a "revival" or "renaissance" would be ridiculous. He carved all his life, my father, myself, others like Willie Seaweed, who was one of the finest artists of his time. There was no revival.[43]

In 1974 First Nations political leader George Manuel and writer Michael Postuns implied that both death and revival views were colonialist in nature, aimed at denigrating the social and political accomplishments of First Nations peoples since the advent of a European presence in British Columbia:

> The renaissance of today is the fruit of the accumulated labour of our grandfathers. If it appears that we are only now awakening and discovering a new strength, it is because the current climate of political, social and economic forces is allowing what was always beneath the surface to emerge into the light of day.
>
> Above all, the appearance that we are only now coming alive is an illusion created by the press and public institutions, who have for so long warped, distorted, and falsified the story of our resistance.[44]

It is significant that Manuel, once president of the North American Indian Brotherhood, tied the concept of "cultural renaissance" to larger social developments. It is precisely this kind of wider self-conscious contextualization that is missing in Northwest Coast art history and that this book seeks to address.

In explaining this absence, Aldona Jonaitis underlines "certain central assumptions"[45] behind some of the early anthropology of the Northwest Coast. It has been commonly assumed

> that Native people had, prior to contact, lived in unified, cohesive communities and shared common values; that the inherent perfection of their culture disintegrated as the overwhelming forces of the dominant society caused first a decline and then the disappearance of their traditions, including art; that on the northern Northwest Coast in particular, the loss of artistic competence was reversed only when individuals from outside the cultures rediscovered earlier stylistic conventions.[46]

Jonaitis then warns that, "by depicting Native peoples as succumbing to the forces of acculturation, such representations implicitly grant ... the dominant society a cultural hegemony over those it colonized."[47]

Nelson Graburn adds that, "even though Fourth World peoples may call themselves nations ... they have neither the autonomy nor the institutionalized power to define their own national symbols, arts, and culture."[48] Bound by the paternalism of the Indian Act, First Nations peoples have been represented through the inter-related institutionalized discourses of anthropology, museums, and art history. Valda Blundell argues that "certain representations encoded in anthropological discourse recur in the media ... because anthropology has been constructed in the West as the primary producer of knowledge about so-called 'primitive' peoples. Anthropologists and their texts constitute ... 'accredited sources' and 'primary definers' of social phenomena regarding native Canadians."[49] There is a continuum of representation of First Nations arts that also reflects a wide range of interests and concerns in non-First Nations society. While anthropologists, like social reformers, were frequently sympathetic with the peoples and societies they were studying, their work, as part of this larger totality, was often compromised.

As can be seen, the representation of First Nations societies is and has been disputed territory. The conflicting meanings of those poles in Stanley Park or, more generally, the notions of decline, revival, and continuity are strategic interventions in the understanding of First Nations peoples and their position in Canadian society. They are statements from a complex number of voices, asserting, negotiating, and disputing the various representations and counter-representations of Northwest Coast art and, through it, of First Nations peoples. I agree with Jonaitis's argument that these assumptions of purity and disintegration in First Nations culture have created absences in the discourses of art through ensuring that discussions have centred solely on "classic" notions of form and iconography.

The mythic tropes of decline and revival confirmed the authority of state institutions and those individuals who formulated the discourse of Northwest Coast objects from within them. Continuity and the appropriation of the revival concept could be used to stress or legitimize contemporary First Nations leadership and political claims. Making sense of the contradictions in the discourses around these objects calls for an understanding of the historical specificity of the discourses and their shifts, or, as Nicholas Thomas puts it, of the "ruptures ... that mark the emergence and displacement of particular ways of constructing others and relating to them."[50]

At the heart of these ruptures are the different ways of understanding, first, Northwest Coast societies, and, second, their relation to *official* Canadian "culture." As anthropologist Virginia Dominguez notes, culture is extremely socially significant because we so often make strategic social and political interventions by invoking it.[51] Dominguez further asserts that culture is implicated in "nationalist visions, nationalist ideologies, and national identities."[52] This is exemplified in the state funding for Northwest Coast objects in the 1960s and, as I shall demonstrate, even earlier. In an argument that I believe is borne out by the development of Northwest Coast art discourse in British Columbia, Dominguez suggests that governments assert their say over the shape of their populations' cultures because they link the idea of culture with respectability, unity, and the minimization of divisiveness – a link critical to international perceptions of national images.[53]

The narratives for Northwest Coast "culture" are thus unstable, at least in part, because of the contested nature of these same nationalist visions, ideologies, and identities. The very notion of "culture" is problematic because, since Boas, the term has commonly suggested "sameness and shared understanding" when applied to non-capitalist societies.[54] For Northwest Coast objects, discursive conflict demonstrates that sameness cannot be assumed. Furthermore, the history of twentieth-century Canadian culture clearly demonstrates the great challenge, perhaps even impossibility, of constructing unitary symbols for a multicultural nation with such a complex colonial history.

For example, the idea of the passing of First Nations societies is the result of the lingering effect of social evolutionary ideologies popular among Euro-Americans in the late nineteenth century and the belief in the expiration of so-called primitive cultures before the dynamism of a European-derived industrial modernity. These are the same underlying ideologies that, prior to the Great Depression, informed assimilationist policies in both Canada and the United States. While totem poles and other Aboriginal objects could be seen to symbolize a unique Canadian identity, within non-Aboriginal contexts they were specifically meant to refer to an imagined Canadian past, to suggest what Canadian culture no longer was (although modern Canada had no place for the Aboriginal meanings behind the poles' original production).[55]

Walter Benn Michaels argues that the Native American is a nationalist trope in the United States, and one could argue the same for First Nations with regard to Canada and its supposed uniqueness when compared to other international industrial nations.[56] According to Marvin Cohodas, "the modernization paradigm operates here: with homogenized global capitalism and labor relations characterizing the modern present, 'cultures' that distinguish national identities are located in 'primitive' or 'traditional' past jeopardized by contact with (read: exploitation by) the modern west."[57] Thus, by the end of the First World War, there was discussion about promoting Northwest Coast objects as a positive aesthetic contribution from the "Indian" past to the Canadian present.

There is clearly a fundamental contradiction in the function of totem poles and other objects within Aboriginal lineage and Euro-Canadian museum systems.[58] "Objects are not what they were made to be but what they have become," writes Thomas,[59] drawing attention to what he calls a "promiscuity of the object"[60] in which meaning is externally impressed by the context within which the object is presented and received. In this sense, then, meaning is not static. Objects are valued and used not for what they are as material forms but, rather, for the meanings applied to them.

One key issue, then, is *how* things become, and specifically how (and why) Northwest Coast things have become, "Canadian." This is where a history of objects, what Igor Kopytoff calls a biography of things,[61] becomes useful because it fleshes out the issues that are at stake in the becoming, in the movement of meaning around a thing or a set of things. It brings into account the idea of multiple audiences and multiple makers of meaning, where a society is not an autonomous group but, rather, a collection of competing groups. In this light, knowing who makes "culture," whose interests this culture serves, and who represents other cultures is crucial to understanding the conflicting assertions of meaning with regard to objects – to understanding what and how objects become.

In another example, after the Second World War, the federal government abandoned the Anglo-conformity of the era of the potlatch ban as the paradigm for national culture. Assimilation was replaced with integration and the notion that non-British social groups could simultaneously hold on to aspects of their "native" modes of expression and still be considered "good Canadians."[62] Furthermore, influential politicians, like Lester Pearson and Brooke Claxton, argued that if Canada were to fulfill a significant international political role in the postwar era, then it would be in the government's interest to promote Canadian identity through "culture" – both domestically and internationally.[63]

In British Columbia, in the early 1950s the University of British Columbia and the provincial government joined together with a number of private corporations and their executives to form the Totem Pole Preservation Committee. The objective of the committee was not only to salvage and preserve totem poles (which was also the intention of projects in the 1920s), but also to use museum collections in conjunction with living "traditional" pole carvers in order to establish a carver training program and to resurrect Northwest Coast "art." Indeed, this was the beginning of Halpin's "enthusiastic revival."[64]

Both the Cranmer potlatch prosecutions and the activities of the Totem Pole Preservation Committee of the 1950s were tied to efforts to "modernize" British Columbia. However, they followed quite different strategies from one another. The potlatch ban was assimilationist, justified by a social evolutionary vision of Canadian society that privileged a particularly British worldview. In theory, the activities of the Totem Pole Preservation Committee recognized non-British contributions to national culture and allowed for the public expression of non-British forms of identity. Both the Cranmer prosecutions and the preservation committee implicitly supported a predominantly non-Aboriginal social and economic order in that they refused (or failed) to recognize the contemporary function of First Nations objects in the lineage and potlatch systems. Taken together, they also supported Thomas's view of the use of culture: "In effect, modernity itself can be understood as a colonialist project that both the societies internal to Western nations, and those they possessed, administered and reformed elsewhere were understood as objects to be surveyed, regulated and sanitized."[65]

However, Thomas goes on to argue that

> it is essential at the same time to recognize that government is not a unitary work but heterogeneous and partial, and moreover that the meanings engendered by hegemonic codes and narratives do not exist in hermetic domains but are placed at risk, revalued and distorted through being enacted and experienced. In colonial encounters, marked not only by struggle but also by misrecognition and by disingenuous compliance, the risks are very real indeed. It is vital, then, to make explicit the efforts to govern that are present in particular fields of colonial representation, without ever assuming that this government is stable and secure.[66]

This book traces Northwest Coast objects as tropes in the emergence of Canada's national culture by looking at a series of representational projects that articulate some of the different positions vis-à-vis the meaning and uses of Northwest Coast objects – positions that are part of the larger struggle to determine a social position for First Nations peoples within Canadian society. In many ways the period between 1922 and 1961 is a rich one. I am not disputing the notion of decline by reciting what survived – the spirit dance masks of the Coast Salish groups,[67] the syncretistic gravestones that appear among the northern groups,[68] the masks and poles of the Kwakwa̱ka̱'wakw, or what Joe David refers to as the "rebel masks" of the Nuu-chah-nulth.[69] Rather, I am examining the negotiation of meaning around objects used in public projects in order to highlight their symbolic uses. And while formalism and iconography have been the strongest currents in Northwest Coast art discourses, their intensive use has marginalized a number of works from the period I am discussing and has obscured the political relations they engender. The multiple meanings apparent in the different ways that these objects have been discussed indicate that there are many ways of approaching this material. I do not intend to preclude these other approaches (indeed, I do use visual analysis when necessary to the discussion); however, I use a documentary approach in order to foreground material that has generally been marginalized in these discourses.

I emphasize the use of Northwest Coast objects in public projects for two reasons. First, the stories, songs, and other performances involving objects used in potlatch ceremonies are considered to be the private property of lineage groups and the holders of specific positions within them. I have no status within this structure and do not want to transgress this concept of ownership. Second, I want to avoid the tendency to conceive of First Nations cultures as isolated from non-First Nations cultures; rather, I argue that the interaction between these cultures was the occasion for an expansion of function and (especially) meaning in Northwest Coast object production.

I have also chosen to limit myself to textual sources. I wanted to rely not only upon the objects, but also upon publications, newspaper accounts, written objectives, and unpublished memoranda and correspondence. Although oral history is always valuable, I believe that interviews, which would have provided forty- or fifty-year-old reminiscences, would have complicated my reading of these written sources. My strategy is to demonstrate the rich presence of First Nations voices within these archival and published sources. It is for this reason that I have chosen to emphasize textual history over ethnography.

While it is well known, for example, that Mungo Martin and other carvers participated in museum projects, they have never been examined within the larger, highly contested context of Canadian identity and national "culture." This book does not present a First Nations perspective;[70] rather, it attempts to show how public display constituted an opportunity for negotiation between local, provincial, and federal governments and First Nations peoples. *Tales of Ghosts,* therefore, explores historical experiences and the shaping of artistic discourses concerning First Nations in British Columbia and their relation to Canadian identity.

By using archival sources (such as the Hawthorn and Duff Papers located in the University of British Columbia Museum of Anthropology Archives; the Duff Papers located in the Royal British Columbia Museum; the Sapir and Barbeau correspondence files in the Canadian Museum of Civilization; the correspondence and field reports available on microfilm through the Indian Affairs Black Series; meeting minutes and scrapbooks of the Art Historical and Scientific Association in the Vancouver City Archives; and the Duff, Raley, and British Columbia Indian Art and Welfare Society Papers in the British Columbia Archives), I am able to examine the ideologies at the heart of art history's discursive parameters.

Contrary to primitivist constructions of "traditional" Northwest Coast societies as unchanging, the concept of power and its visual manifestation as transforming and transformative was not alien to Northwest Coast political leaders. That objects may be misrepresented for economic or social gain within Aboriginal contexts is both recognized and limited by the potlatch and lineage systems, where individual and group rights to recite certain histories and to display associated images have been controlled and disputed. The recognition of multiple meanings and the ability of objects to represent political goals does not necessarily indicate a radical conceptual break due solely to the circumstances created by Euro-Canadian colonialism (although colonialism did create contexts for shifts in meaning). That First Nations peoples have participated in transforming the meanings of Northwest Coast objects in an attempt to assert their own power should surprise no one. The concept of transformation has long been celebrated within their own private and public spaces.[71]

2
The Cranmer Potlatch and Indian Agent Halliday's Display

The race has waned and left but tales of ghosts,
That hover in the world like fading smoke
About the lodges: gone are the dusty folk
That once were cunning with the thong and snare
And mighty with the paddle and the bow;
They lured the silver salmon from his lair,
They drove the buffalo in trampling hosts,
And gambled in the tepees until dawn,
But now their vaunted prowess all is gone,
Gone like a moose-track in the April snow.
But all the land is murmurous with the call
Of their wild names that haunt the lovely glens
Where lonely water falls, or where the street
Sounds all day with the tramp of myriad feet ...

– Duncan Campbell Scott[1]

Although in 1935 the Reverend George Raley would write of the objects of the Northwest Coast as "Canada's first contribution to the world of art,"[2] they had not long been considered as such. Their transformation into "art" in Euro-Canada's public understanding was gradual, prompted through a number of projects that sometimes had conflicting objectives. And before they were seen as "art," they were presented in non-Aboriginal public displays as "antiquity." In 1905, summarizing public sentiment and the basis for public policy in his poem "Indian Place Names," Duncan Campbell Scott wrote that "the race has waned ... now their vaunted prowess all is gone."[3]

Because ceremonial objects contributed to the construction of status and the hierarchical organization of access to resources through the potlatch system, reconfiguring the objects as "antiquity," as part of the past, effectively denied the continuing importance of Aboriginal political structures. Although not all Euro-Canadian projects centred on First Nations objects had this denial as their primary objective, an important early display associated with the Cranmer potlatch prosecutions certainly did.

The potlatch ban of the late nineteenth and first half of the twentieth century was part of a larger policy of assimilation. The repression of ceremonialism discouraged participation in traditional rites and, at least in theory, subverted Aboriginal modes of leadership. This opened the way to the inculcation of British social customs and values through Christianization and enforced education. The reconfiguration of objects previously associated with the potlatch into objects of antiquity served two purposes: first, it paralleled the overtly repressive strategies of the potlatch ban by suggesting that the objects no longer held a viable role in First Nations societies; second, the objects could be appropriated and presented as part of a mythical Canadian past now useful in symbolizing Canadian identity. While normally the connection between the repression of ceremonialism and the appropriation and presentation of First Nations objects as Canadian was obscured by the fact that officials from different arms of the state were responsible for different aspects of the process, William Halliday, the Indian Agent based in Alert Bay, both prosecuted and adjudicated the potlatch ban and then catalogued and displayed seized objects before shipping them to the national museum in Ottawa. He did this at the instigation of his superior in the DIA, Duncan Campbell Scott. The distance between repression and appropriation was never so slim as it was in the Cranmer potlatch prosecutions, the subject of this chapter.

The Kwakwa̲ka̲'wakw Potlatch and Its Persecution

The research efforts and collecting activities of Franz Boas and the most oppressive implementation of the Canadian government's potlatch ban focused upon the same group of people, the Kwakwa̲ka̲'wakw – commonly referred to, prior to the 1980s, as the Kwakiutl.[4] Boas, through his collecting, research, publications, exhibitions, and his organization of Kwakwa̲ka̲'wakw performances at several world fairs, did much to bring the Kwakwa̲ka̲'wakw to prominence in Euro-American consciousness. While the potlatch had technically been prohibited since 1884, initial attempts at prosecution were largely unsuccessful.[5] The Kwakwa̲ka̲'wakw in particular were perceived as openly resistant to both the ban and to the introduction of Christianity and were thus the target of renewed attempts to stamp out the potlatch following the First World War.[6] Duncan Campbell Scott, who had written "Indian Place Names" in 1905, rose to the position of deputy superintendent of the Department of Indian Affairs in 1913.[7] He introduced amendments to the Indian Act in 1914 and 1918 in order to expand the definition of the potlatch and to facilitate the prosecution of potlatch participants.[8] This led directly to the arrest, conviction, and imprisonment of participants in a potlatch hosted by Dan Cranmer at Village Island in 1921.[9]

Arguments both for and against the potlatch were often made in economic terms.[10] In 1874 George Blenkinsop, an agent with the Indian Reserve Allotment Commission, suggested that "these people are the richest in every respect in British Columbia and were a proper disposal made of their immense gains they could furnish themselves with every comfort they could possibly wish for."[11] Apparently the Kwakwa̱ka̱'wakw participated enthusiastically in the colonial economy. "Kwakiutl economic achievement was motivated by potlatching and sustained and increased potlatching," writes Helen Codere. "The 'stream of wealth' of which the Kwakiutl speak was at once the measure of their successful integration with the new and expanding economy and the motive for their success."[12] "The lack of 'progressiveness,'" she concludes, "was not a lack of industriousness, but a failure to be industrious for the right reasons, in the context of the values of the whites."[13] The economic argument against the potlatch was deeply rooted in a disjunction between the potlatch's social function and the authority that officials such as Scott and Halliday presumed necessary for the development of Canadian capitalism.

Scott, Halliday, and a number of other officials saw the potlatch as a symbol of Kwakwa̱ka̱'wakw resistance to their authority and, therefore, as "the great stumbling block in the way of progress."[14] Barbeau quotes S. Cook, "an educated and shrewd Indian woman,"[15] who argued that "the Kwakiutl [would] not own allegiance to the government as long as the potlatch prevails: it excludes all other forms of government."[16] Indeed, the various ceremonies referred to under the term potlatch validated the hierarchical ranking of groups and individuals, ordering both social relations and the access to and exchange of both natural and supernatural resources.

The Kwakwa̱ka̱'wakw consisted of thirty autonomous groups (termed "tribes" by Codere) when the potlatch ban was first introduced. Each group had its territory, winter village, and several sites occupied seasonally, and each consisted of several corporate kin groups, anglicized as *numaym*, or *numayma*.[17] The *numaym* was a social division that traced its crests back to a supernatural ancestor. Through its lineage history, each *numaym* had claims to physical property, such as house and food resource sites, and to crests and titles that existed in a multitude of forms (from designs on house fronts, poles, posts, and feast dishes to privileges such as the use of certain betrothal ceremonies, songs, house names, and titles).[18] The properties were "not mere names, titles and privileges"[19] but, rather, related to a corpus of ancestral myths and, therefore, "spiritual goods, representing essential spiritual qualities of founders and ultimately of all ancestors."[20]

Myths, writes Halpin,

> tell of a primordial age before the world became as it is now, a time when finite divisions between humans, animals, and spirits had not yet been created and beings could transform themselves from one form to another – humans could become animals by putting on skins, animals could become humans by taking them off, humans could marry animals and spirit beings. All realms of existence (water, earth, sky, and the land of the dead) were interconnected by beings who could pass among them. It was a time when everything was possible, when all boundaries were fluid and forms were plastic; a time when the fundamental opposites of life – natural/supernatural, man/woman, life/death, human/animal, hunter/hunted, eater/eaten – were interchangeable aspects of each other. It was a time when cosmic power accelerated the natural processes of change into miracles of transformation. It was a time now lost but remembered. It was a world now gone, but one that people recreated in art and ritual. Through ceremonial and artistic re-enactment of their heritage, through dance, song, and ritual acting, people maintained continuity with their genesis.[21]

The celebration of interconnectedness, of the fluidity of boundaries, allowed for the acceptance of the possibility of trans-generational transfers of power associated with names and titles. The recreation of myth time was an act that metaphorically validated the contemporary leadership structure through the re-enactment of mythical histories. An important aspect of potlatching, then, was the negotiation of social positions, prestige, and authority; the relations they constructed; and the right of access to resources they generated. With recitations of lineage histories and the transfer of social positions, the potlatch was also crucial with regard to expressing and mediating conflict resulting over contradictory claims.

Because of a gender distinction between how the characteristics that contributed to status were conveyed, the alliance between lineage groups through marriage was extremely important to consolidating and expanding both collective and individual spiritual and terrestrial wealth.[22] Halliday, in particular, objected to traditional Kwakwa̲ka̲'wakw marriage ceremonies because they were arranged between *numayms* to facilitate the transfer of important ceremonial rights, sometimes pairing an older man with a much younger woman. Halliday saw Kwakwa̲ka̲'wakw weddings and potlatches as closely connected and believed that, if such marriage ceremonies could be stopped, then "the potlatch would lose its chief feeder."[23]

Halliday was at least partially correct. Charles Nowell described his relationship to his father-in-law (Lagius) in potlatch terms, demonstrating that following potlatch etiquette was essential, at least in certain families, to being a "good" Kwakwa̲ka̲'wakw individual:

> Any time I feel like giving a feast or a potlatch after I was married, I get my own money and give it to Lagius, and he give it back to me to give a feast or a potlatch. This for the honour of my children, and most times he add some of his own money to make it more. And when I give the feast or potlatch, I say the money comes from him. After my child was born I did this, and every time a child of mine comes to the time when the baby begins to eat, I do this. Any time the child begins to play and gets hurt, I give money to Lagius and he gives it back to me, and I give it away to wipe the blood of the child's wounds. A good son-in-law would do this to the wife's father.[24]

Thus, in the late nineteenth and early twentieth centuries it is impossible to disengage any of the ceremonial privileges, myths, names, and crests from the overall structure of Kwakwa̱ka̱'wakw society. Social status engendered in potlatching was based on Kwakwa̱ka̱'wakw perceptions of both the structure and interrelationship of human, natural, and supernatural realms. Part of this included the management of resources and territories according to the *numaym* system, which, in theory, reflected a cosmic order.

The person identified as most responsible for the organized resistance of Christianized Kwakwa̱ka̱'wakw to potlatching in Alert Bay in 1921 was described in a confidential letter to Barbeau as "a very clever woman, who is a lieutenant of the Church. This woman has no high position in the potlatch, but she is in high power with the Church. It is quite apparent that if the Indians abandon the potlatch and go into the Church, she would be a leader among them."[25] State assimilation efforts and the refutation of the potlatch system on the part of some Christian converts created serious conflict with those who continued to assert rank through potlatching. This was because the violation of the chiefly hierarchy was perceived, at least by non-Christianized members of the chiefly classes, as a disruption of the natural as well as of the social order.[26]

Despite Halliday's moralistic objections and the inroads of evangelical Christianity, potlatching may have been accelerated by the establishment of permanent European settlements in British Columbia.[27] The introduction of trade goods and wage labour enabled more people to hold larger potlatches. Population depletion due to the spread of infectious diseases resulted in empty *numaym* positions, which encouraged "a flexible and opportunistic use of every possible means of filling the positions and using them in potlatching."[28] Drucker and Heizer even report that the "introduction of the element of outwitting the agent gave an added zest. It is quite clear that the potlatch became even more esteemed and cherished, acquiring overtones of defiance of the unwelcome authority of the agent, defiance of the laws of white civilization that the Indians felt were closing in on them."[29] And, as Scott tabled amendments to facilitate the enforcement of the potlatch ban, many Kwakwa̱ka̱'wakw continued to assert their right to a ceremonial system that reproduced their authority. The Cranmer potlatch, "the largest ever recorded on the coast,"[30] was a climactic confrontation between two holders of authoritative positions and two modes of constructing authority.

The Cranmer Potlatch

The Cranmer potlatch was part of the marriage ceremonial cycle for which Halliday had expressed such dislike, and it included the transfer of rights to Winter Ceremonial dances.[31] As Chaikin and Cole point out, "the potlatch was ... Emma Cranmer's 'repurchase,'[32] followed by (Dan) Cranmer's distribution of the goods received from his wife and her family as well as more of his own."[33] With at least 300 guests, the festivities lasted five days. The first two days consisted of Dan Cranmer's repayment of earlier loans and the transfer of property from Emma Cranmer's side. This included Billy Assu's payment of $2,000 in blankets and gift for the rights to a *xwexwe* (*Qweeqwee,* in Sewid-Smith's transcription) dance and names. Hanuse, acting for Emma Cranmer, gave Dan Cranmer canoes, furniture, and other goods. In addition, a copper[34] changed hands several times before ending up as Dan Cranmer's property along with $3,000 cash. He also received sewing machines, bracelets, and money. At the conclusion of this paying back, Herbert Martin danced the *hamatsa* and James Knox the *q'ominoqa*.[35]

The next section, which deals with what Cole and Chaikin refer to as Cranmer's "giving away," is described by Dan Cranmer himself in *An Iron Hand upon the People:*

> He gave pool tables to two chiefs ... Assu received a gas boat and $50 cash. Three more gas boats were given away and another pool table. Dresses, shawls and bracelets went to the women, sweaters and shirts to the young people. For the children, small change ... Then came blankets, gas lights, violins, guitars, basins, glasses, washtubs, teapots, boxes, three hundred oak trunks, sewing machines, gramophones, bedsteads, bureaus, and more cash. Finally on Christmas Day, the fifth and last day of the ceremony, came the sacks of flour. (Angermann recorded "about 400" sacks, Cranmer recalled 1000 at three dollars each.)[36]

Daisy Sewid-Smith, in *Prosecution or Persecution* (1979), transcribed her recording of Mecha (Herbert Martin, brother to artist Mungo Martin). He was an important potlatch participant and described the activities involved, particularly the transfer of the rights to the ceremonial names and dances:

> You will now listen to what happened to Pul-na-Qwa-Lus Walkus (Dan Cranmer) when he Num-bun-gil-ha-lud (To do everything together.

> Feasting and Potlatching were usually held separately but because of the continual threat of imprisonment it was done together). In that great thing he did. When Zoh-la-lee-tlee-louq (the late Emma Cranmer) completed their marriage contract at Village Island ...
>
> They invited the Kwakiutl (Fort Rupert), invited the Mamalillikulla (Village Island), Tla-wee-jees (Turnour Island), Da-naoq-douk (New Vancouver), the four clans of the Ja-wah-da-nooq (Kingcome Inlet). They all came to Village Island ... Zoh-la-lee-tlee-louq (Emma Cranmer) asked me to go to Hamatsa, so I went. The people were all gathered at the house of Hanuse at Village Island. The dancing began. I went out to dance when they sang for me. I danced and then everybody danced. It was finished. The dancing was finished for the night. Next day we danced all day and night. Yeh-koo-cla-lus (Emma Cranmer's other name) completed her marriage contract to Gwa-gwa-duk-ka-la (Dan Cranmer). She gave as part of her dowry to him the Qwee-Qwee dance (the Qwee-Qwee dance was given as part of her dowry by Chief Billy Assu of Cape Mudge). Jooq-jay-sah (Harry Glendale) was in one mask and his younger brother Kum-kah-kaw-weed (George Glendale) was in the other. Somebody would yell, Wooee! and they were the people that got arrested ... Without our knowledge Kenneth Hunt was writing names down ... Little did we know that we were going to be arrested. Gwim-kah-ness (Sam Matilpi) was paying his security. High-yahlth-kin (John Whonnock) was speaking. His wife was the Potlatch recorder. She was recording securities given to the women ... Recording as they were given something. They gave things away. Gwa-gwa-duk-ka-la (Dan Cranmer) gave trunks, pots, pans. Gave away all kinds of things ... That is what you call Num-bun-gil-ha-la (at the same time) what he did.[37]

Royal Canadian Mounted Police sergeant Donald Angermann investigated and charged the principals involved. During the trial Halliday shared the bench with A.M. Wastell. W. Murray of the McTaggart and Ellis law firm represented the defence.[38] Historian Tina Loo outlines the three "logics of dispute" in the Kwakwa̱ka̱'wakw defence. First, they invoked tradition, suggesting that they stood outside Canadian law and, therefore, could not be legitimately prosecuted.[39] Second, they drew analogies between their ceremony and those practised by the Europeans. The most obvious example of this was Christmas, which, like the potlatch, is a social and spiritual ceremony, linking the present with the past and celebrated through gift-giving.[40] Finally, and most disingenuously, they argued that the potlatch was an economic transaction and, therefore, was in accordance with Canadian laws of obligation.[41]

In the end, Halliday would have none of the complicated arguments against prosecution, and the defence altered the four initial pleas to guilty after hearing the strength of Angermann's case. They then presented an agreement indicating that they would no longer potlatch; this agreement was signed by the defendants and some fifty others. Angermann would not accept this compromise, claiming that several accused had already signed similar agreements and were now again before the court.[42] Instead, he suggested the need for "more tangible evidence of good faith";[43] namely, the surrender of potlatch paraphernalia by all members of the Kwawkewlth agency. The decision that now lay with some 300 people who were present at the Cranmer potlatch was either (1) to go to prison during the beginning of fishing season, which would pose a severe financial test for heads of families (and a possible burden for the government), or (2) to surrender the physical embodiments of the encounters of their ancestors with the supernatural world (objects symbolic of contemporary prestige and status); to quit entirely the public practice of transferring, perpetuating, celebrating, and legitimizing the powers gained through these ancestral encounters; and to assist Euro-Canadian authorities in suppressing this practice among their neighbours and family. By 31 March, all the decisions had come in. The Lekwiltok of Quadra Island, the Mamalillikulla of Village Island, and the Nimpkish of Alert Bay surrendered their coppers and dancing gear. "I guess it was like paying a fine so that they would not go to prison," said Ack-koo (Agnes Alfred). "They paid with their masks."[44]

Seven offenders refused to pay this price: Jim Hall of Karlakwees and six more from Fort Rupert. In April Angermann pressed charges against a further seventeen people who were present at the Cranmer potlatch and three who were active in potlatches on Harbledown Island the previous January and February. Five were given suspended sentences because they had played minor roles or signed the agreement. Of the remaining fifteen, all opted for the Oakalla Prison Farm in Burnaby, Vancouver's immediate municipal neighbour to the east. Of the twenty-two whom Angermann accompanied south on 10 April 1922, twenty-one had been given two-month sentences, with Nimpkish Charlie Hunt receiving six months for his second conviction.[45]

Emma Cranmer, as a member of the Nimpkish band, had submitted her paraphernalia and signed the agreement. Nonetheless, she was "in a prison of her own for she blamed herself for what happened and continually wept over it."[46] "Emma tried to offer herself to go in the place of the women arrested, but she was refused," writes Sewid-Smith. "She took it upon herself to see to the needs of the prisoners out of her own earnings from the cannery. She followed them to Vancouver. She supplied their needs and waited for their release ... and she paid for all their expenses,"[47] which included providing food as well as covering street car fares, restaurant and hotel bills, and the steamship tickets back to Alert Bay.[48] Despite Emma Cranmer's dignified and responsible actions, an event aimed at transferring spiritual and terrestrial property between lineage groups and cementing the social position of the participants involved had turned into a public catastrophe.

The Halliday Display

The surrendered potlatch regalia and coppers were put on exhibit at the Alert Bay parish hall and could be viewed upon paying an admission price of twenty-five cents. Halliday charged admission in order to cover the price of the hall,[49] but this seems particularly ironic, given that Alert Bay was a cannery town in the heart of Kwakwa̲ka̲'wakw territory and, therefore, at the heart of the potlatching controversy.

Two photographs (one of which is attributed to Halliday) in the Royal British Columbia Museum's (RBCM) Visual Archives illustrate how Halliday's display of the seized objects exemplified Nicholas Thomas's assertion that colonial authorities viewed colonized societies as "objects to be surveyed, regulated and sanitized."[50] In Halliday's photograph an unnamed man, identified as a "paid orator" from the Cranmer potlatch, poses in front of a white sheet in the parish hall (see Figure 2). He wears a crest-displaying carved headdress and a button blanket, both of which are normally worn on ceremonial occasions. He holds his coppers slightly away from his body

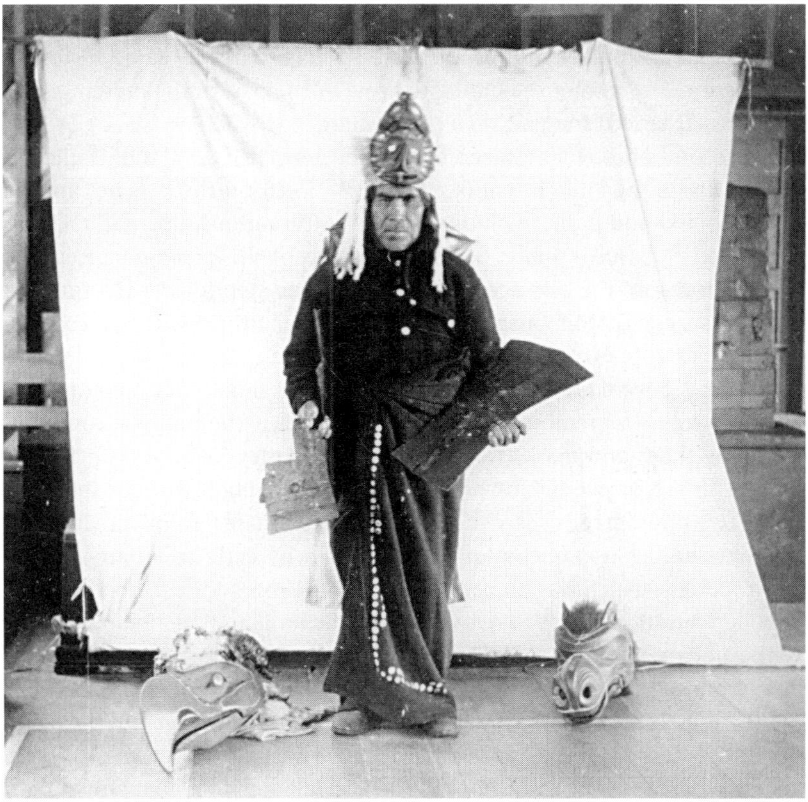

2 A participant of the Cranmer potlatch poses showing his ceremonial regalia.

to the front, so that the camera audience can see them, and two masks lie by his feet. The mask on his right is a thunderbird headdress, and the one on his left is a wolf (both are worn in the Winter Ceremonials).[51] Perhaps intended as a record of the last time such regalia was actually worn, this representation is strikingly eloquent. Although this man is dressed in symbols of the myth-time origins of his *numaym* (symbols that served to perpetuate ancestral powers), the absence of the enacting songs, lineage myths, ritualized dance and gesture – indeed, the very anonymity of the individual photographed – displaces and disempowers both the objects and the human histories to which they refer. While the photograph is silent concerning Aboriginal views of the potlatch, its practices, and its paraphernalia, it speaks volumes about Euro-Canadian intentions to recontextualize potlatch objects within a Euro-Canadian environment, presenting them as touristic/anthropological representations of the past. The silence of Aboriginal views is significant in the context within which the photograph was taken and the regalia seized. The photograph represents an intermediary step during which the meaning of the paraphernalia was reconfigured, transformed from sacred tool for the reaffirmation of a cosmic and social structure into the signifier of a past now beyond retrieval. While both Kwakwa̱ka̱'wakw and Euro-Canadian understandings of these objects share the same historical time period, the former celebrated the role of the past *in* the present while the latter distanced the past *from* the present.

The second photograph, taken by the Reverend V.S. Lord, is of Halliday's display inside the church hall (see Figure 3). Piled on the benches are the various masks and props, including masks of the various supernatural birds of the sky: *Hux̱whukw* and crooked beak masks of the *hamatsa* dances.[52] In this photograph, the displacement is carried one step further than it is in Halliday's "paid orator" image. With the absence of the owners, all connection to contemporary life is erased. In this sterile space the masks lie as if decapitated. Severed from the enlivening body of ritual, they are now only trophy heads – a premonition of their new life in the national museum. "Dancing robes and masks without dancers," writes Ki-ke-in (Ron Hamilton) in his recent poem "Box of Darkness," are "symbols without spirits."[53]

The two photographs share the same "indeterminate terrain"[54] that Annie Coombes argues was uncomfortably occupied by early twentieth-century anthropology, which was "at pains to justify its existence on a broadly based popular educational level, a rigorous scientific level and on a practical level as the helpmate of the state."[55] Since colonized societies and the objects they produced were necessarily destroyed by the process of colonization, it was the duty of those at the forefront of modernity's intrusion into the societies of the "less advanced" to vigorously record what colonialism displaced. The photographs lent scientific support to Halliday's actions, providing a visual record of the objects he seized. While the objects themselves were

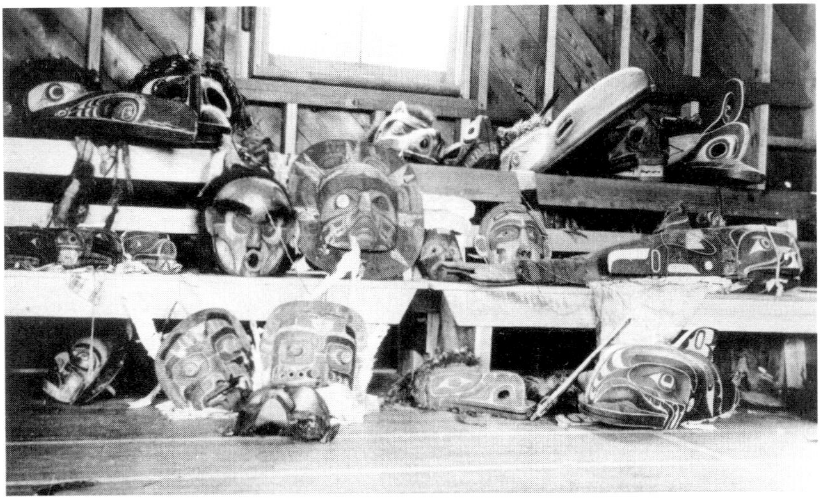

3 Potlatch paraphernalia exchanged for suspended sentences on display in the church hall, Alert Bay, 1922.

trophies that were partly symbolic of the success of Halliday's anti-potlatch campaign, their new metaphorical significance lay in allusions to the displacement of Aboriginal traditions by Western modernity and in modern science's "altruistic" preservation of them, first in the form of photographs and then later in the form of their physical storage on museum shelves.

Halliday had been instructed by his superiors to ship all the material to the national museum in Ottawa; however, before finishing crating, he sold thirty-five pieces for $291 to the American collector George Heye, founder of New York's Museum of the American Indian.[56] It is curious that Heye, who was from New York, would have been in Alert Bay at such a fortuitous moment. It is possible that he was given inside knowledge by someone in British Columbia. Halliday received a reprimand for this, especially as he sold the material to an *American* collector. "The Department is at a loss to understand your action in disposing of them without authority, more especially in view of the fact that they are to be taken to the United States, when they should have remained in a Canadian museum," wrote J.D. McLean, Scott's assistant, to Halliday in September 1922. "Your explanation as to obtaining a good value for them is not considered sufficient to justify this unwarranted action. I presume, however, that the articles are now beyond recall, but on no consideration are you to dispose of any of the rest."[57]

The remaining seventeen cases, not including the coppers (see Figure 4), were appraised in Ottawa by museum anthropologist Edward Sapir at $1,456. Many anthropologists, including Harlan I. Smith and Edward Sapir of the National Museum of Canada, Franz Boas of the American Museum

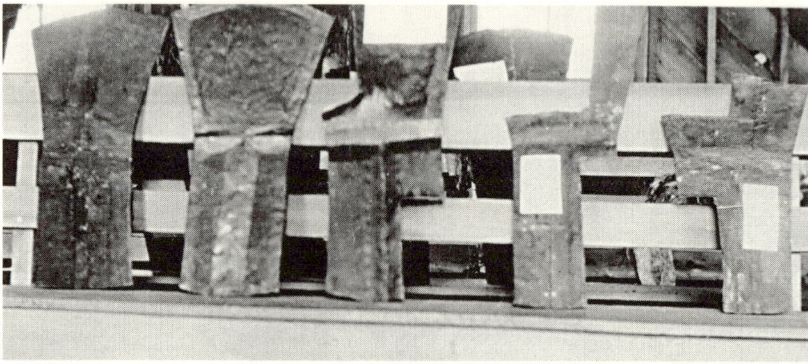

4 Kwakwaka'wakw coppers on display in the church hall, Alert Bay, 1922.

of Natural History, C.F. Newcombe of the British Columbia Provincial Museum (BCPM) in Victoria, and John Swanton of the Smithsonian Institution, were outspoken in their opposition to the potlatch ban, arguing against the economic and moral implications of such legislation.[58] However, part of Sapir's job was to appraise the objects and then to receive them for storage and display at the museum in Ottawa. Caught in Coombes's "indeterminate terrain," Sapir and the others found themselves in the "ambivalent position [of being] simultaneously critic and advocate of government policies."[59]

Sapir's valuation was deemed entirely inadequate by the surrendering families, but no compensation at all was given for the coppers.[60] Sapir himself, perhaps aiming to depress the prices of the objects (which, given that his financial resources were more limited than were those of private collectors, seems quite possible) like Heye, said that he considered his own total "a very moderate figure from the standpoint of an ethnological museum."[61] And Halliday responded to Kwakwaka'wakw dissatisfaction by suggesting that any argument over value rested on differences in opinion and the market demand for older objects: "Some of the things for which good prices were paid, the ordinary individual would not consider worth anything at all, while some of the things were more or less new and though in many instances were much better looking, they only brought fair to low prices, as to those learned in the antiquities of the Indians they had little historic value."[62]

This contradictory mix of historical and financial valuation was not the result simply of a difference in opinion rooted in market conditions, but also of assimilation. Being based on assimilation, the implementation of the anti-potlatch sections of the Indian Act affected First Nations object production and display in a number of ways. First, state officials denied the valuation system of Kwakwaka'wakw society by refusing any appraisal based on potlatch economics or symbolism; rather, they provided their own appraiser in Sapir, who, as seems clear from Halliday's recollections, in turn valued the potlatch objects according to the criteria of the curio/museum commodity market. The seemingly contradictory roles that Euro-Canadian authorities played within this framework of valuation is further demonstrated by Halliday, who, on the one hand, enforced assimilationist state policy in his position as Indian Agent and, on the other, dealt seized objects on the commodity market.

Second, the Cramner prosecutions signalled the active participation of state officials in the reconfiguration of First Nations objects. While the national museum had been collecting such objects since its inception, nowhere are the political implications of this reconfiguration so clear or so active as in Halliday's exhibition. What Halliday explicitly demonstrated was that the conditions of display, particularly the motivation informing the display, controlled the acceptance or denial of the ideological value of the objects. Integral to the social systems of the Northwest Coast, these potlatch ceremonies controlled the display of the objects and generated the production and acceptance of social position validated by a cosmic order. By refusing this ceremonial context, the Canadian state denied the social positions the potlatch generated within First Nations communities. Halliday's display forcibly demonstrated the Euro-Canadian ability to appropriate First Nations possessions, whether masks, land, or labour. The fact that he could easily sell some of them emphasized that what was most at stake was control, and this implicitly negated any concept of land or resource ownership associated with the objects. Further, the physical movement of objects from First Nations to state hands, from British Columbia to Ottawa, was a potent symbol of the movement of First Nations peoples from autonomy to subjugation and dependence. In this movement, the objects went from being symbolic of the inheritance of both tangible and intangible property to being symbolic of the people and lands brought under Euro-Canadian control.

The reconfiguration of Aboriginal objects and the potlatch thus contributed to the creation of a new social position for First Nations people within Canada. Whether as art or as antiquity, First Nations objects retained commercial value. First Nations individuals could continue to produce these objects, but only as commodities. Of course, First Nations had produced objects for commodity exchange at least since European contact. As commodities, these objects propelled an active and beneficial (especially for the Euro-Canadian dealers) market. But the Halliday display asserted that the symbolic value that the potlatch invested in both the object and its owner was now vestigial. This worked to secure the status of First Nations as a new labour class and, in conjunction with the potlatch ban, to maintain Anglo-Celtic political hegemony by asserting a new law of the land. All this occurred at a time when non-British immigration was perceived as a threat to the interests of Canada's primarily British bourgeoisie.[63]

Both a poet and an administrator, Indian Affairs Deputy Superintendent Duncan Campbell Scott took a personal interest in First Nations objects. In 1922 Sapir forwarded a list of the objects seized and shipped to Ottawa directly to Scott, complete with indications of which objects were selected by the national museum. C.T. Currelly of the Royal Ontario Museum had contacted Scott prior to the objects' arrival, requesting examples for the "other large Museum of Canada,"[64] so it seems Halliday's charge of the objects having "little historic value" was not shared by Currelly, Sapir, or Scott. By January 1923 Sapir had further divided the newly indexed collection into three groups: the first for the national museum, the second for the Ontario museum, and the third containing "those that we suggest putting aside for your own use."[65] All the masks were valued and invoiced at a total of seventy-four dollars and sent to Scott at the end of February 1923,[66] whereupon they began their new life as trophies in his Department of Indian Affairs office.

Scott was careful in departmental correspondence and took pains to make sure that the material he requested personally was properly invoiced, and he certified "that the prices charged [were] fair and just, to meet the requirements of the Auditor-General's office."[67] A bird mask with four interchangeable mouth-pieces[68] owned by J. Kalokwami was added to Scott's request, and Scott had a voucher issued immediately. However, Cole points out that some Kwakwa̱ka̱'wakw do not remember receiving compensation. Henry Bell, for example, insisted that he packed six masks to Halliday's boat, although Cole suggests that only three were inventoried[69] and, in the list sent to Scott from Sapir (and now available through the Canadian Museum of Civilization archives), only two are recorded.[70] There seem to be a number of discrepancies associated with the inventory. At some points extras are included, while at others objects are identified as "not found." And there are yet other objects for which ownership is in doubt.

However, there appears to be no uncertainty concerning the coppers. Quite simply, no payment was ever made. In May 1923, Sapir asked Scott whether "the purchase of the Coppers is still pending ... or would you instruct me to consider them as already the property of the Victoria Memorial Museum?"[71] He went on to suggest assembling data on the coppers, presumably through interviews with their former owners, although it is hard to imagine why they would cooperate in such a matter. Sapir's ultimate goal was the publication of an associated bulletin. Scott hardly acknowledged this in his secretary's responding letter, ending the correspondence with the ambiguous comment that he "would be glad to discuss the matter ... personally"[72] with Sapir. In the end, Scott must have felt that adequate compensation had already been issued.

Scott's attitudes exemplify the ideology of social progress in 1920s Euro-Canadian society. The notions of a "fatal impact" and the disappearance of

First Nations societies in the evolution towards European modernism appeared simultaneously in both Euro-Canadian artistic expression and government strategy. The nostalgic tone of the myth of the "Vanishing American" in Scott's poetry contributed to DIA policy. Scott actively suppressed First Nations ceremonies while, in his poetry, implying that the people themselves were gone, their landscape now empty and ripe for development, their history now available to legitimate European presence.

Yet, although the concept of British social progress informed the discourses of Canadian art and law, its influence was unstable, and, given Canada's growing post-First World War independence from London, its acceptance was increasingly uncertain. There were growing contradictions in Euro-Canada's approach to First Nations peoples. Even Scott was clearly interested in First Nations societies and their modes of creative expression. As Stan Dragland writes in his literary history *Floating Voice*, a "difficult puzzle ... [is] how to reconcile Scott's attractive and apparently humane poems and stories about Indians ... with the dreadful legacy of his administration of Indian Affairs."[73] The short solution to Dragland's puzzle is that, upon further analysis, there is no contradiction. Scott was interested in First Nations societies only as part of the romanticized past, not as part of the contested present. His literary construction echoed his administrative policy by reinforcing the image of colonial displacement.

Scott's own ambivalence – his desire to study, celebrate, and simultaneously suffocate Aboriginal ways – mirror larger conflicts in the process of Canada's colonization and the projects of construction that supported it. Scott's activities affirm Thomas's argument that "colonizers have also frequently been divided by strategic interests and differing visions of the civilizing mission; ... frequently split ... between impulses to define new lands as vacant spaces for European achievement, and a will to define and collect and map the cultures which already possessed them; and in the definition of colonizers' identities, which had to reconcile the civility and values of home with the raw novelty of sites of settlement."[74]

Prosecutions for potlatching continued through the late 1920s. Other groups, notably the Nuu-chah-nulth of Vancouver Island and the Gitxsan of the upper Skeena River Valley, also saw convictions. Agent G.C. Mortimer charged Gitxsan potlatchers John Smith and Tom Campbell in 1931. Smith received a one-month suspended sentence while Campbell received three months (later suspended on the condition that he no longer participate in such events). Mortimer's reasoning for the harsher sentence for Campbell was that he was the "I.W.W. type,"[75] referring to the International Woodworkers Union, one of the labour unions that gained prominence with the rise of socialism in British Columbia immediately after the First World War and again during the Great Depression (a time when over 18,000 men in the province were housed in relief camps).[76]

The Cranmer potlatch has come to epitomize the enforcement of the potlatch ban. While Halliday and others proclaimed the passing of the potlatch with the Cranmer arrests, this was far from the truth. Upon his release, Mecha (Herbert Martin) gave a grease potlatch[77] at the oolichan fishery in Knight Inlet – "so that I may, as we use to do in ancient times, cleanse those that were put in prison with me"[78] – and then distributed almost 4,000 gallons of oolichan oil, from Blunden Harbour to Alert Bay to Newitti.[79]

There are numerous other stories about how many people on the Coast either adapted the potlatch after 1922 (e.g., splitting the giving and dancing portions of the celebrations in order to circumvent the restrictions of the Indian Act or simply holding smaller potlatches in hidden or more remote locations).[80] Drucker and Heizer stress that potlatching continued despite administrative pressures against it, and they attribute lulls in potlatch activities in the 1930s to economics (e.g., the Great Depression and the fishers strike of 1936).[81] The ban did not destroy the potlatch. The production of objects for the potlatch continued and even contributed to the creative development of three of the now best known Kwakwa̱ka̱'wakw artists of the 1930s and 1940s: Charlie James, Willie Seaweed, and Mungo Martin.[82] Because of the socio-political chasm consequent upon the enforcement of the Indian Act and its various amendments, the meanings pertaining to Northwest Coast objects constructed within museum contexts differed significantly from those constructed within potlatch contexts.

When First Nations ceremonies involved Euro-Canadian dignitaries, the threatening and supposedly regressive nature of the potlatch or any other First Nations event was dissipated, being replaced in public conception by a sense of quaint, colourful nostalgia. The potlatch and the objects used in it were not the issue; rather, government officials were more interested in assuming control over when these kinds of ceremonies could be held and what their intent would be. The harshest result of the ban was the attempted replacement of Northwest Coast social structure (and its methods for controlling and acknowledging social status and resource ownership) with British modes of authority; this, in turn, was part of a larger program aimed at expropriating and securing the continental land base for development and providing a pliant labour force. Convenient by-products of the potlatch ban were the increasing frequency with which First Nations people converted to Christianity and the intensifying commoditization of Northwest Coast ceremonial objects.

Of course, a vibrant market for First Nations objects already existed; and, indeed, their commodity value may have saved such objects from large-scale destruction. A number of people participated in the curio market while engaged in the enforcement of the potlatch ban. Halliday's sale of goods to Heye after the Lekwiltok, Mamalillikulla, and Nimpkish had turned over their paraphernalia is one example of this. Powell collected for the American Museum of Natural History[83] and Angermann turned up at a meeting of the Vancouver Art, Historical, and Scientific Association in 1926 (only four years after the Cranmer prosecutions) with $250 worth of Alert Bay objects for sale.[84] And for Scott, whose real passion, Titley suggests, was the arts – his position as deputy superintendent of Indian Affairs being "a mere source of income"[85] – the shipment of seized paraphernalia to Ottawa must have constituted an instance of passion coinciding with income.

3
Totem Poles in Stanley Park

Assimilation strategies and the removal of potlatch paraphernalia and totem poles to museums on the eastern side of the continent all seemed to confirm that the past uses for such objects had ceased. The objects could now be used in the construction of a local identity that was important to the promotion of tourism, immigration, and investment. By the 1920s, after four decades of collecting activities on the part of museums and curio shops, of tourist steamship lines running the Inside Passage from Olympia to Skagway, totem poles had become a pervasive, primitivist symbol closely associated with the region.[1] At the same time as Scott's intensified implementation of the potlatch ban and the national museum's involvement in the relocation of the seized Cranmer objects represented a heightened interest in the federal regulation of these objects, civic leaders throughout the Pacific Northwest recognized the utility of the totem pole with regard to advertising the success and identity of their new centres. And totem poles in a city setting suggested how life on the Coast had "progressed" from primitive village to urban modernity. With civic growth, more municipal agencies began to explore the possibilities of purchasing and re-erecting crest poles and houseposts.

Vancouver had rapidly ascended to the position of western Canada's commercial hub by the 1920s.[2] A construction boom, the expansion of commercial services, and an active social life all added to Vancouver's identity as the modern heart of the northwestern section of the continent (despite or through its rivalry with neighbouring Seattle). The first local, permanent totem poles outside either museum or Aboriginal contexts in Canada thus occurred in Vancouver, where the placement of "antique" Kwakwa̱ka̱'wakw totem poles in Stanley Park, across Coal Harbour from the Canadian Pacific Railways station and at the Burrard Narrows entrance to the harbour, constituted a highly visible modern/primitive juxtaposition near the heart of the city.

However, this project was additionally significant because of Squamish resistance to initial plans for a full, reconstructed Kwakwa̱ka̱'wakw village and their demands for the acknowledgment of a living Squamish presence in the park. It also contributed to the regulated federal control of totem poles and other Northwest Coast objects by provoking Ottawa's decision to designate totem poles a *Canadian* heritage resource and, thus, preventing other cities from following Vancouver's example.

Totem Poles in Stanley Park

Even before the erection of totem poles in Vancouver, Stanley Park had historical importance for local residents.[3] It was charted by Spanish explorers in the 1790s and was believed to be where George Vancouver met with local Squamish (Halkomelem Salishan-speaking) peoples.[4] It had been declared a government reserve in 1859 when war between Britain and the United States appeared imminent, and it was the site of five small logging operations from the 1860s to the 1880s. One of the earliest monuments in Stanley Park was an imitation classical temple made of cedar and fir – popularly known as Lumberman's Arch – that had been originally erected in

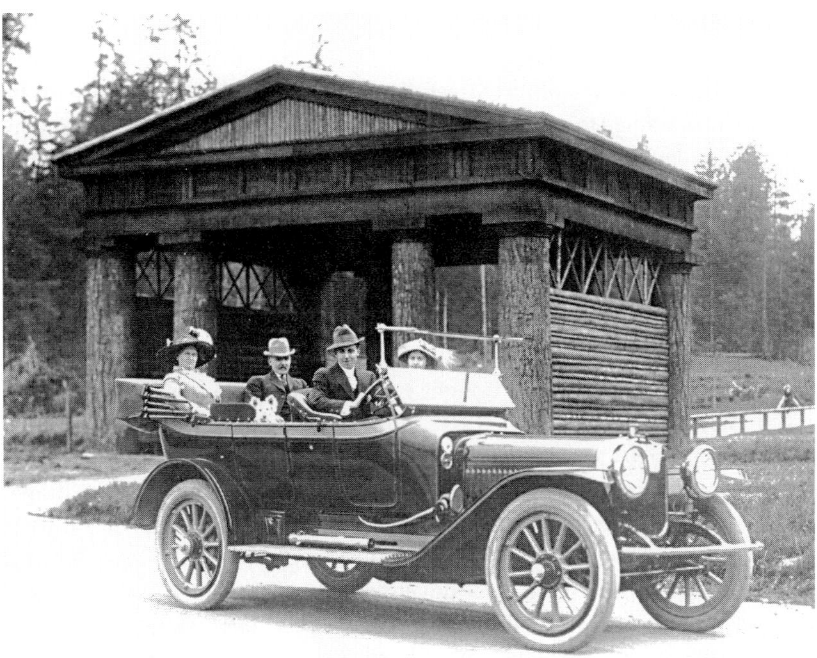

5 This is the original Lumberman's Arch, erected in Stanley Park. A second Lumberman's Arch replaced the dilapidated original and was relocated to Stanley Park in 1913.

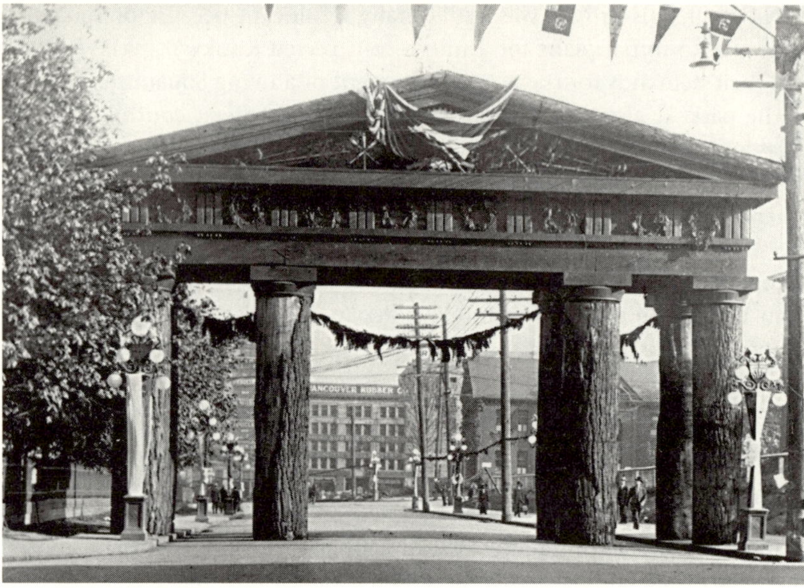

6 Lumberman's Arch in its original location at Pender and Hamilton streets, ca. 1912.

1912 at Pender and Hamilton Streets (see Figures 5 and 6) as a tribute to the visiting Duke and Duchess of Connaught and then moved the following year to Stanley Park.[5]

The new site for Lumberman's Arch was located on top of a large shell midden excavated around the turn of the century.[6] It had also been home to a historic Salish village known as XwayXway.[7] XwayXway's residents had been relocated during the smallpox epidemic (between 1888 and 1890), shortly after Stanley Park's official 1887 opening. Most of the houses, including a central lodge called "Tay Hay,"[8] were burned to the ground. The three surviving houses were bought for twenty-five dollars each and were razed in 1900.[9]

Prior to the relocation of Lumberman's Arch, Stanley Park had been left as a natural reserve. Grandiose plans for the park's development were drawn up in the two years preceding the First World War, although not all the city's residents agreed on the direction this development should follow (or even whether the city should develop the park at all). As Robert A.J. McDonald argues, the public debate that erupted over plans for the park was divided along class lines and played out in the realm of public "culture," where the "upper stratum sought to foster art, music, science, and intellectual discourse as a means to counter the city's 'busy commercialism.'"[10] The re-erection of Lumberman's Arch, a monument imitating classical form in local materials, resulted from the local support of the City

Beautiful movement, which advocated the taming of the park,[11] just prior to the First World War.

The focus for Vancouver's City Beautiful movement became Coal Harbour, which was close to the growing city centre and was plagued by a deteriorating bridge and foul-smelling tidal flats. In 1912 the Vancouver Board of Park Commissioners hired respected British park designer Thomas Mawson to propose improvements. Although ultimately hampered by compromises between disagreeing civic groups, Mawson's plan, with its proposed changes to Stanley Park,[12] nonetheless put Coal Harbour and the surrounding periphery at the centre of the city's attention and led to the creation of playing fields and the erection of a number of monuments. The movement continued in spirit after the First World War, when the Art, Historical, and Scientific Association of Vancouver (AHSAV), a group described by MacDonald as "more British than the business community as a whole,"[13] proposed the erection of more "historic" monuments in Stanley Park on the peninsula at the north side of Coal Harbour.

With its membership interested in the creative expression of both British Columbia's past and present, AHSAV maintained a social Darwinist understanding of Vancouver's culture. When the organization was founded in 1894, for example, the distinction between art (as something European) and antiquity (as something "Indian") was clear. Its constitution proposed that its primary objectives were:

> To form a collection of paintings and works of art as a nucleus of an Art Gallery;
> To hold from time to time a Loan Exhibition of paintings and works of art;
> To form a Museum of Antiquities, especially of the remains of Indian life in British Columbia and America.[14]

Through the organization's incorporation under the Benevolent Societies Act, 1901, and its absorption into the city's political system as a quasi-municipal institution in 1903, the separation between past and present, between "Indian" and "modern," was enshrined.

In 1921, without thought to any possible conflicts with contemporary First Nations peoples, the AHSAV proposed to obtain and re-erect "an original Indian village and Hudson Bay [sic] Trading Post in Stanley Park."[15] A committee was appointed to sort out any funding problems and to arrange ways and means with various connected public bodies and the Hudson's Bay Company. Funding was, of course, a major focus for the committee, but the association enthusiastically instigated the planning procedures, being confident that "the scheme, if successfully carried out, would be a great attraction to Stanley Park and of great educational value in illustrating Indian and other early life."[16]

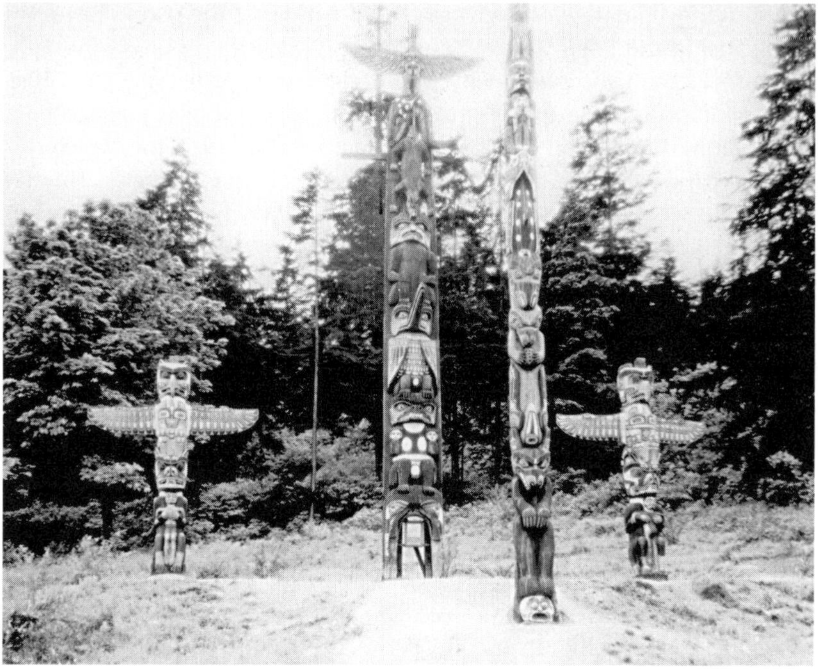

7 Kwakwaka'wakw poles and houseposts erected opposite Lumberman's Arch, Stanley Park, ca. 1923.

By January 1923 two free-standing poles and two houseposts (see Figure 7), purchased by Mrs. Schooley (an association member) for $764, arrived in Vancouver.[17] The two houseposts were carved by Charlie James (Yakutlas)[18] (see Figure 8) and originally belonged to Tsaweenok of Kingcome Inlet, where they served as interior supports for a house cross-beam.[19] Both houseposts depict a thunderbird with outstretched wings supported by a grizzly bear of equal size holding a smaller male figure. Furthermore, along with a replica of the Wakius pole, Edward Curtis used these houseposts as set props in his 1914 film *In the Land of the Headhunters*.[20]

One of the two free-standing poles was also carved by James and belonged to Kingcome Inlet chief Sisaxo'las (also spelled "Sisa-kaulas") (see Figure 9), although Nuytten reports that it originally stood in front of a large communal house in Alert Bay.[21] The pole relates to the story of Se-wid[22] and contains six figures. From top to bottom these are: Qolus, "with her folded wings, ... the sister of Thunderbird";[23] Chief Tla-Wunum-Qolus, an ancestral figure; Killer Whale; Sea-Otter "shown eating a sea egg,"[24] or sea urchin,[25] which Gunn writes "was the symbol of fertility and ... usually represented at nuptial ceremonies";[26] Sea Bear; and a human head, "the open mouth representing a rival who had spoken against Sisaxo'las – and who had been 'pushed down' – to the bottom of the pole."[27]

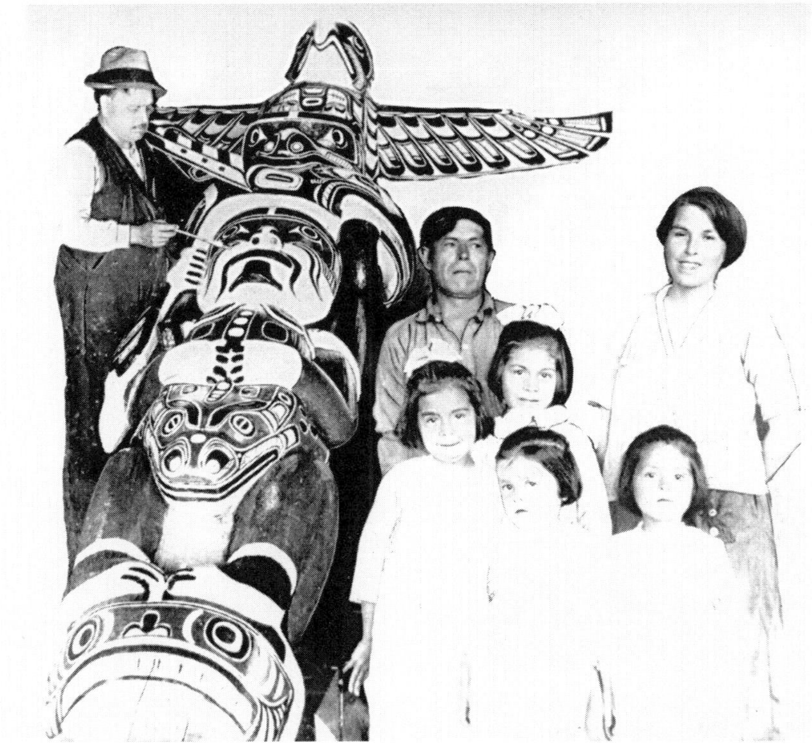

8 Charlie James and family, ca. 1936.

The second free-standing pole (see Figure 10) belonged to Wakius (variously spelled "Wakyas," "Wakiash," and "Wakias"), was carved by Yurhwayu, and was raised as the central frontal pole of a communal house in Alert Bay in 1899 after a potlatch distribution of 350 blankets. It was the first fully carved large pole erected in Alert Bay[28] and was immortalized in several paintings by Emily Carr. From top to bottom, the seven figures are: Thunderbird; Killer Whale; Wolf; an ancestral figure called Nan-wa-kawie (The Wise One);[29] Huk-Huk, or Hoh-Hox;[30] Grizzly Bear; and Raven. Raven originally had an enormous beak that served as the entrance to the Wakius house. The pole had been fitted to the facade of the original house in Alert Bay. Giant wings and a tail were also painted on the house front itself, connecting the pole to the house in an integrated composition that combined both two- and three-dimensional form.[31]

In Stanley Park, AHSAV temporarily erected the poles near Lumberman's Arch so "that visitors and tourists may have the opportunity of inspecting them."[32] In their original context the poles – like names, stories, and other crests – related to the hierarchical standing of individuals within the *numayms*. They were indicative of socio-economic rank as determined by

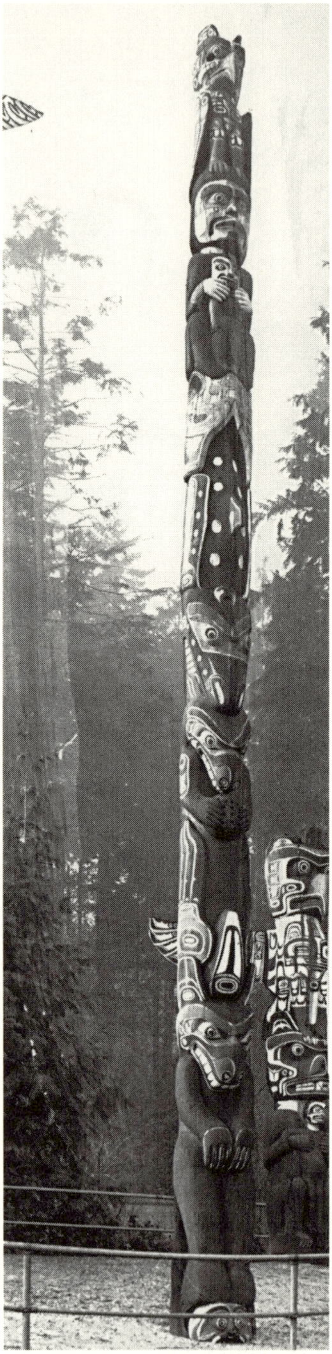

9 Sisaxo'las pole, Stanley Park, ca. 1925.

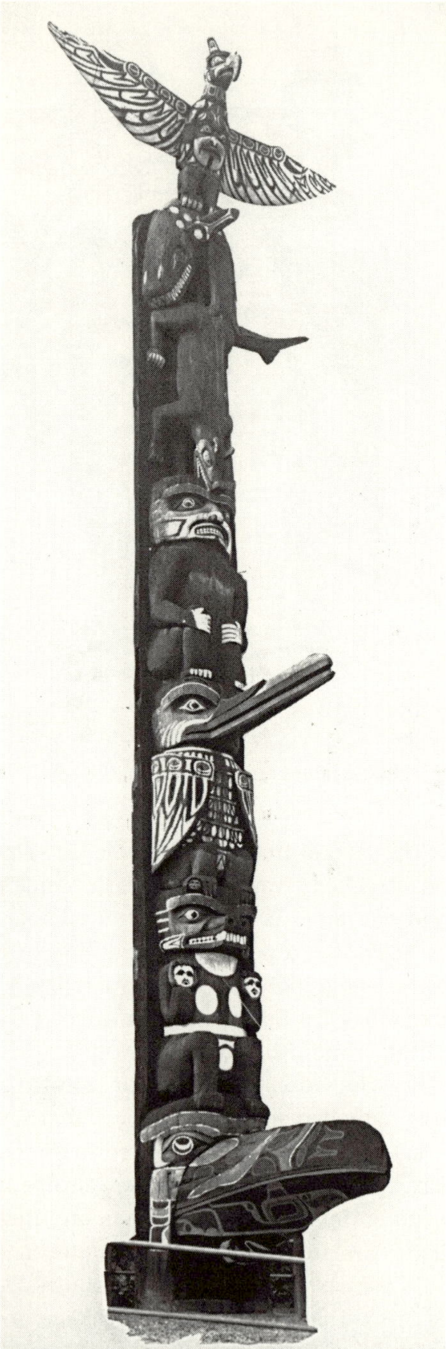

10 Wakius pole, Stanley Park, ca. 1925.

the inheritance of rights to ceremonial prerogatives and as negotiated through the potlatch system. This is clearly demonstrated by the inclusion of a potlatch rival in the Sisax̱o'las pole. Boas wrote that house frontal poles were chiefly prerogatives that included carvings of figures relating to ancestral legends,[33] as exemplified by the Nan-wa-kawie figure on the Wakius pole. He further reported that a "totem pole with various carvings is described only once and this description was called forth by a totem pole standing in front of the house in which the tale was told."[34] It was in this way that the owner of the pole and the crests it represented legitimized his/her right to display them as his/her property. The poles and houseposts purchased for Stanley Park also included crests – such as thunderbird, Qolus, and Huk-Huk, or *Hux̱whukw* – associated with the Winter Ceremonials. Boas states that these particular carvings were "a substitute for carved house dishes."[35]

Even when they were moved within the Kwakwa̱ka̱'wakw communities (e.g., from Kingcome Inlet to the cannery town of Alert Bay), the poles and houseposts were still associated with a specific kin group through their attachment to the house structure of a ranking member of a particular *numaym* (see Figure 11). As references to lineage histories, they also asserted the place of origin of these individuals and *numayms* (perhaps even the relationship between *numayms,* given the possibility of marriage references in the Sisax̱o'las pole and the inclusion of crests associated with the Winter Ceremonials – crests that were frequently transferred from father-in-law to son-in-law as part of the marriage ceremonies). All this created some sense of order in the movement from peripheral, outlying villages to the centre of a new economic order at Alert Bay.[36]

The relocation of the poles to Stanley Park thus separated them from specific locational references that related to their role as indicators of rank. Within the European understanding of First Nations objects as something unique deriving from the past, the construction of meaning that occurred when the poles were moved to Stanley Park obscured the historic lineage meanings that would still have been apparent to most Kwakwa̱ka̱'wakw residents of Alert Bay.

Although touristic in intention, the relocation of the poles was based on the same ideological understanding of Northwest Coast societies (i.e., as part of the past) that was evident in much of the anthropological writing of the time. The conflation of different societies and linguistic groups into one "totem pole culture" is exemplified by the crest poles of the "distant Kwakiutl" being placed in Stanley Park and thus contributing to the erasure of physical reminders of the local Salish (who did not conventionally raise free-standing poles)[37] and their claims to the park and other parts of the city. This temporal and spatial conflation of distance, which is akin to anthropologist Renato Rosaldo's imperialist nostalgia, where the "innocent

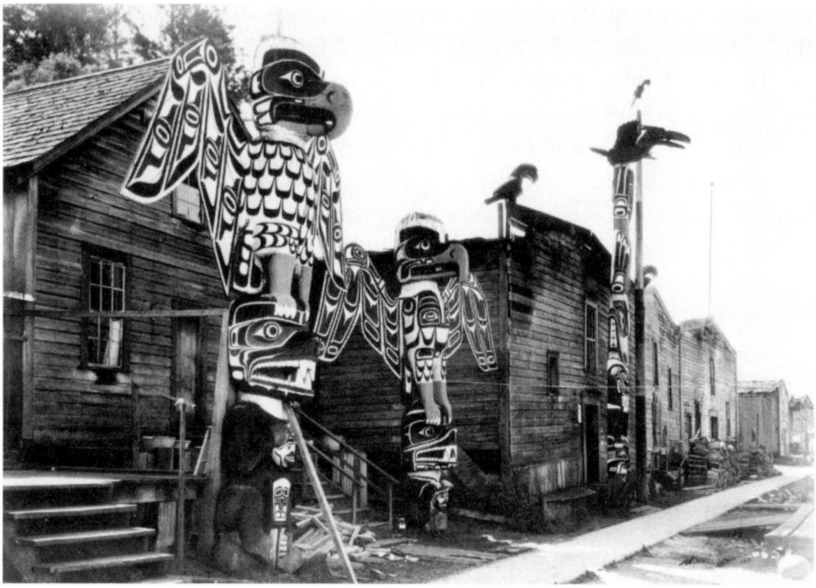

11 View of the boardwalk in Alert Bay with houses facing the beach front, ca. 1925.

[colonial] yearning"[38] for an unaltered colonized society conceals the colonizer's "complicity with often brutal domination"[39] (like the razing of XwayXway), provides the groundwork for a pacific, artificial history in which the "Indian" becomes a unique, geographic trope.

Less history than geographic symbol, the poles now became the tangible manifestations of an imagined past in Vancouver's unified social memory – a past that legitimized AHSAV and established a powerful colonial metaphor for the "modernization" of British Columbia. AHSAV's original intention to place the poles in a village next to a reconstructed Hudson's Bay Company post indicates an interest in inserting a First Nations presence within a tableau of Western historicity. The juxtaposition of the crest posts with the classical "civilized" style of Lumberman's Arch, and with downtown Vancouver just across the bay, accomplished this.

There were likely a number of reasons for the Kwakwa̲ka̲'wakw to sell the poles, depending on the individuals and families involved. At that time it was easy to suggest, given the government suppression of the potlatch, that these sorts of objects no longer served a purpose within Kwakwa̲ka̲'wakw society, that their redundancy rendered them available for sale. However, although pressures related to Canadian colonialism (e.g., Christianization) contributed to the sale of objects, as we have seen, throughout the mid-twentieth century potlatching continued, often in private rather than public contexts.[40] Consequently, within certain First Nations circles, potlatch-related objects retained symbolic currency. It is possible that certain individuals even re-channeled money from the sale of the poles and other objects back into the potlatches or, given some of the economic strains of the 1920s, into more pressing concerns, like boat purchases or simply getting a family through a financially difficult winter.[41]

Furthermore, as Boas indicates, the recitation of the associated story was only presented once and within a controlled context.[42] The material manifestation of the prerogative can then be seen as secondary to the inherited *right* to the prerogative and its validation through a potlatch, although such objects were indeed vital to acts of social reproduction, fixing relations of inheritance and hierarchy in material form. Codere reports that the "Kwakiutl are also alleged to have ... gone on paying for or trafficking in the coppers deposited in the ethnological collections of the museums of North America."[43] Bill Holm, discussing Willie Seaweed's sale of masks to Charles Newcombe and the BCPM in 1914, argues that

> selling masks, which represent noble prerogatives, to outsiders might seem to be a strange act for a conservative chief steeped in the traditions of his people. Yet it seems never to have been really troublesome for the Kwakwa̱ka̱'wakw. A fine mask was and is prized, especially if it is an heirloom, but it is the right to display it, derived from ancient tradition, that is jealously guarded. Outsiders will not claim that privilege, and new masks can be made.[44]

For some individuals the location of objects was not as important as was the right to the associated titles. In addition, prestige may well have been associated with enshrining a family monument in an urban, non-Kwakwa̱ka̱'wakw setting and, thereby, extending the awareness of individual and lineage accomplishments to those outside the Kwakwa̱ka̱'wakw communities. Continuing to celebrate and validate crests within the underground Kwakwa̱ka̱'wakw potlatches after 1922, some individuals may have seen the sale of a pole as a chance to simultaneously achieve economic gain and to assert the importance of the history of their particular *numaym*. This is another example of the contestation and negotiation of meaning surrounding Northwest Coast objects in the twentieth century.

The re-erection of the poles also resulted in a certain amount of prestige for AHSAV. The display favoured by the association was facilitated by the province's vast store of natural resources and its increasing economic power. There was no need to commission model replicas, as Boas and Swanton had done for the American Museum of Natural History in New York. Instead, AHSAV proposed to buy or simply to reconstruct an entire village within the vast park land of Stanley Park. And while Aldona Jonaitis suggests that, in New York, the target audiences for the hegemonic intentions of the

American Museum of Natural History were specifically non-Anglo-Saxon immigrants,[45] the AHSAV sought to construct its life-size tableau in a place frequented by Vancouver's entire population and visible to anyone entering or leaving the city's main port. The poles of Stanley Park, erected by a sub-association of the municipality, were to become part of Vancouver's physical profile, as millions of visitors to Vancouver can now attest.

Negotiations between AHSAV and the Squamish Band

The AHSAV executive's minutes clearly indicate the importance of obtaining unaltered structures. The original intention was to simply manufacture a facsimile village.[46] However, this was soon followed by the discussion of a more ambitious plan involving the purchase of the village of Alert Bay in January 1924 (only two years earlier the site of the Cranmer potlatch prosecutions) as at least one of the directors questioned the authenticity of the poles already purchased and argued that the facsimile "village as proposed ... would be of no real value."[47] This plan was never realized. "It requires little effort of the imagination to satisfy the mind that no single, pure example could now be found standing, and in a fit condition to be removed and re-erected,"[48] wrote the Reverend John Goodfellow of AHSAV's attempts to remove the entire cannery town to Stanley Park in 1925.

The plan to erect a "totem pole" village using the notorious Kwakwa̱ka̱'wakw, whose public reputation as being symbolic of the whole coast had been bolstered by Boas's studies, the Curtis film, and the Cranmer potlatch, was sunk in 1925 by the Squamish people. Andrew Paull, translator for the McKenna-McBride Commission in the Salish territories, current secretary of the Allied Indian Tribes of British Columbia, and future president of the North American Indian Brotherhood,[49] called a meeting with Department of Indian Affairs agent C.C. Perry and members of the AHSAV Indian village committee.[50] After the rise of the pan-Indian political organizations, non-Aboriginal committees had to negotiate with and accommodate them. According to minutes of the meeting, Paull cited Squamish objections, stating that the proposed spot was where Chief Capilano had welcomed Captain Vancouver and that, therefore, it was significant to the history of the Squamish people: "It was here that the Squamish kept their best fighting men, Medicine men and the place where all the Tribal Dance masks were made; in fact, it was far the most important of all their village sites."[51] It was Squamish land, and the Squamish did not want a Kwakwa̱ka̱'wakw village. They had no objections to a mixed village or to unattached poles, but they wanted the living Squamish to be recognized.[52] It also seems that the Squamish leaked news of the meeting to the local media, with the result that AHSAV funding drive dried up. The four poles already purchased were erected and then turned over to the care of the city's parks board.[53]

While AHSAV members bickered among themselves over the "authenticity" of their purchases and proposals, the reference to a historical Squamish presence had more immediate implications. Through the 1920s there was a problem with squatters in Stanley Park, especially on Deadman's Island on the south side of Brockton Point, in Coal Harbour itself. At the same time, one resident, known popularly as "Aunt Sally," still remained at the old XwayXway village site on the opposite side of the point, facing out towards Burrard Narrows. When the parks board request for a lease to Deadman's Island was approved in January 1929, the park authorities sought eviction notices to clean the park of its "unwanted" residents. Aunt Sally was the only Stanley Park resident able to establish a legal right to live in the park as she was able to prove she had lived at XwayXway for more than sixteen years. Her property was subsequently purchased on behalf of the Parks Board by philanthropist W.C. Shelley for $15,500.[54]

In the end, the village idea was never realized, although the Vancouver Parks Board has since bought, commissioned, and erected a number of other free-standing poles, moving them all south to Brockton Point in 1963.[55] Ironically, given the construction of First Nations societies in the Stanley Park project as something of the past, Aunt Sally legally claimed the right to live near Lumberman's Arch and the newly erected poles. In addition, the two houseposts and one of the free-standing poles were carved by famed Kwakwa̲ka̲'wakw carver Charlie James, who died eleven years *after* their erection in Stanley Park. AHSAV members, who wanted "to make the model Indian Village as much as possible like the original habitations of the Indians in very early days,"[56] had erected poles carved by a *living, contemporary* carver. The AHSAV project contributed to the creation of a modernist paradox; that is, that "a culture" can "appear to have disappeared while its members continue to exist"[57] – a paradox that, due to its conceptual instability, was destined to implode.

4
Northwest Coast Art as National Heritage: Two Federal Projects of the Late 1920s

Euro-Canadians were beginning to realize that the nation indeed possessed a "resource as important to ... Coastal British Columbia as the pyramids are to Egypt or the ruins of ancient Rome to modern Italy."[1] That this admission also came from the United States was an important, if problematic, point. While it was good that Americans and, especially, American tourists might be interested in this aspect of culture in the North, the depletion of a *Canadian* heritage resource had been a concern to some in British Columbia's small intellectual community at least since the beginning of the twentieth century. Douglas Cole quotes archaeologist Charles Hill-Tout, who, in 1901, "counted himself as 'one of those who never cease to regret' at the passing of so many treasures to the United States and felt it 'a serious reflection upon the Province' that anyone wishing to study the region's aborigines 'must go to New York to do it.'"[2]

By the standards of Hill-Tout and his concerned colleagues in British Columbia, Ottawa's participation in museum collecting in the province must have seemed tardy. The national museum was not established until 1910, although collecting for it had begun earlier. However, after the First World War Ottawa's interest in the Northwest Coast heightened. The removal of the Cranmer potlatch paraphernalia to Ottawa bolstered the national museum's collection significantly, and the museum's presence in British Columbia increased dramatically from 1924 to the beginning of the Great Depression in 1929. Two of the most important projects from this period – the in situ preservation of totem poles along the new Canadian National Railways (CNR) line in the Skeena Valley and an exhibition of traditional Northwest Coast objects alongside the modernist paintings of Emily Carr, A.Y. Jackson, and a number of other well-known American and Canadian contemporary artists – are the focus of this chapter. In promoting Northwest Coast objects not only as antiquity, but also as art and heritage, Marius Barbeau played an important role in both national museum projects. Continuing the construction of Northwest Coast objects as part of the past, these projects furthered the federal government's interests by promoting tourism in the west. After the Cranmer potlatch and the removal of poles to Stanley Park, the projects also reaffirmed government control over the objects' location and meaning.

A comparison of these projects illustrates how the national museum sought to balance its roles as scientific-educational resource and helpmate of the state. In addition to promoting Canadian business interests through touristic representations, the construction of First Nations objects as art lent a sense of prestige to the museum's collection and, therefore, to its activities. While both railway and gallery projects supported similar ideological constructions of First Nations objects within an evolutionary narrative, and while both projects were smaller, linked components of a broader-based strategy to encourage industrial development, the *Exhibition of Canadian West Coast Art, Native and Modern* (hereinafter referred to as the *West Coast* exhibition), was instrumental in bolstering the public perception of the national museum, its specialist staff, and its programs by philosophically legitimizing the objects contained within its spaces.

Totem Pole Preservation Project

While, prior to 1910, Canadian museums had done some piecemeal collecting, by 1909 British Columbia's provincial museum was able to hire C.F. Newcombe to reorganize its ethnological collection and to publish his *Guide to the Anthropological Collection of the Provincial Museum*. Government revenues more than doubled between 1909 and 1911.[3] In 1911 the museum provided Newcombe with a $3,000 collecting budget.[4] Although Newcombe paid specific attention to acquiring monumental poles for Victoria, this local collecting effort was short-lived, collapsing, along with the provincial economy, in 1913.[5]

Around the same time, Ottawa's role in assembling museum collections from British Columbia also took a significant turn. In 1910 the Victoria Memorial Museum, which would later become the National Museum of Canada, opened in the nation's capital. One of Boas's doctoral students from Columbia University, Edward Sapir, was hired as the first chief of the museum's anthropological division. Sapir pursued a strong collecting policy, and, in moves that would directly contribute to the strengthening of the museum's focus on British Columbia (especially after the First World War), he hired Harlan Smith, Marius Barbeau, and Diamond Jenness.

Cole calls Barbeau "the most aggressive collector" of the three. Born in 1883, Barbeau grew up in rural Quebec and enjoyed a privileged education, studying law at Laval University and then, under a Rhodes scholarship, anthropology at Oxford. Even while out on national museum-funded fieldwork, Barbeau collected privately for such competitor institutions as the American Museum of Natural History, the Heye-owned Museum of the

American Indian in New York, and the Royal Ontario Museum.[6] He also wrote about the use of First Nations subjects and other nationalistic "folk" motifs as the basis for a modern, patriotic Canadian art[7] – an idea that paralleled John Gibbon's later idea of a mosaic as being the appropriate post-assimilationist model for modern Canada.[8] In 1927, the same year as the *West Coast* exhibition, Barbeau helped organize a festival of French-Canadian folksongs and dances at the Château Frontenac in Quebec City. Intensely proud of his accomplishments, Barbeau later wrote: "I say that I had a happy career ... because I succeeded in what I thought I should do, and I had the best judgment ... because I was a specialist in those subjects."[9]

The emergence of institutions of "culture" at both provincial and federal levels, and their shared interest in assembling collections specifically from the Northwest Coast, stimulated a competition over whether these objects were matters of provincial or federal patrimony. In the 1920s the federal government dominated this informal competition as it sought not only to consolidate its authority in western Canada, but also to assemble a distinctive national identity for both domestic and international consumption.

While the First World War interrupted American and Canadian collecting efforts alike, the interest in Northwest Coast objects as examples of *Canadian* heritage intensified after 1918. During this period the objects were tied to the growing issues of Canadian political and cultural independence. The federal government demanded the international community's acknowledgment of Canadian nationhood, and it used the 1919 Treaty of Versailles and the creation of the League of Nations to assert a foreign policy independent from Britain's.[10] National identity was still in flux during the 1920s, with many unsure how Canada could simultaneously maintain its imperial connections and forge its own national path.

This uncertainty was exemplified in Anglo-Canada's response to First Nations societies and their objects. On the one hand, government policy in the 1920s ruthlessly stressed Anglo-conformity, not only for First Nations peoples, but also for the 800,000 non-Anglo-Saxon immigrants[11] who had come through Minister of the Interior Clifford Sifton's 1896 "open door."[12] In 1928 British Columbia premier Simon Fraser Tolmie announced: "We want British Columbia British and nothing else."[13] On the other hand, Northwest Coast objects had already proven to be attractive Canadian symbols – symbols in which American and European museums had expressed an interest and over which officials of the various levels of Canadian government therefore felt obliged to exert control.

Rumours of the purchase and export of five Kwakwa̲ka̲'wakw poles in 1924 seem to have galvanized the resolve of the federal authorities. Further investigation led to the realization that these poles were to remain in Canada. Two of them had been promised to the Vancouver parks commissioner and were destined for Stanley Park.[14] Rebellious potlatchers and avaricious foreign museums were thus not the only threats to Ottawa's control over objects and their meanings.

Charles Stewart, commissioner of the Department of the Interior, in a response to Sir Arthur Conan Doyle's plea for the poles' preservation, equated the efforts of the Art, Historical, and Scientific Association of Vancouver with those of foreign museums and announced the federal government's novel solution:

> It is true that prohibiting their export destroys the Indians' best market and so helps protect the poles, but a number have lately been sold within Canada and placed in public or private parks where they present a more or less incongruous appearance. We have come to the conclusion that the best method will be to try and re-awaken the interest and pride of the Indians in the remains of their former art and to enlist their cooperation in preserving the poles where they are.[15]

However, while members of the federal government professed a desire to preserve the poles and to reawaken an "interest and pride" in a "former art," their reasons were "utilitarian and pragmatic."[16] As art historian Ann Morrison argues, in this wide-ranging federal project, "native artistic production was ... 'redeemed' as part of Canadian art history, and ... seen as an available source for decorative design motifs that could be used for the production of manufactured and industrial products, made entirely in Canada."[17] While Morrison specifically connects the national gallery's 1927 *West Coast* exhibition to the use of Northwest Coast objects as a source for commercial designs, this connection is even more far-reaching. It can be seen to include other federal projects, like the preservation scheme in the Skeena Valley and Harlan Smith's accompanying film, *The Tsimshian Indians of the Skeena River of British Columbia*, as well as the printing of a 1925 stamp bearing the image of a totem pole. All of these projects were intended to promote tourism along the CNR line, which led through the Skeena Valley to its western terminus in Prince Rupert, which was also the northernmost major Canadian port and, not coincidentally, a stop on the steamship line from Olympia, Washington, to Skagway, Alaska.

The preservation project began in the fall of 1924 with ethnologist Barbeau being sent to survey poles in Kispiox, Hazelton, Hagwelget, Kitsegukla, and Kitwanga. He was sent by a committee that included Duncan Campbell Scott, deputy superintendent of Indian Affairs; Charles Camsell, deputy minister of mines; J.B. Harkin, commissioner of Canadian national parks; Barbeau's senior at the museum, Edward Sapir; and Barbeau himself. The museum's Harlan I. Smith was sent to the Skeena Valley the following year to supervise the preservation of poles, beginning in Kitwanga. All the costs were paid by the DIA, and the CNR provided materials and a special engineer,

T.B. Campbell[18] ("Totem Pole" Campbell as he was later referred to by the Victoria newspaper known as the *Daily Colonist*).[19]

Of course, the CNR had a vested interest in the project, given that its passenger line ran adjacent to the villages and poles in question. The Skeena line and its Pacific terminus, Prince Rupert, were originally built in 1913 by the British-owned Grand Trunk Pacific Railway. It went into receivership at the end of the First World War and was taken over by the federal government in the autumn of 1919.[20] The federal government's ability to shape the patterns of tourism and development was an important motivation for the program. The *Montreal Gazette* called Kitwanga "the showplace of northern British Columbia and, next to Niagara Falls, the most photographed spot in Canada."[21] Cole quotes Smith's assertions that "steps should be taken to save *in situ* or guard until that can be done totem poles at Kitwanga, the best on the C.N. line route or they will go as did those at Alert Bay, the best on the steamship lines."[22]

The federal government was under considerable pressure to turn the now publicly owned company into a profitable enterprise, and tourism was one component of its plan to do so.[23] The federal government saw the poles as an important tourist attraction and, therefore, as essential to the development of the transportation infrastructure that connected northern British Columbia overland to Edmonton and the east, and along the coast to Vancouver and the mainland United States in the south. Purchases of poles, such as AHSAV's from Alert Bay (for Stanley Park) and the 1923 sale of a Gitxsan pole to New York's American Museum of Natural History,[24] directly threatened the financial viability of the plan by relocating the attractions away from the steamship and train lines and thus funnelling tourists away from the new regional development in the northwest.

It was also important, in this development scheme, to secure government authority over land distribution and the utilization of natural resources. The potlatch ban served this objective in that it attempted to erase Aboriginal modes of authority and resource control. The reconfiguration of the poles as touristic reminders of a "primitive" past also increased the commodity status of ceremonial objects. As touristic signposts, the poles were no longer territorial markers or indicators of leadership status. In this sense, then, the federal display projects of the 1920s furthered the intentions of the Cranmer potlatch prosecutions and Halliday's post-trial exhibit.

The priority given projects whose purpose was to secure monuments (i.e., the poles) for tourist consumption rather than to encourage the production of objects as a source of local employment indicates how much Scott and the others in Ottawa wanted to construct Northwest Coast objects as something of the past rather than the present, as items of leisure rather than of commerce. Nonetheless, as early as 1925 Smith suggested activities aimed at promoting the contemporary production and marketing of local Aboriginal "art" during his fieldwork in Kitwanga. Barbeau had proposed the formation of a national totem pole park in the Skeena Valley. It would be called the Indian National Park of Temlaham and would coincide with the 1928 publication of *The Downfall of Temlaham*,[25] Barbeau's fictionalized account of the so-called 1888 "Skeena River Uprising." Along with the establishment of the national park, Smith advocated developing souvenirs as tourist attractions. His suggestions included the sale of miniatures, jewellery, and other curio items, but his passion was his own plaster-cast replicas of pole parts. "Anyone wishing to put himself through school or university," he wrote to Scott, "with $5.00 worth of tools and $10.00 worth of plaster could turn out one of these plaques per day before breakfast for several weeks."[26] And while one of Smith's plaster casts made its way into Scott's departmental art collection,[27] the promotion of a contemporary arts industry was discussed only briefly and never in detail. Smith asked Scott, "Should I vigorously encourage manufacture and sale as souvenirs of baskets, blankets, paddles, etc. and all such artistic things as they may make in the future?"[28] However, Scott was not interested in directing departmental resources towards this kind of activity.

As for the preservation of the poles themselves, "the initial step was to gain the goodwill and consent of the Indian owners of the poles," wrote Smith in a 1926 project summary published in the national museum's annual report. "This was not easy, for they were unfavourably disposed toward white men in general, and particularly toward Government officials."[29] And while Smith failed to mention specific legislation that might have displeased the Gitxsan owners, he did list a series of grievances, some of which, he suggested, were "no doubt real, some imaginary."[30]

> The white men had settled on their land and were pushing the Indians more and more to the wall; they had built canneries on the coast that were destroying all the fish; they were cutting all the best timber in the country so that within a few years none would remain for the Indian; they sold whisky in Government liquor stores and put the Indians in jail when they drank it. A few years ago, they had prohibited the erection of totem-poles; why did they wish now to preserve them?[31]

As Smith admitted himself, this was a difficult position to explain. "Much tact and patience were necessary to answer these and other objections the Indians raised to any interference with their poles, but in the end most of the difficulties were happily overcome."[32]

With permission from the pole owners, Smith hired labourers, found gravel and hauled it to the sites, cut wood poles to reinforce damaged crest poles, obtained permission to relocate some of the poles next to the rail lines, and trimmed the tops of trees that may have obscured the view from passing

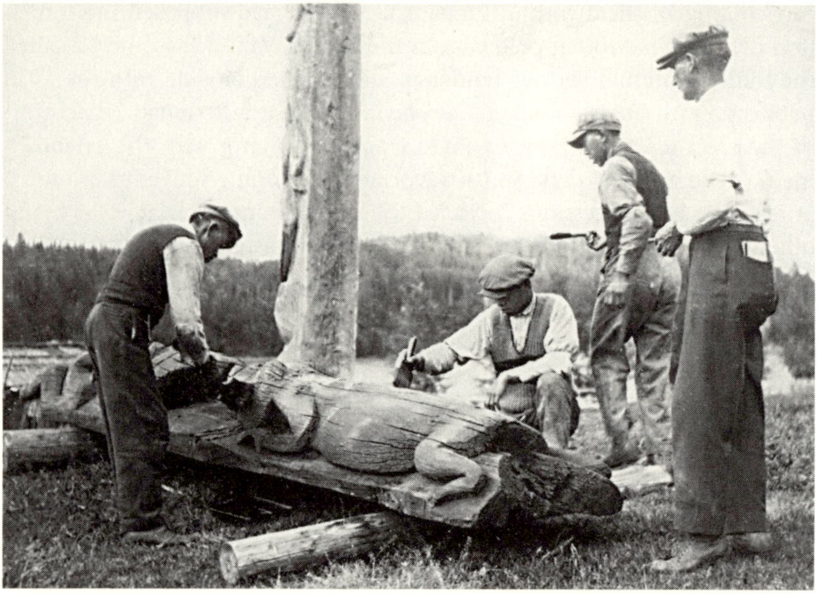

12 Labourers repaint Gitxsan poles for preservation in the Skeena Valley, ca. 1925.

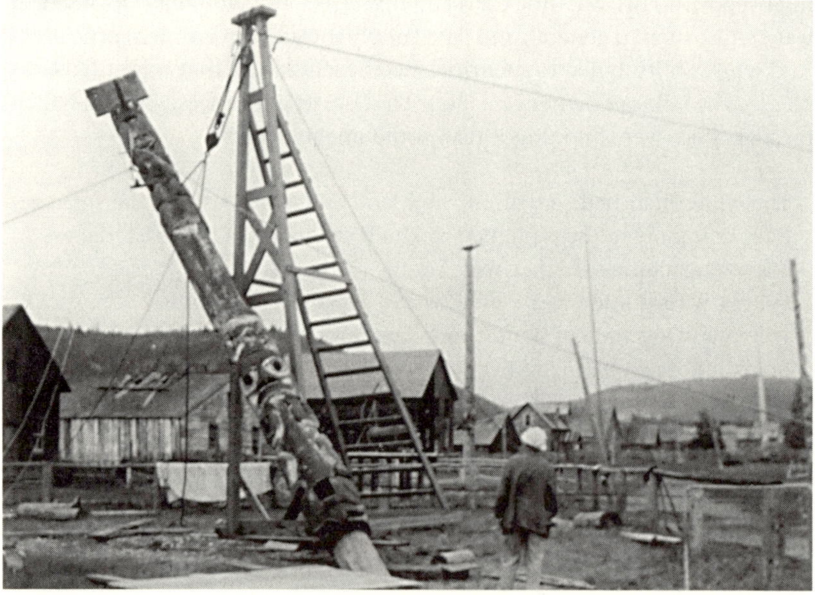

13 Gitxsan pole re-raised as part of preservation project, ca. 1927. The exact location is unknown, but it is likely Kitwanga.

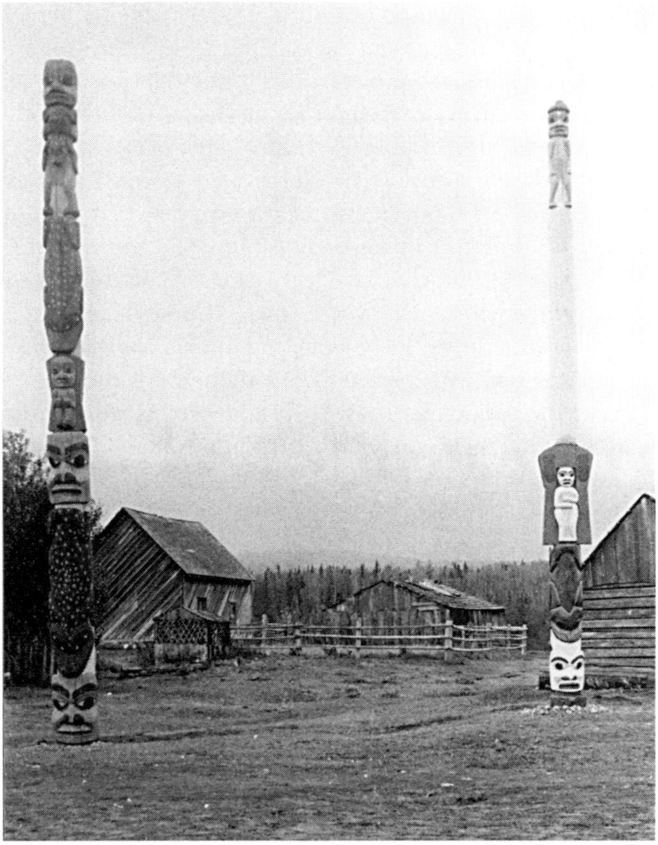

14 Poles repainted and re-set in the preservation project, ca. 1927.

trains (see Figures 12 through 14). He also made plans to erect "show signs so tourists may have chance to see poles at each place where in sight of trains"[33] and labelled the restored poles.[34] The field seasons of 1925 and 1926 saw the restoration of sixteen poles in the villages of Kispiox and Kitwanga, but Smith's optimism about the situation was short-lived.

Two incidents in 1926 contributed to the increasing difficulty of Smith's work and resulted in legislation that, in theory, echoed the project's preservationist intentions and, in practice, ensured that Ottawa's control appear all the more urgent. The first incident occurred in April 1926, when Wallis A. Olen of Clintonville, Wisconsin, contacted first Harlan Smith and then Diamond Jenness (Edward Sapir's replacement as chief of the anthropology division at the national museum) about purchasing a crest pole. Jenness then contacted Scott concerning the legality of shipping poles outside of Canada without government authorization.[35] Scott replied that "unfortunately there is no legal authority preventing the shipping of these totem poles outside of Canada but I do not think it is advisable for Mr. Olen to be made aware of this."[36]

In the second incident, Chief Seamadaks (sometimes spelled "Semideck" or "Semidec") of Kitwanga (see Figure 15), the village in which Harlan Smith was working, sought to sell a pole for $330 and ten masks for an additional $70 to cover medical expenses. The North West Biscuit Company of Edmonton was the potential buyer, and Scott's own direct correspondence to Seamadaks had little effect in dissuading him.[37] By the end of the same month, Jenness and Scott had drafted legislation that extended government jurisdiction over the poles, making it illegal to tamper in any way with any "Indian grave-house, carved grave-pole, totem-pole, carved house-post or large rock embellished with paintings or carvings"[38] without government permission. In the various rewrites, Scott and Jenness worded the legislation specifically to include control of First Nations individuals.[39] This gave the DIA veto power over the sale of any pole on reserve land and thus, in tandem with the government's ability to declare sites and objects part of Canada's national heritage, the power to control the destination of all poles. Once again the authority of the DIA under Scott asserted itself and disempowered First Nations peoples. According to Cole:

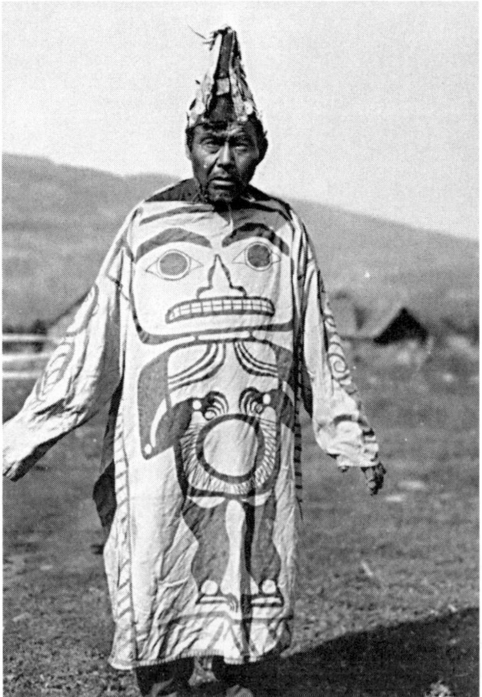

15 Chief Seamadaks, ca. 1927.

> Where enforceable, this prevented private sales, but did not seriously impede sales to public institutions. Nor did it affect exports. Indian Affairs policy – and National Museum advice – was that poles should be preserved *in situ* where they were potential tourist attractions, but where they stood far off the travel routes, as at Cape Mudge or in the Nass valley, they should be in museums. If Canadian museums could not afford them – and in the 1930s few could – they should be allowed to be sold abroad.[40]

In the cases of both Seamadaks and Olen, the government halted initial sales. The Seamadaks pole would come back to haunt Scott, however, and is perhaps indicative of how Smith and the other workers associated with the Totem Pole Preservation Committee failed to gain the trust and cooperation they claimed in their correspondence. Seamadaks first refused to grant permission for anyone to touch his two poles in Kitwanga, the one village where Smith had had some semblance of success. Furthermore, in 1929, despite an ownership dispute internal to Kitwanga and rooted in the intricacies of the Gitxsan potlatch system, Seamadaks went ahead and sold the pole to the Hudson's Bay Company for $300.[41] To add insult to injury, the removal of the pole was carried out under the supervision of the CNR engineer T.B. Campbell, without the permission of the DIA.[42] Scott was forced to grant permission for the pole's sale after the fact because of his own employee's failure to notify the department. Scott and the committee were further caught because, if they had themselves bought the pole and preserved it on site, then they would have been forced to pay not only for any new poles they wished to conserve, but also for the ones they had already finished.[43]

The amendment to control pole sales coincided with a second 1927 amendment to the Indian Act, this one aimed at blocking First Nations abilities to further claims to land within the judicial system. First Nations individuals and groups now had to gain written permission from the DIA before hiring a solicitor. This effectively resulted in a ban on land claims activities and was in direct response to petitions made by the pan-Indian political organization known as the Allied Tribes of British Columbia (under the leadership of Andrew Paull and Peter Kelly, and the legal direction of Arthur E. O'Meara, an Ontario lawyer and Anglican minister associated with the primarily Euro-Canadian group Friends of the Indians). The Allied Tribes were responding to the government's reneging on the First Nations right to consent to or deny reserve cut-offs as outlined in the provincial-federal McKenna-McBride Agreement.[44] Together, these amendments, along with the Cranmer potlatch prosecutions, represent a multipronged federal attack on Aboriginal leadership structures and an attempt, throughout the 1920s, to consolidate federal authority. One of the results of these attempts was a heightened tension between Aboriginal and non-Aboriginal groups.

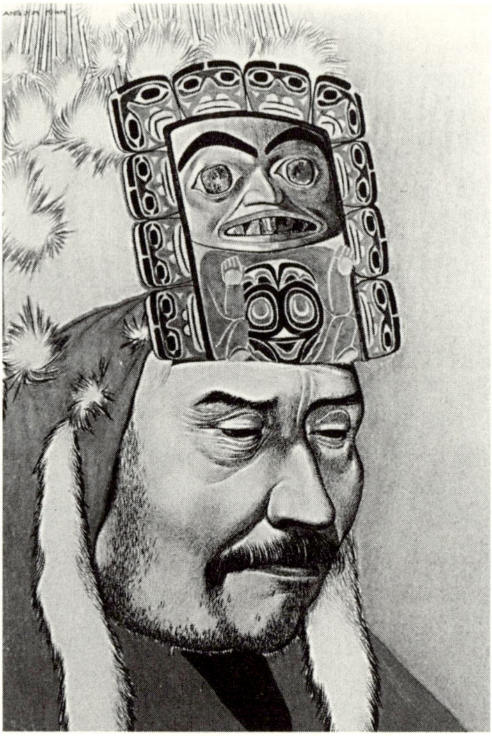

16 Portrait of Tom Campbell by Langdon Kihn.

When Smith and the crew moved on to Kitsegukla in 1927, they were handed a protest petition signed by fifteen Kitsegukla chiefs and were forbidden to touch any of the poles. The blame for this came back to Tom Campbell of Hazelton (who, when arrested for potlatching in 1931, was described by Agent Mortimer as the "I.W.W. type"). Campbell, whose portrait was painted by Langdon Kihn (see Figure 16) and included in the 1927 exhibition,[45] refused to let Smith touch two of his poles, claiming that they had been cut down by provincial road crews and that he had not yet received compensation for them. Edgar Hyde, the local Indian Agent, laid the blame for this on "'propaganda spread by Tom Campbell,' who alleged that the government intended to move villages and give the old ones to the railway 'and other such nonsense.'"[46] In one letter, Hyde wrote that "Tom Campbell is one of the worst agitators in the Agency known as such to both Indians and Whites alike, he is very bitter towards the White people and any kind of government and gives vent to his feelings when opportunity affords."[47] Smith also singled Campbell out as a troublemaker, citing as problems: "too much home brew, the unsettled land question, broken promises by an earlier photographer, white jealousy at not being hired for the work, a missionary's opposition to preservation, and the Indians' fear that the government would own the poles if it spent money preserving them."[48]

When the people in Kitsegukla heard of Seamadaks' successful sale, all the poles in Kitsegukla went up for sale.[49] Ironically, the collecting activities of committee member Barbeau undermined the ability of the committee to realize its objectives. In 1927 Barbeau was also collecting for the Royal Ontario Museum. He bought nearly $1,000 worth of objects more than the museum had budgeted for as he was certain he could sell the surplus at a profit to Heye and the Museum of the American Indian in New York.[50] As Cole writes, Barbeau's career "was now launched as a collector in 'a purely personal' as well as official capacity."[51] When Barbeau offered $600 for a pole on the Nass River and was turned down, he began negotiating an offer for $1,000.[52] The price of each pole in Kitsegukla then went to $1,000, a price deemed unacceptable by the federal Totem Pole Preservation Committee, especially after it had managed to preserve poles in Kitwanga and Kispiox without any payment at all.[53]

Smith then moved down to Kitselas Canyon, a village not included in Barbeau's initial 1924 report. Barbeau was opposed to the restoration of the poles at Kitselas, even though Smith noted that all fifteen poles could be seen from the rail line. Cole reports that Barbeau sought to undermine Smith's work, perhaps in order to secure his own ability to deal independently in poles that were listed as being away from the villages in the 1924 survey, since Barbeau was actively acting as an agent in the sale of totem poles outside his capacity with the National Museum.[54]

As with the Kwakwa̲ka̲'wakw, so with the Gitxsan: their reasons for participating in the preservation program or for selling their poles and other objects varied. Increasing financial difficulty, for example, contributed to certain sales. In 1927 Barbeau was successful in freelance collecting partly because of the "failure of the 1927 fishery."[55] The sale of older poles may also have been one way of funding a cycle of potlatches for the next generation of Gitxsan leaders.

The non-Aboriginal perspective on the preservation can be glimpsed in Smith's film (see Figure 17), *The Tsimshian Indians of the Skeena River of British Columbia*, the making of which one of Smith's responsibilities to the museum during the preservation fieldwork and which is discussed in detail by Rosalind Morris.[56] The opening title reads: "The Canadian National Railway speeds through the mountain walled valleys of British Columbia toward the land of the Tsimshian, where totem poles and costumed Indians recall the glories of a vanished past."[57] Morris, although apparently unaware of the film's relationship to Smith's work for the preservation committee, argues that the film's travel motif was a device intended to emphasize the distance of the Tsimshian from the film's non-Aboriginal audience. Travel in the film operated both spatially and temporally,[58] a process physically

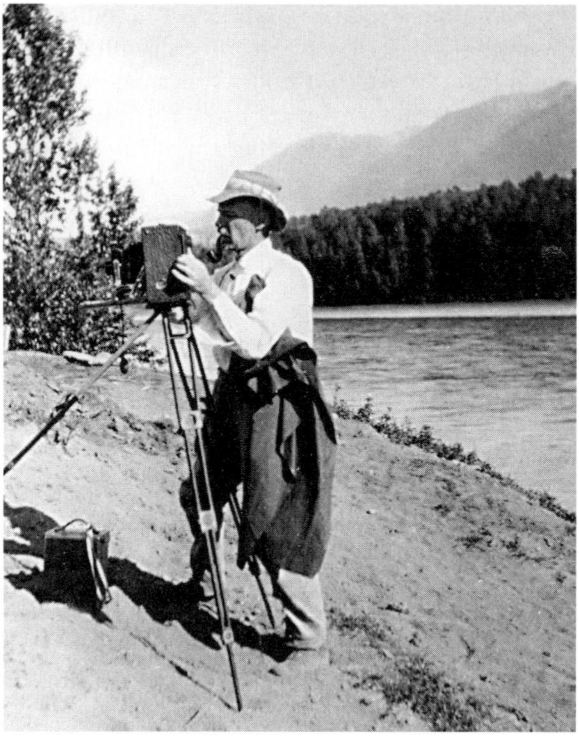

17 Harlan Smith filming poles in Kitwanga for the CNR, 1927.

replicated in train travel. Through the results of Smith's preservation efforts, travelling through the valley and viewing the preserved poles was akin to travelling back in time. What the project offered in terms of attracting visitors to the region, then, was a "trope of travel ... at one with those accounts of exploration and discovery that so entertained the previous generation."[59] Morris's paradox of simultaneity, "the contradiction ... of cultural disappearance and physical survival,"[60] which disrupted the narrative of social evolution, was mediated by the idea that the past could function within a modernist framework: as heritage resource or as commodity. It was for this reason that Scott and the rest of the committee in Ottawa could brook no challenges from Vancouver, Edmonton, or the American museums. The "inauthentic" erection of these "heritage" monuments outside their place of origin would undermine the ability to control the location and meaning of the objects and, therefore, their usefulness with regard to constructing a particular vision of "modern" Canada and being a resource for the railway and other tourism industries.

Because owners were demanding $1,000 for every pole on the reserve before consenting to preservation work, only two more poles were preserved following the disastrous 1927 field season.[61] Cole suggests, I think shortsightedly, that the Gitxsan were primarily concerned with sharing any economic benefit received by the railway. Even in 1927 this would only have amounted to a small benefit when compared to the overall value of the poles, with their connections to the ownership of inherited territories and resources – especially considering the scope of Euro-Canadian plans for the region between 1904 and the end of the 1920s.

At this point, Gitxsan resistance differed from both Squamish and Kwakwa̱ka̱'wakw resistance. With the Cranmer potlatch, land rights were not so explicitly at stake as they were with the Stanley Park and Skeena Valley projects. The suggestion made by government officials that their intention was to preserve the Gitxsan poles for future generations obscured their primary concern, which was to use the poles as tourist attractions and so facilitate the valley's industrial development. Furthermore, the erection of Kwakwa̱ka̱'wakw poles on land claimed by the Squamish was a kind of intrusion. Yet much of Gitxsan resistance can be related to the clash between the vibrant social significance the poles still served within Gitxsan communities and the attempt of federal authorities to control Gitxsan political and social life (and that of the Coastal peoples in general) through the potlatch ban, the prohibition of land claims activities, and the prohibition of pole sales. While the demand for such substantial amounts for the poles may have been a symptom of the problem, the root of the problem was the duplicity of Euro-Canadian officials. The most common complaint from the Gitxsan villages was that, if the government spent money on the poles, then the Gitxsan themselves would no longer own them. State officials argued that they were simply keeping the owners' memories alive, yet they repeatedly blocked sales of which they did not approve. One might ask what the point of ownership is if the owner does not have the right of disposal, either through sale or transport. What, if anything, did "ownership" mean in this kind of definition?

The National Gallery and the *Exhibition of Canadian West Coast Art, Native and Modern*

Morris's paradox of simultaneity was fashioned in the realm of "fine art" as well as in the realm of anthropology. The success of Canada's modernist contributions to the colonial art exhibitions in London in the early 1920s led to French requests for a representative exhibition in Paris in March 1927 and may have inspired Barbeau (along with the general interest in expressing Canadian identity through the painterly documentation of the land) to recruit artists to depict the Skeena Valley.

The French requests resulted in a show that was, in part, organized by Eric Brown (director of the national gallery) and held at the Musée du Jeu de Paume. It included modernist paintings by Brown's favoured Group of

Seven as well as by people like Homer Watson, Maurice Cullen, Clarence Gagnon, J.E.H. MacDonald, and James Morrice. The landscape content was of course inescapable and was supplemented by a selection of Northwest Coast sculpture[62] and fabrics contributed by national museum director Collins at the suggestion of Duncan Campbell Scott,[63] who was again using his position in the DIA to further his passion for the arts. A critic with *Figaro Artistique* noted that the Northwest Coast objects were "really unusual and handled with undeniable skill. They will interest the curious."[64] Furthermore, the exhibition's inclusion of Northwest Coast objects was in line with the government's policy of using the Aboriginal products of British Columbia to advertise the country.

That primitivism would play an important role in the self-definition of a new, essentially European, industrialized state exemplifies Daniel Miller's assertion that, "since meaning is often defined through oppositions, dominant groups may often be found not only to construct material representations of their own interests, but also to project models of those which they define themselves in opposition to."[65] And while, as an artistic strategy, this is most closely associated with Paris around the time of the First World War, the specific use of Northwest Coast material in conjunction with the modernist treatment of the *Canadian* landscape distinguishes the project as distinctively Canadian. Modernism, especially with references to primitivistic oppositions, signifies membership in an international capitalist industrial modernity. The premodern operates as the negative defining the positive space, as a geographic trope, and as the foundation upon and over which the industrial state is built. To employ such a strategy in the cultural heart of France, claimed by the state as one of Canada's own founding societies, is a coming-of-age statement. The fact that Canada was internationally asserting itself as culturally distinct coincides with an important shift in its relationship with Britain and the British Empire.[66]

A similar show, this time focusing exclusively on British Columbia, opened at the national gallery in December 1927. In retrospect, it should have been an auspicious opening since it was the first time the National Gallery of Canada had put Canadian First Nations "art" on display, let alone included a living First Nations painter with a selection of Canada's best known and most critically accepted modern artists. The *Exhibition of Canadian West Coast Art, Native and Modern,*[67] under the cooperative direction of the gallery's Eric Brown and national museum ethnologist Marius Barbeau, collected anonymous Northwest Coast ceremonial objects from the museum's shelves, objects borrowed from other Canadian institutions (especially the Royal Ontario Museum), works by the recently deceased Haida carver Charles Edenshaw and living Coast Tsimshian painter Frederick Alexie (a protégé of Barbeau), and paintings by members of the Group of Seven, Paul Kane, Annie Savage, Florence Wyle, Walter J. Phillips, Charles Scott, F.M. Bell Smith, Langdon

Kihn, Peggy Nichol, and Emily Carr to offer a statement about the development of Canadian art. Much of the exhibition's intention centred on creating a visual mosaic through combining ethnic streams into a contemporary expression, giving new painters an artificial historical pedigree – a pedigree that said something about the spirit of the country. It was not so much about Northwest Coast "art" as it was about the utility of First Nations objects and the landscape to the construction of a new, unique, and wholly Canadian artistic style.

Then again, perhaps it was sadly appropriate to the marginalized position of First Nations peoples that the opening was poorly advertised and even more poorly attended, despite the national museum's 1927-28 *Annual Report* and its suggestion that the exhibit "proved so successful that it was shown later in Toronto and in Montreal."[68] "It was horrid," wrote Carr in her diary at the time: "No invitations were sent out except to a few artists and those in the building. Others were angry at getting no cards or notices except the eleventh hour general invitation that came too late to be taken."[69] Carr criticized the general lack of recognition accorded to her nationalistic paintings – a lack that she attributed to poor organization and sparse attendance. "Dominated by dead England and English traditions," she lamented, "they are decorating their tombstones while living things clamour to be fed."[70] And this she took personally, since she had woven her own sense of artistic self so tightly into the leaning, picturesque crest poles, tumbled old villages, and the forests of the Coast. "They all say I have more of the spirit of the Indian than the others ... I loved the country and the people more than the others who have painted her. It was my own country, part of the West and me."[71] The inclusion of named First Nations artists like Alexie and Edenshaw, apparently not noticed by Carr in the throes of her own anxieties, has since become an obscure, albeit telling, footnote in the history of Canadian art.

Canada's Diamond Jubilee, which was in 1927, seemed entirely the right occasion upon which to install in Ottawa an exhibition with historicist references and with a bold inclusive statement about Canadian artistic identity. It now also seems a chillingly ironic occasion for such an exhibition, given the then recent adoption of Sections 140 and 141 of the Indian Act and the suppression of both potlatching and land claims. Brown, Barbeau, painters like A.Y. Jackson and Edwin Holgate, Canada's "worthwhiles," "people who," in Carr's words, "really count and are shaping a nation[,] ... all so big and broad ... so proud of the bigness of their country, so anxious to probe its soul and understand it,"[72] sought a vehicle for expression in Northwest Coast subject matter. And, in doing so, they carved out an artistic metaphor for First Nations peoples that mirrored the federal government's assimilationist policies. "Enough ... remains of the old arts," wrote Brown in the catalogue preface, "to provide an invaluable mine of decorative design which is available to the student for a host of different purposes and possessing for the Canadian artist in particular the unique quality of being entirely national in its origin and character."[73]

The catalogue illustrates the mechanics of the exhibition's construction. Following Brown's preface, Barbeau sketches a brief introduction establishing the international stature of "West Coast Indian Art," then he comments on the notions of content and function. The catalogue itself is then divided into two basic sections, seemingly according to a loose chronological arrangement, with the first providing partial explanations of object categories and the second listing, without explanation, the Euro-Canadian paintings of the Group of Seven and the others. The difference between the two parts is characteristic of the difference between art and anthropological exhibits, with anthropological displays designed to educate and art exhibits assuming a prior knowledge appropriate to the connoisseur class. What makes this catalogue special is the juxtaposition of these two modes within a single work.

The installation itself was more integrated, with paintings being displayed side by side with ceremonial objects, thus implying both stylistic affinities and a hierarchy. The Aboriginal objects, although prominent, were arranged in display cases and in museum-like groupings that reinforced the sense of the Euro-Canadian depictions as something of the present and the "artefacts" as something of the past. In this way, the exhibition's curatorial strategy privileged the modernist paintings.

On the one hand, affinities contributed to the inspiration of modernist painters, on the other hand, they legitimized Northwest Coast objects as art. The *West Coast* exhibition can be viewed within the context of early attempts to explain and to institutionalize "primitive art," and it begs for immediate comparison with Franz Boas's *Primitive Art*,[74] which was published the same year. Like Boas, Barbeau chose to emphasize the aesthetic refinement of the northern Coastal groups, whose "artists have left works of art that count among the outstanding creations of mankind in the sphere of plastic or decorative beauty."[75] However, Boas constructed the objects as art in order to prove the "equality," or "civilization," of the people who produced it; consequently, his text operated on a metonymic level, with objects standing for the originating nations. Boas does not seem to have been concerned with using the Aboriginal "premodern" to construct American nationalism.

The way in which Brown and Barbeau utilized the objects of the Northwest Coast as sources of inspiration for modernist painters echoed the modernist "discovery" of African and other non-Western arts in Europe just prior to the First World War. Marianna Torgovnick describes this process and its implications:

> A group without an "art" and "aesthetics" can be thought to lack "culture" and "political integrity;" it can then be "discovered" and "developed" by "superior" groups, that is those with both "art" and "culture." Any challenge to the designation of "art" for African, Oceanic, and Native American pieces thus flirts dangerously with modes of thought that made the appropriation of land from primitive peoples possible.[76]

Despite the shared strategies of equating beauty with art, an evolutionary hierarchy was more important to the structure of the *West Coast* exhibition catalogue entries than it was to Boas's *Primitive Art*. Within the object categories, a subtext of differing creative sophistication ranks both the objects and their producers. Haida model poles, with "their refined stylization coupled with a touch of feeling and realism, and the clever grouping of figures along the slender shafts, disclose the outstanding characteristics of Haida art at its best."[77] Tsimshian and Haida masks "both varieties belong[ing] to the northern nations ... are often from the hands of the best carvers."[78] The hierarchy descends from the north to the south. Thus, "the southern tribes, on the other hand (the Kwakiutl and the Nootka) could not boast of like refinement,"[79] their style "is either a degenerate form of the northern art or, else, it represents an early stage, beyond which the southern West Coast tribes did not advance."[80]

Towards the end of the first catalogue listing, Edenshaw appears in an introduction to Haida argillite carvings, which, according to the text, emerge after 1850, "when the white strangers showed their interest in native souvenirs."[81] The best of the argillite poles are attributed to Edenshaw and his "faithful Tlingit slave" who "spent much of their lives in friendly rivalry, carving figures of all kinds."[82] Charles Edenshaw, a Haida carver (ca. 1839-1920), lived and worked at Massett, Skidegate, Port Simpson, and Kasaan.[83] He was commissioned by Boas and, through John Swanton, the American Museum of Natural History to prepare a series of model poles and houses that, as Jonaitis argues convincingly, became the stylistic paradigm for "classic" Haida art.[84] Furthermore, Boas makes a number of references to Edenshaw in *Primitive Art*, either through illustrating Edenshaw's work or through discussing his explanations of specific images.[85] The catalogue's recognition of Edenshaw, although cursory at best, was essential, given this kind of international attention.

The last four entries of the first section cover the gradual bleeding from one group into another. Bracelets, made from hammered "Mexican" dollar coins,[86] are singled out as a nineteenth-century innovation. They are followed by two of Alexie's paintings (one of which had been purchased by A.Y. Jackson and then loaned to the exhibit), identified by Barbeau as "an old Tsimsyan half-breed [sic] of Port Simpson"[87] (see Figure 18). Frederick

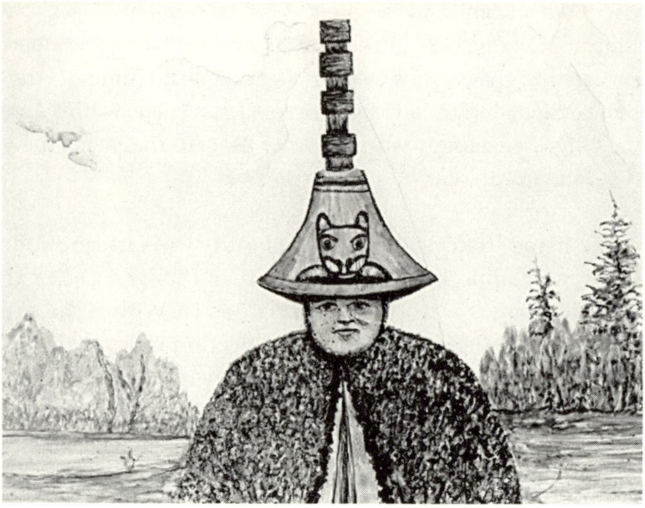

18 Lantern-slide painting, by Frederick Alexie, of a historic chief in Port Simpson, ca. 1912.

Alexie was born in Port Simpson in 1853.[88] His father was part of a small group of Iroquois brought to the Pacific coast in the 1830s by the Hudson's Bay Company. His mother was a Coast Tsimshian, thus Alexie belonged to the *gispawadwada* clan of the Giludzar Tsimshian. According to Barbeau, he was trained as a *halait* carver and was responsible for the production of *naxnox,* or secret society paraphernalia;[89] however, in 1934 Viola Garfield described him as "a good natured, highly volatile and imaginative person" with "little formal training in painting and drawing, either by white or native teachers." She thought that his paintings were "done in a stilted manner with very little regard for perspective."[90] According to Barbeau:

> The two paintings by Fred Alexee[91] might be placed among the primitives of Canadian art here exhibited. They are worth special notice. In European countries primitive paintings have been prized for their naivete, their charm and the historical perspective which they confer upon the development of art. In Canada this category has so far eluded search, if we except Indian art pure and simple.[92]

Barbeau later added:

> The totem-like features and plastic treatment of the figures shown here belong partly to the art of the North West Coast Indians and partly to the conceptions of the white people within the fold of the church. This blend of two cultures ... is a rare accident at the frontiers of two worlds. It makes his paintings and carvings exceptional, fascinating, significant.[93]

Through his inclusion of Alexie, Barbeau opens up a new facet to the narrative of social evolution. Alexie's paintings are used to mediate the myth of cultural extinction and the physical survival of First Nations peoples by serving as a stepping stone from the old to the new, from "primitivism" to "modernity." Alexie becomes the missing link, bridging the Aboriginal past and the Euro-Canadian present. In the catalogue text there is no mistaking the tone and tense of most object descriptions. They are works of the past. Both tense and tone change during the examination of Alexie, who was part of the present and who thus seemed an appropriate bridge to the next two entries on Carr. Carr's objects (other than her paintings), in turn, bridge the first section with the painting list of the second.

The entries on Carr's hooked rugs and pottery begin with the statement: "Miss Carr has spent many years among the Indians and has succeeded in getting them to revive many of their native arts."[94] While this endows Carr with an authority and influence that she did not possess, her relationship with the "Indians" is then legitimized with the statement that "she has received the name of Klee Wyck – (She who laughs)."[95] This, of course, was a nickname and had nothing to do with the acquisition of a ceremonial name. Yet commercially, identification with the marginalized "primitive" was good for Carr's modernist image, reinforcing her own position outside the bourgeois status quo and firmly placing her within Canada's new avant-garde – a position that, according to Morrison, Barbeau also supported by picking up

> Carr's own statements about her "discouragement over the utter lack of public interest" in her work in Victoria which resulted in Carr discontinuing after 1914. This was not, in fact, the case, since Carr had been painting and exhibiting since 1924, but the myth of "discovery" was connected to a Cinderella syndrome in which the talented woman painter was rescued from oblivion by a member of the patriarchal elite, a myth in which both Carr and Barbeau participated.[96]

The exhibition was an important one. Not only did its strategy of affiliation legitimize the use of First Nations subjects as a *Canadian* theme and promote contemporary Euro-Canadian artists working in this direction, but it also raised the profile of Northwest Coast objects, moving them from the steamship boardwalk vendors and curio shops to the national gallery. Barbeau's own interest in Alexie and his decision to include him in the exhibit broke the paradigm of First Nations as past and Euro-Canadian as present, and it signalled a tentative but growing recognition of the possibility of contemporary First Nations *art*.

5
The New Deals: George Raley and Depression-Era Reform in British Columbia

The Great Depression dramatically influenced the development of Native American touristic industries in both the United States and Canada. During the American presidential administration of Franklin D. Roosevelt, the social reform ideals of the 1920s became officially entrenched as public policy under the direction of John Collier, commissioner of Indian affairs. In Canada, however, the impact of the Great Depression smothered any further major participation on behalf of governmental institutions in the collecting or display of Northwest Coast objects until after the Second World War. Not only did the Depression wreak economic havoc on First Nations communities, but the cash-strapped federal government could no longer afford its museum programs. The perception with which many middle-class non-Aboriginal Canadians were left was that the state had abandoned its fiduciary responsibility.

In Canada, the vacuum in museum activity was filled by missionaries and educators seeking to extend the reconfiguration of First Nations objects to include the sale of contemporary "Indian art." This chapter examines how, within the social debate centred on the welfare and education of Aboriginal peoples first in the United States and then in Canada, the economic crisis brought about by the Great Depression fostered the use of Aboriginal objects as a primary resource. Ultimately, this led to a shift from promoting Native American and First Nations art as a product of the past to promoting it as a product – indeed, an industry – of the present. This strategy had an enormous influence on the shape of museum and other institutional activities from 1945 on.

Mandatory industrial training for First Nations boys had been common in residential schools since the 1880s, and it emphasized the role of resource-based wage labour in "modern" Canada.[1] British Columbia's resource industries (e.g., logging, mining, and salmon fishing and processing) still provided adequate employment (and investment return) in the 1920s, when Scott, the DIA, and the Canadian National Railways took an active interest in the province's totem poles. Since the pre-First World War collecting craze had passed, more money could be made on the boats or in the canneries – industries that intersected well with pre-colonial Kwakwa̲ka̲'wakw economic pursuits[2] – than in labour-intensive souvenir carving. And so, although Scott was certainly interested in First Nations objects, he never deemed it necessary to promote their current production. For those in Ottawa, "Indian art" was nothing more than inspiration for the creativity of "modern" artists. It seems that Scott believed his own poetry – that "the race has waned and left but tales of ghosts"[3] – or, as Marius Barbeau wrote more bluntly, "the art now belongs to the past."[4]

But the "Vanishing American" paradigm weakened in some circles in the 1920s, and the Depression demonstrated how much of a failure it had been as the source of policy, both in Canada and the United States. Not only were First Nations peoples social "outcasts,"[5] stated Diamond Jenness in 1934, but "economically they [were] an encumbrance."[6] With the near financial collapse of the Canadian government and widespread unemployment after 1929, crisis conditions stimulated calls for sweeping systemic reform, and this suggested that, by overhauling the DIA, the Canadian government could relieve itself of an "encumbrance." These calls were formulated in terms of state intervention for the sake of the economy, and, in terms of "Indian" policy, the focused upon First Nations objects, which were saleable because of their association with Aboriginal tradition and premodern heritage. The election of liberal governments in North America hastened the adoption of Keynesian theory, with its emphasis on a state-managed economy and its rhetorical use of pluralism as a model for national intra-group cooperation. In both Canada and the United States this was a time of transition – a time when these countries shifted from a policy of assimilation to a policy of integration, when the maintenance of Aboriginal heritage within the framework of state capitalism became both possible and desirable.

Provincial lobbying activities centred on the arts in British Columbia after the onset of the Depression took a tack quite different from Scott's. This lobbying called first for the provision of encouragement, opportunity, and limited training for First Nations practitioners and, second, for the creation of "Indian-mindedness" among the art-consuming general public. These programs, like George Raley's efforts at encouraging government support for the arts or the British Columbia Indian Arts and Welfare Society's attempts to systematize both art consumption and art production, have been ignored in academic studies of First Nations art. Nonetheless, they were important with regard to pressuring different levels of government to create programs that enshrined Aboriginal history as a continuing, positive force in modern life. In short, they heralded the proclamation of a cultural "renaissance" in the provincial totem pole salvage and carver training programs of the 1940s and 1950s.

It was in this restructuring phase that the political nature of contemporary First Nations public art became evident, for it was then that its ability to attract public attention was recognized and utilized. Not only did the Depression affect how state officials approached Aboriginal arts, but it also indirectly expanded the public uses of these arts, including, for First Nations, resistance to the intent of the Indian Act.

Social Reform in the United States and the "Indian New Deal"

The relocation and preservation of poles in Canada during the 1920s were not isolated incidents. In addition to the collecting activities of the large municipal museums of New York and Chicago, a number of Alaskan efforts prior to the Depression focused upon the preservation of Tlingit poles. As early as 1890 a public park had been created around a cluster of poles at the village of Kiksadi, where the Russians had won control of Sitka in 1804.[7] In an attempt to prevent vandalism, in 1910 President William Howard Taft issued an executive order making this park the Sitka National Monument.[8] Another presidential proclamation in 1916 created the National Monument of Old Kasaan, a Haida village on Prince of Wales Island that was abandoned around the turn of the twentieth century.[9] In 1920 Alaskan judge James Wickersham began a movement to preserve totem poles at Port Tongass, including, most notably, the so-called "Abraham Lincoln totem,"[10] a pole erected in 1867 and containing a portrait of the American president as its top figure.[11] The same year James Gordon Steese, president of the Alaska Road Commission, was granted $200 to raise and repaint fallen poles at Sitka.[12]

Between 1921 and 1938, organizations and service clubs such as the Wrangell Chamber of Commerce and the Ketchikan American Legion Post carried out sporadic restoration efforts. Walter Waters of Wrangell purchased and removed a number of poles from villages on the west coast so that they could sit outside his Bear Totem Store in Wrangell. Waters's "preservation" activities included the use of rock salt to prevent dry rot, the removal of rotted wood, the refilling of cavities with concrete, and repainting.[13] Although none of these individual projects matched the scale of the Smith-supervised project in the Skeena Valley, collectively they illustrate a shared concern for totem poles specifically and for First Nations "art" generally as a regional symbol and, hence, as a tourist attraction.

These efforts in Alaska echoed earlier efforts in the Southwest.[14] In his detailed survey of the Indian Arts and Crafts Board, Robert Fay Schrader reports that the American government had been interested in promoting Native American arts and crafts as early as 1863.[15] The interest, writes Schrader, initially stemmed from "an increasing concern over the effects of industrialization on the quality of everyday life ... As the years passed, however, the Indian Office came to emphasize the development of Indian crafts into manufacturing industries. Contrary to the popular emphasis on arts and crafts as an antidote to the effects of industrialization, the motivation behind the federal government's ... role in Indian arts and crafts was a desire to industrialize the Indians."[16]

Pueblo ceramics had gained notice with the westward expansion of Euro-America in the last third of the nineteenth century. The completion of the Santa Fe Railway in 1880 and the military defeat of the southern Plains people contributed to Santa Fe's reputation as a tourist destination. Marketing efforts by J. Walter Fewkes, Hewett and Chapman of the School of American Research, the Museum of New Mexico, the Museum of Northern Arizona, the Fred Harvey hotel chain, and individual traders like C.G. Wallace and Thomas Keam all helped to establish craft production (most often for tourists) as an important economic pursuit in the Southwest. By the 1920s the works of ceramicists like Nampeyo and Maria Martinez, which were based upon historical or archaeological models, were commanding significant prices. These people were sustained at least in part by the institutional efforts of the School of American Research and the Santa Fe-based Indian Arts Fund.[17] However, good markets had also opened up for basketry, Navajo textiles, silver jewellery, Pueblo kachina carving, and easel painting. As an industry, Southwest Native American art had shown great growth potential. Ruth Roessel, for example, points out that, in 1930, the value of Navajo weaving alone stood at $1,000,000, up from its 1890 value of $30,000.[18] Furthermore, the concerns of Euro-American artists and intellectuals, who were attracted by the vitality of Southwest production, played an important part in shaping attitudes towards not only Native American art, but also Native American social reform.[19]

The vitality of Pueblo and Navajo "cultures," as exemplified in the thriving crafts market, was seen to contradict the myth of the Vanishing American. It was here, suggests Brian Dippie, that the "revolutionary idea of Indian continuity and survival"[20] was best represented. It was also here that the state could simultaneously address two of its primary functions: accumulation and legitimization. The ideas of the arts and crafts, and the growing anti-assimilationist sentiments of liberal Euro-Americans, served as sources for a major national policy shift instigated by the inauguration of Franklin Delano Roosevelt in 1933 – an event that increased the promotion of Tlingit and other Native American arts and set models for similar programs in Canada.

The fundamental idea behind Roosevelt's presidential platform, his so-called New Deal, involved an increase in state participation in economic management as a way of combatting the effects of the stock market crash and the consequent spiral of international responses that were affecting the American domestic economy. With the financial disarray brought about by the Depression, increased state interventions facilitated American business, including the business of art, and also soothed class and ethnic divisions. Under Roosevelt, the protectionism of the 1920s and early 1930s was replaced with strategic social expenditures, which were considered to be part of a managed economy. This was the birth of welfare statism in North America.[21] The promotion of Native American arts was part of the wider program of soothing ethnic divisions through the reform of the educational curricula.[22] The federal government in the United States encouraged art production in the schools as both a means of recognizing Native American cultures and of stimulating their economic independence.

John Collier, one of the most outspoken of United States Indian policy opponents, was selected commissioner of Indian affairs immediately after Roosevelt's election. In 1934 Collier announced the United States Bureau of Indian Affairs policy agenda as the economic rehabilitation of Native Americans, principally on their own lands; the organization of tribes so that they could manage their own affairs; and civil and cultural freedom and opportunity for Native Americans. These objectives were more or less realized with the introduction of the Wheeler-Howard Indian Rights bill in 1934. Sometimes called the Indian Reorganization Act or the Indian New Deal, it suspended the allotment policy of the 1887 Dawes Act and instituted limited forms of self-government. It advocated the gradual phasing out of boarding schools and the incorporation of a spirit of cultural relativism into the school curriculum.[23] A subsection entitled "Special Education for Indians" declared it "to be the purpose and policy of Congress to promote the study of Indian civilization and preserve and develop the special cultural contributions and achievements of such civilization, including Indian arts, crafts, skills, and traditions."[24]

In the Indian New Deal, arts-related education and research, and the infrastructure for marketing and distribution, came together under state management. Not only did the state continue to encapsulate all aspects of Native American life within its bureaucracy, but it also, for the first time, sought to market Native American heritage. This strategy hinged upon a new understanding of the American nation, one that at least rhetorically sought to include ethnic diversity as part of the American experience. American federal officials encouraged this diversity through education, concentrating more directly on what was understood to be Native American "culture," and the call to Euro-America to experience bicultural enjoyment through the consumption of Native American products. These efforts represented an attempt to bridge different segments of the United States and, in this sense, they demonstrated a shift away from assimilation towards integration and the maintenance of ethnic identity within the context of loyalty to the American state. The ingredients of the American melting pot were now expected to maintain their distinctive flavours rather than simply to disappear into a homogenous stew dominated by the Anglo-Saxon majority.

Consequently, markets could open for unique luxury items that would be produced within these ethnically distinct pockets and then consumed in the rest of "modern" America.

This emphasis on the promotion of Native American "culture" would have a significant influence on the development of Native American arts. The creation of the Indian Arts and Crafts Board under the Wheeler-Howard Indian Rights bill in 1935 institutionalized the production of Native American arts. The Indian Arts and Crafts Board further realized state intervention in the business of "Indian art" in its attempts to manage the problems of production, marketing, distribution, and quality control.

The board cooperated directly in important exhibitions of Native American objects as fine art at the Golden Gate Exposition in San Francisco in 1939 and at the Museum of Modern Art in New York in 1941. Under the curatorial direction of René d'Harnoncourt (the general manager of the Indian Arts and Crafts Board hired by Collier) and Frederic Douglas (curator of the Denver Art Museum) these exhibitions went a long way to establishing an understanding of this material as "art" and to promoting contemporary Native American artists like Hopi painter Fred Kabotie.

In southeast Alaska, the Indian New Deal resulted in a public works program under the supervision of Frank Heintzelman of the Forestry Service, whose objectives were to "salvage, re-carve and relocate at least a selection of the region's disintegrating totem poles into prescribed Totem Parks."[25] The Civilian Conservation Corps made available $127,000 to hire Alaskan Aboriginals for the project.[26] According to Polly Miller:

> News of the undertaking first reached the public through the Indian Affairs newssheet, *Indians at Work*, which explained that old skilled native carvers were employed to give technical direction and to instruct younger Indians in the art, most of whom had no knowledge of it. Clusters of these poles "restored with faithful accuracy," now stand in public parks at Saxman, Totem Bight, and Klawock.[27]

The project contributed to a greater non-Aboriginal appreciation of the contemporary accomplishments of Native Americans. The 1941 *Indian Art of the United States* exhibition in New York, which was "aesthetically dominated by the arts of the Northwest Coast,"[28] was especially influential.[29] Sponsored by the United States National Museum, and with contributions from the Royal Ontario Museum, d'Harnoncourt and Douglas established their mandate, which was to improve the reception and consumption of "Indian art" and to encourage the appreciation of Indian achievement under New Deal policy. Improving the reception of Indian art involved reiterating the mythic connection between Native Americans and the American landscape within a modern context. "Indian art from coast to coast actually recreates the land, America, in every one of its countless variations," wrote d'Harnoncourt and Douglas. "Indian art not only has a place but actually fills a concrete need in the United States today. Its close relationship to America, the land, and its unexplored wealth of forms offer a valuable contribution to Modern American art and life."[30]

While Canadians were slow to follow the example of the Indian New Deal, a regulated and controlled market for First Nations art seemed to address two important social concerns in Canada. First, the promotion of First Nations heritage at least superficially encouraged a more inclusive attitude towards First Nations people and provided a focus for the public discussion of other issues, such as health and welfare. Second, the encouragement of the arts as a viable economic pursuit could somewhat alleviate the numbing poverty associated with reserve life in Canada and, thus, hasten the economic assimilation of First Nations peoples. Shortly after Collier's appointment as United States Indian commissioner, reformers in Canada began citing American policy as a model for new directions – a call that would take First Nations art in British Columbia in a different, albeit related, direction.[31]

George Raley and the Call for a Canadian New Deal

While the early to mid-1920s saw an economic high in British Columbia, the financial collapse of October 1929 paralyzed the provincial economy. With the international demand for primary products in severe decline, resource-oriented regions like British Columbia were the hardest hit.[32] The building trade and lumber industries fell into disorganization. Reversals in the mining, lumbering, and fishing industries accompanied a glut on the world wheat market. By 1930 the Okanagan fruit industry had suffered serious setbacks and western Canada's unemployed flooded Vancouver, which was already swollen with 7,000 unemployed men, in search of a climate that was milder than the Prairie winter. In 1931 there were 237 relief camps in British Columbia, housing one-third of the "relief men" in Canada. Accusations of government and relief mismanagement flew as the provincial deficit soared to $165 million by 1933, and the ranks of the provincial unemployed numbered 100,000.[33] Ormsby describes Vancouver in the 1930s as a "shabby and battered city, more scarred by the depression than any other city in Canada."[34] The situation for First Nations in British Columbia was further aggravated by the already limited economic opportunities on most reserves, widespread racism, intra-Canadian emigration and the consequent increase in competition for seasonal work, and an inequity in relief payments.

Of course, the severity of this economic crisis was not limited to British Columbia. The response to the Great Depression became the central political question of the 1930s and has affected government structure in North America

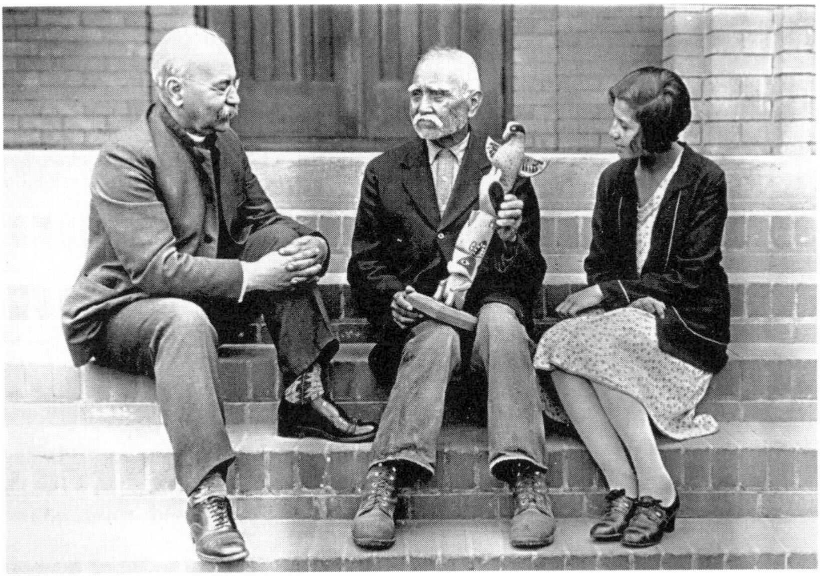

19 Rev. George Raley (left) with Chief Sepass and his daughter, 1934.

ever since. In 1930 the two options open to the Canadian government have been characterized as (1) the maintenance of the status quo policy of laissez-faire economics and (2) the adoption of a Keynesian state-managed economy in a guise similar to that adopted by Roosevelt's New Deal. For Canadians, the American New Deal not only served as a model, but it also both legitimized social reform efforts and provided hope. American developments demonstrated that reform could, indeed, be successfully implemented.

In British Columbia, the Reverend George Raley (see Figure 19) was the first to attempt to follow the Indian New Deal lead. Raley was born in Barnsley, England, in 1864 and came to Canada in 1882. In 1893 he was appointed Methodist missionary to the Haisla community of Kitamaat, where he printed and published the periodical *Na-na-kwa* (Dawn of the West Coast) from 1898 on. From 1904 to 1914 he was the superintendent of the Port Simpson District, which included all the area north of Alert Bay. In 1906 he transferred to Port Simpson, and in 1914 he became the principal at Coqualeetza Residential School in the Fraser Valley. He retired to Vancouver in 1934, and the bulk of his collection, assembled primarily in Kitamaat and Port Simpson during the collecting craze of the late nineteenth and early twentieth centuries, went to the University of British Columbia in 1948. Raley died in 1958.[35]

As principal of the Coqualeetza Residential School in Sardis, Raley was part of the system; however, especially after his retirement in 1934, he also advocated the reform of the DIA and how it managed the "Indian problem."

The Coqualeetza school itself was something of an anomaly – a Protestant missionary school in a Roman Catholic zone that would count such important future political leaders as George Manuel[36] and Peter Kelly[37] among its alumni. Raley, like Collier, focused upon reforming First Nations education, and he combined this reform spirit with his own personal interest in First Nations heritage.

Raley is important in a number of different ways. He was well known around Vancouver. During the 1930s his large, comprehensive collection of Northwest Coast material served as Vancouver's de facto municipal museum, and it provided significant portions of the Northwest Coast collections now housed at the Royal Ontario Museum and the University of British Columbia's Museum of Anthropology. He also exemplified a growing dissatisfaction with the management of the DIA and articulated the ideological arguments and promotional strategies discussed during the Depression. His actions further demonstrate the increasing difficulty of the independent, amateur, and volunteer cultural organizations in realizing their objectives. In the cash-strapped society of the 1930s, these organizations looked to the state for reformed leadership. However, the state was absorbed by deficit and welfare payments, and, initially, it instigated government restructuring only to solve its own financial crises.

Raley's Canadian Indian Arts and Crafts Board

Raley combined writing with more practical activities when promoting provincial and national arts programs. He wrote texts centred on his vision of a "revival of Indian art and handicraft as a welfare movement,"[38] echoing, albeit not consciously, the calls of Harlan Smith in Ottawa in the 1920s and paralleling similar developments in the other provinces.[39] And he was the first major figure to attempt to implement a handicraft guild organization to aid in the marketing of First Nations objects in British Columbia. His concern stemmed, first, from his intimate knowledge of reserve poverty and of what a social obstacle it was and, second, from his dismay at the prejudice-driven unwillingness of Anglo-Saxon Canada to bear what he saw as its paternalistic responsibility for the full economic assimilation of First Nations peoples. "Apart from Government and Church aid in medical, educational and missionary service," he wrote, "comparatively little has been expended on the economic problems of the Indians."[40] He contributed his own collection to public displays, and his activity with AHSAV saw the confluence of a number of circumstances in the promotion of individual artists, something that was crucial to the foundation of any successful revival or promotional program.

Raley began this line of pursuit in the early 1930s, at the height of the Great Depression. Influenced by Roosevelt's developing New Deal policy in the United States, Raley was also aware of the contemporary state encouragement of arts and crafts associations and other cottage industries in Britain, and he thought that it should be possible to adapt these programs to Canada's economic problems. In discussing art, his aesthetic sensibilities, and his vision of art as a social tool, he was reiterating well established ideas in the field of arts and crafts.

For Raley, the arts were not simply a historical product: they were also the solution to what he saw as the "Indian problem." Sometime in the 1930s Raley summarized the plight of those producing objects for cross-cultural sale, and he did so through the use of imagery that reflected Depression-era chaos. Choosing a female basket weaver as the symbol of the vulnerability of the curio producer, he wrote:

> The basket-making woman is often seen on the streets of our villages, towns and cities with a clumsily wrapped bundle of baskets for sale. She naturally wants cash, sometimes difficult to get. Rather than not make a sale, she barters them for old, second-hand clothes and learns how to haggle. Now, in the eyes of an intending purchaser the goods are cheapened before they are sold and the Indian woman is led to believe her goods are different from those of the whites and not worth cash, so she has to be content to swap them for food, old clothes or anything. It is not an unusual sight to see an aged Indian near a curbstone market or sitting on the sidewalk in all kinds of weather, or in some other public place, trying to effect a sale. It is neither profitable to the Indian nor creditable to Canadians ... It would be very helpful to the women if this form of labour were organized.[41]

Raley's solution was certainly confined by the colonial vision of First Nations people as lower-class labourers. And, in this sense, the reform he called for was limited,[42] coming from within the ideological system of the mainstream society. The pressures he applied in his attempt to promote change were structured by the bureaucracy of the DIA. An example of this can be seen in Raley's 1934 attempts to confirm funding for an arts program through this department. During this period one can sense, in the correspondence between Raley and Indian agency officials, that the nuances of art versus handicraft versus industry had taken on a certain urgency with regard to the battle for limited public funding. Competition for attention stimulated semantic negotiation. Words like "art," or even "handicraft," ignited public interest, while phrases like "industrial arts" attracted public funding. Raley wrote to Indian Agent Daunt:

> The enclosed copy of the Department's letter ... dated Ottawa April 23rd, states the reason why the Department is not disposed to make a grant of $600.00 to continue the teaching of Indian pupils their native handicrafts such as weaving, basketry, etc.

> It is evident from the wording of the letter my recommendation did not carry weight enough, neither did I persuade the Department of the vital importance of the undertaking. I hope you will forgive me if I write at length to explain more fully the terms of my letter which appear to be vague, to emphasize the need and renew the request for a grant.
>
> I was unfortunate using the term "handicraft arts." The meaning would have been obvious if I had used the term "Indian industrial arts." However, the term "handicraft arts" generally expresses to me, when applied to the Indians of the Pacific Coast, the whole range of cultural activities and industries. In other words, the washing, carding, spinning, knitting, weaving, carving, and bead work, with symbolic Indian designs are "Indian industrial arts."[43]

Canadian social reformers thus faced stiff opposition from both the general public and the administration. Although the Indian Arts and Crafts Board also worked to set up cooperative retail outlets for curios on or near reserves, the American government recognized the general public's resistance to the conception of Native American products as "art," and it used the board for marketing purposes. This is why the exhibitions it co-sponsored included sections on "Indian Art for Modern Living."[44]

Raley advocated a similar approach, but he first had to convince public bureaucrats who were inclined to favour industrial training over arts and crafts, especially with regard to a primarily resource-oriented province, and especially since industrial training had been one of the DIA's goals since the 1890s. His option was to form an independent board without public financing, a difficult task during that era.

In his public lectures and writing, Raley was careful to follow the wording of the arts and crafts movement. He had assembled his own collection at the height of the movement's popularity; presumably, he found its rhetoric personally appealing. He suggested, for example, that the "machine age is ... responsible for the decay of [Indian] handicrafts."[45] His focus on both nature and healing in the arts are also reminiscent of the arts and crafts movement. He defined two kinds of "Indian arts and crafts," both involving "the skilful adaptation and application to some purpose and use of knowledge acquired from nature,"[46] one pre-historic – "natural art in its purity, before any extraneous or foreign influences" – and the other historic, having lost "realistic features" and having become "conventionalized through Asiatic, Russian, Spanish and other European contacts."[47] He stated further that any revival of these arts "as a welfare movement ... would give a new cultural activity with a sense of accomplishment and improve his [the 'Indian's'] social status in the community."[48]

Raley, cognizant of open hostility towards such traditional First Nations pursuits as the potlatch, framed his argument for the promotion of First

Nations art within the concept of historical progression, which was accompanied by state rhetoric pertaining to "modernizing" First Nations peoples through assimilation. "Ignorantly by some, maliciously by others, an undercurrent of propaganda has been maintained to the effect that Indian youth revert to type ... upon their return home" from residential school. "It is true the graduates of our schools have not an easy time of it," writes Raley. "He has grown, the people of his village have not. He has advanced intellectually, the people of his village have been intellectually stationary. He finds a conflicting of ideals." But, Raley continues, applying the arts and crafts idea that the making of art produces better people, "a revival of primitive arts" would lessen rather than increase "the danger of reversion to objectionable customs ... Industries would help socialize the graduate, by a common activity, and re-establish the equilibrium between him and his family and the village group."[49]

In essence, Raley advocated "disappearing" the ancient social order by commoditizing its visual trappings. This was the point of offering "prevocational instruction in weaving, basket making, carving, [and] art designs with Indian motifs"[50] at Coqualeetza. Commoditization and the use of British models of the organization of production were the two pillars supporting Raley's argument that such "industries" did not encourage "reversion to objectionable customs." Raley even demonstrated an almost prophetic understanding of how important a marketing tool Northwest Coast design might prove to be for Canadian business when he cited the Prince of Wales's admonition that "greater attention to the artistic side of industry or design in industry is essential if our manufacturers are to develop their domestic and overseas market."[51]

Raley's primary interest was in expanding the Coqualeetza experiment into a national, state-funded organization. He thought that this should be possible as, in the nineteenth century, the organization of guilds and other supportive associations was an integral part of the arts and crafts movement in Britain and Euro-America. However, he focused his efforts on duplicating and adapting the guild structure in order to promote First Nations objects, particularly in British Columbia.

Raley and Public Display in Vancouver

With his personal interest in collecting First Nations objects, one of the earliest moves Raley made after retiring to Vancouver was to arrange for his collection to be put on public display. This was part of his desire to encourage the understanding of, and aid for, First Nations peoples. In an October 1934 letter to Vancouver city archivist J.S. Matthews outlining the history of his collection, Raley demonstrated an understanding of how the salvage paradigm constructed value and authority in "ethnographic" collections:

> Most of the specimens are of ethnological value. Now, ethnology, as you are aware, is a view to understanding their modes of life, their customs, social organizations, ceremonials, psychology, religion; and in general terms, their cultural background. Only through this study can we appreciate the early life of the Indians of the North West Coast of the Pacific, and be fair to them ...
>
> The opportunity for first-hand information is passing quickly. We have imposed our civilization upon their primitive culture, and are now dependent for our knowledge on the few remaining aged Indians, the scientific records, and museums. It follows that a collection such as mine is symbolic, on a modest scale, of the arts, handicrafts, ceremonies, social life, religion, culture of a race. In the specimens we read the life history of a vanishing race.[52]

According to a 1946 document written by Matthews, in 1934 Mrs. Raley was negotiating the sale of Raley's collection for $3,500 to George Heye of the Heye Foundation in order to cover tax payments. (Heye, of course, is the same "foreign" individual who had purchased objects from Halliday [see Chapter 2].) However, instead, Matthews arranged for Victor Spencer, who was associated with Vancouver's David Spencer Department Store, to purchase the collection at the same price as "enough 'stuff' ha[d] gone out of British Columbia already."[53] Raley would provide for suitable display cases out of the $3,500, and Matthews arranged for the rotunda of the old court house on Georgia Street to be used as the location for this personal museum. In 1937 it was moved to the tenth floor of the newly constructed city hall, presumably as part of the city museum intended by the Art, Historical, and Scientific Association of Vancouver some forty years earlier. The collection later provided a sound basis for both the Vancouver Museum and the University of British Columbia's Museum of Anthropology, despite some disagreement between Spencer and Raley over the amount paid.

Raley seems to have seen the exhibition of the past as a new beginning. He saw public display as a stimulus to sales. Probably due to his experience as an educator and Indian school administrator, he entertained the idea of an active role for art in the economic development of First Nations peoples. For Raley, First Nations art provided mainstream "Canadian" society with a unique luxury product. Raley's vision was very much mired in the British class system. He was, in essence, advocating arts and crafts as a product that First Nations, as a labouring class, could produce for the consumption of a European, presumably British, managerial elite.

What distinguishes Raley from other collectors and ethnologists of his time is that, while he accepted the "invention of heritage" (i.e., the formation of this new social memory and its implications for colonial self-legitimization), he pushed it towards an "invention of art" that was not limited to understanding First Nations objects simply as historical heritage. In his view, the objects also had practical value as vehicles for achieving his vision of the fair and just absorption for First Nations peoples into Euro-Canadian society.

There are thus two aspects to Raley's collection: (1) its assemblage and use within the Euro-Canadian community as a symbol of the past and (2) its utility in the promotion of a *contemporary* commodity market. Since it was focused on curio production, his commoditization campaign was not intended to force closure in the sense referred to by Dominguez, who, when discussing ethnological collections, commented: "The separation of objects from their users and the closure imposed on that separation by the act of sale left museums with objects whose relevance to the cultures they presumably embody is ... a Euro-American invention."[54] Although the value of objects of the past was, as Dominguez notes, an unequivocally Euro-American invention, Raley, like d'Harnoncourt, hoped to manipulate this symbolic value in order to produce new value for newly produced objects that imitated the forms of the past. It is the mainstream desire for this manipulation that makes the commoditization programs of the 1930s, like Raley's proposals, so utterly distinct from such 1920s promotional programs as the national museum projects and AHSAV's Stanley Park village. In the 1920s, under state management, objects like crest poles were transformed into props for the construction of national identity and social memory. Raley was advocating the commoditization of these props, albeit in the altruistic hope of jump-starting an economic outlet for impoverished communities.

The Royal Society of Arts Brief

In 1934, during a trip aimed at drumming up support among a number of circles (including the DIA, museums, and established craft associations), Raley outlined his own revitalization plan in an address to the Royal Society of Arts in Toronto. He had toyed with the basic ideas, particularly the use of the school system to instill both skills and desire in First Nations students, in his work at the Coqualeetza Residential School in Sardis, and, over the preceding two or three years, he had been developing a national scheme.

While praising the stewardship policies of the Canadian DIA, Raley called for a readjustment of policy based, in part, on the example of Roosevelt's New Deal and aimed at the improvement of the economic status of First Nations peoples. He had four reasons for choosing the arts as a focus for this economic improvement: (1) the decline of Aboriginal art from its nineteenth-century zenith was largely due to "the mistaken zeal of the white man, who overwhelmed primitive ideas and ideals with the so-called superiority of all things white";[55] (2) First Nations arts and crafts were distinctively Canadian and were "Canada's first contribution to the world of art";[56] (3) the discontentment found among First Nations graduates "could be remedied by a revival of native arts and regional industries";[57] and (4) such a revival would solve the economic problem, especially if it could be given "a commercial value by means of a permanent market for tourists ... [and] could also be linked with ordinary commercial industries and manufactures, and applied to many commodities of trade both ornamental and useful."[58] Later in his address, he pointed out that most First Nations people could not compete on equal terms with Euro-Canadians, so the arts would be a perfect beginning for economic revival as there would be no competition from Euro-Canada.

Raley notes that some older artisans were still living and that young people continued to be inspired by the "legends, symbols, and monuments of their forefathers."[59] In fact, in his follow-up draft, "Important Considerations Involved in the Treatise on Canadian Indian Art and Industries," he detailed more precisely how many people were still producing what kinds of material in various First Nations communities throughout the province, suggesting that there were at least twenty to twenty-five active, high-quality carvers and citing the continuation of a number of different textile techniques. He also stressed the lack of opportunity on reserves and called for work incentives in the form of financial reward. His plan called for the stimulation of the interest of the elderly artisans, the de-emphasis of distribution as found in the potlatch system, the enlistment of anthropologists and ethnologists "who know where there is real accomplishment and finished work to be found,"[60] and an educational campaign aimed at day and residential schools. In this sense, he advocated strategies followed by Dorothy Dunn at the Indian School in Santa Fe from 1932 to 1937, and supported after 1934 by the Indian Arts and Crafts Board.

However, Raley also called for the education of the Euro-Canadian public through various media outlets in an effort to create what he called "Indian mindedness towards primitive Indian crafts."[61] He further advocated securing the cooperation of railway and steamship lines, suggesting the use of a demonstration car on the main rail transport lines. This could all be accomplished under the formation of the Canadian Indian Handicraft Arts Association or Guild, which would be organized with an official patron or patroness; a board of directors; an executive with chairman, secretary, and treasurer; branches with committees for each province; and life, honourary, and annual memberships.[62]

A fundamental objection raised to Raley's plan, cited by Raley himself,[63] was that the program could be incorporated into the existing structure of the Canadian Handicrafts Guild. Just as, previously, Raley had argued that welfare support differed for Euro-Canadians and First Nations, respectively, so he argued that the artistic situation for these two groups also differed and that, therefore, First Nations needed an organization other than the guild. Raley insisted that Indian arts be segregated from the mainstream so as to minimize competition, and he wrote briefs and resolutions calling for the preservation of these handicrafts, frequently citing the "dangerous" example of the Japanese imitative mass-production of First Nations designs.[64] In addition, Raley had found that the guild's forays into the marketing of First Nations objects was feeble. In the guild's efforts "there was nothing to suggest Canada had in its borders a great zone of primitive culture."[65] He also pointed out that a craft store that the guild opened in Vancouver was thin in its exposure of First Nations work and that it closed due to its failure to turn a profit. Raley must have also felt that the necessary start-up funding for his comprehensive vision would come from the DIA. This government support would dwarf any paltry amount available from the guild and, therefore, necessitated a distinct arts and crafts organization.

His plan went beyond these two treatises to the actual writing of a resolution for the Canadian Indian Art and Handicraft Guild, although if it was ever actually formed, its impact was minimal. It did not result in any broad marketing campaign or in any major commissions or sales for individual artists. Alice Ravenhill's British Columbia Indian Arts and Welfare Society, formed only four years after Raley's Royal Arts Society address and following the guild structure closely enough to indicate an awareness of Raley's intentions, was to have a much more significant impact.

6
Alice Ravenhill and the BCIAWS

Although Vancouver had achieved a reputation as British Columbia's commercial centre before the Great Depression, it was not where government policy decisions were made. For this reason alone, Raley's lobbying activities had a strike against them. Anyone seeking meaningful change had to somehow align him/herself with the circles of political power in either Ottawa or Victoria, centres of government locked in a seemingly endless series of disputes over jurisdiction. Policy disagreements regarding "Indian" administration dated back to British Columbia's entrance into Confederation.[1]

Reform of the system of education was a widespread concern in British Columbia[2] and provided an avenue by which the provincial government could establish some semblance of control over the policy of Indian administration and the destiny of First Nations peoples in that province.[3] With education a provincial matter and the Department of Indian Affairs a federal ministry, the education of Aboriginal children satisfied no one. Once again, because First Nations "art" was the one attribute of First Nations societies constructed in a positive light by public institutions like the museums, it proved to be a useful tool in generating non-First Nations public support for educational reform efforts. The most successful reform lobby to promote First Nations art, and the focus of this chapter, occurred in Victoria and can be traced to the organizational efforts of Alice Ravenhill and the British Columbia Indian Arts and Welfare Society between 1935 and 1948. In contrast to Raley, who wanted to use the educational system to encourage the production and consumption of First Nations arts as a means of economic integration, Ravenhill sought to use the production and consumption of First Nations arts in order to better the educational system, making it both more relevant and more accessible to First Nations children.

Ravenhill and the Importance of the BCIAWS

Ravenhill was instrumental in forming the Society for the Furtherance of British Columbia Indian Arts and Welfare, later shortened to the British

Columbia Indian Arts and Welfare Society (BCIAWS), in December 1939/January 1940. The BCIAWS is significant because it followed the goals and corporate organization for a voluntary association (as advocated by Raley in 1935) as well as, by the mid-1940s, some of the objectives then being pursued by the British Columbia Provincial Museum. The BCIAWS formed an important link in the transition of First Nations arts promotion from voluntary organizations (in the 1930s) to state institutions (in the 1940s). Ultimately, the BCIAWS may have succeeded where Raley (at least in his association with AHSAV) failed, partially because of its proximity to the provincial social elite in Victoria.

Ravenhill was thus an important figure in the professionalization of the field of First Nations art; she contributed to the definition of an occupation – "Indian artist" – that was, in the 1950s, allocated professional status within the public "cultural" institutions of British Columbia. During the 1940s and 1950s museums and universities sought to establish a monopoly over the title and practice of specific "professional" practitioners as well as to exert control over entry and training. The BCIAWS played a significant role in developing an infrastructure that would, in the 1950s, link the three main components of a formalized art market: producers of objects, consumers of objects, and producers of knowledge about the objects. The BCIAWS's utilization of museum collections and its participation in educational projects simultaneously informed producers and consumers about standards of performance as well as about form and materials, thus serving, over the next three decades, as the basis for promotion and marketing. This, in essence, established the ability of state officials to define the criteria used for determining what constitutes "Indian" art and, therefore, who could be an "Indian" artist. By aligning itself with the British Columbia Provincial Museum (BCPM), the BCIAWS supported and legitimized state control over the social distribution of knowledge about First Nations objects, thus also contributing to the ongoing attempt to deny Aboriginal modes of authority and leadership.

Ravenhill and Educational Reform

Alice Ravenhill was born in England in 1859 to an upper-class family. On the periphery of Britain's royal web, Ravenhill was fluent in the intricacies of a social order accepted and reproduced by the Victorian English upper class.[4] "The stream of social life into which I was born has almost petered out," she lamented near the end of her life. And despite the problems created by Victorian industrialization, the problems that were the focus of her professional life, Ravenhill believed that the positive attributes of her generation were passing with that stream of Victorian social life. "With it has disappeared to a great degree the atmosphere in which I was reared, with its sense of responsibility for the advantages enjoyed, of the paramount duty of serving others, of self-control and reticence, of dignified endurance of reverses, of respect for authority and law, of cheerful self-sacrifice, and of dogged perseverance to gain desired ends."[5] With this idealized British worldview, she adapted her training and experience to the social welfare of British Columbian First Nations.

As a young woman in England, Alice Ravenhill received a County Council Lectureship from the National Health Society. She participated in a growing government-sponsored infrastructure that was intended to maintain healthy work and home living conditions, particularly among the lower classes, through the provision of education. This included both basic health practices, domestic technical training, and workplace inspection.

Ravenhill emigrated to Canada in 1910, living at Shawnigan Lake on southern Vancouver Island before moving to Victoria. She became involved with First Nations arts when she was approached by the provincial women's institutes in 1926 to provide guidance with regard to adapting First Nations designs to the making of hooked rugs, a craft pursuit Victoria resident Emily Carr had also been involved with at around the same time. Ravenhill was, by her own admission, ignorant of the subject and turned to her neighbour W.A. Newcombe, a biologist with the BCPM and the son of C.F. Newcombe (who was primarily responsible for assembling the Aboriginal objects collection at the museum). By the time Ravenhill felt confident enough to talk about the subject, the women's institutes had turned their interest elsewhere, and she was left with a growing collection of First Nations-based needlework designs that were being sold in a commercial store in Victoria. She also had both a steadily growing interest in First Nations arts and a concern that the federal system of education had failed First Nations children.[6]

Ravenhill's official involvement was instigated with the BCPM's 1934 receipt of a Carnegie fund grant for public lectures. These lectures covered a variety of natural history topics,[7] with Ravenhill's primary responsibility being both adult and children's lectures on the Indian handicrafts of British Columbia. The attendance for such lectures, which provides an idea of the program's popularity, hovered around 300 per lecture for children's classes and eighty for adult classes.[8] This kind of program was becoming increasingly popular in museums throughout both the United States and Canada. Ravenhill's interest in unconventional educational techniques was particularly suited to the changing interests of museums. Malcolm Knowles suggests that accessibility was becoming an urgent concern for museums, with previous museum-based educational programs tending to "please the staff and reflect their professional interests rather than please the public and take into account their interests."[9] The public programs, stiff, formal, and organized according to academic principles, were not bringing in the operating funds. "This view began to change," continues Knowles, "as a result of the economic pressure brought on by the depression of the 1930s,"[10] although it had been a concern of the museums even earlier, as is indicated by the popularity of Harlan Smith's public lectures at the national museum in the 1920s. "As contributions from wealthy patrons diminished, museums became increasingly dependent upon public support. Accordingly, the 'curriculum' of the museums began to broaden."[11] The BCPM then took a more functionalist role. In this new curatorial attitude it became a repository of knowledge that could be applied socially for the apparent benefit of the larger community. By 1940 the BCPM broadened its display strategy to include the construction of Thunderbird Park adjacent to its main building, making its collection of poles (assembled primarily by Newcombe prior to the First World War) a highly visible outdoor public landmark in the city's downtown centre.

Ravenhill and the BCPM Publications

In 1936 Ravenhill gave an introductory presentation to the Victoria Normal School on First Nations peoples in British Columbia. This turned out to be a stepping stone to a number of larger projects. "I learned ... that an eight weeks' course on our B.C. Indians had been recently included in the grade school curriculum, without any authentic guidance being provided for the teachers who had to give it," she wrote in her memoirs. "I ventured to take this up with the Provincial Department of Education and after some months was entrusted with the difficult task of summarizing this unusually intricate subject in a bulletin limited to 30,000 words. To do this was a clear case of 'fools rush in.'"[12] Nonetheless, the result was *The Native Tribes of British Columbia*, published in 1938 primarily for each grade school in the province but also including an extra run-off of a few hundred copies for sale to the general public. It was the first school text to examine specifically the First Nations of British Columbia, and this in itself qualifies the book as a significant step. Furthermore, while Ravenhill culled the elder Newcombe's 1909 *Guide to the Anthropological Collection in the Provincial Museum* for photographs from the Northwest Coast, her book did not suffer from the same bias towards both the Coast and carved Coastal objects, normally thought of as men's arts, as did many of the later books on the same subject. Instead, she attempted to give a fuller idea of the "lost cultures"[13] of the entire province, directing her attention to interior peoples and women's textile arts as well as to the usual material.

The Native Tribes of British Columbia outlined Ravenhill's position on First Nations societies and their relationship to "modern" Canada. While this position is indistinguishable from much of the popular and academic writing of the period, it significantly reinforced the strong hold exercised by Euro-Canada's paternalistic sense of fiduciary responsibility towards all aspects of First Nations life. She states unequivocally that "these people were three thousand years behind the standard of European culture at the close of the eighteenth century"[14] and that their "backwardness"[15] (here she follows the ideas of her acquaintance Diamond Jenness)[16] was due to the "physiographic formation of the continent";[17] the "unsuitability of flora and fauna for agriculture";[18] and, perhaps most tellingly, First Nations peoples' own lack of "mechanic instincts."[19] This idea, made official when the Ministry of Education adapted and widely disseminated her book as a school text, also sets up what Ravenhill calls Euro-Canada's "deeper sense of responsibility towards backward races" and the desire, if not the obligation, "to make amends, when opportunity offers, for previous misunderstandings."[20] The question of responsibility then led to Ravenhill's primary role in the formation of the BCIAWS.

The BCIAWS and the BCPM's attainment of a Carnegie grant for Ravenhill's involvement in the mid-1930s formed an institutional intersection for educational reform interests in British Columbia. Ravenhill and the BCIAWS emphasized educational reform as an answer to the "Indian problem." Based on the American Indian New Deal model, their ideas of artistic promotion and the encouragement of cultural pride was intended to enable First Nations children to open the door to an Anglo-Canadian way of life. By the mid-1930s the BCPM was producing materials and displays intended to complement the provincial school curricula. The museum was attempting to respond to what its administration perceived to be the needs of the society. The salvage paradigm, which guided the accumulation of objects for museum collections as contributions to scientific prosperity, was giving way to a farther-reaching educational purpose. In addition to its participation in education-related projects with the BCIAWS, by the mid-1940s the museum was also exhibiting, for example, selected works from children's Saturday morning art classes at the Vancouver Art Gallery and installing a panel series on "Indian life" in the rotunda of the provincial legislature.[21]

The crux of Ravenhill's call for policy change was that Euro-Canada had not sufficiently understood and exploited either the potential contributions First Nations peoples could make to the economy or how much it could enjoy First Nations products. The line between assimilation (the replacement of Aboriginal identities with a British worldview) and integration (which would allow aspects of First Nations identities to be commoditized in order to further the modern Canadian economy) was a subtle one.

Through these school-related projects, Ravenhill gained considerable power with regard to shaping public thought about First Nations societies. Although it may have seemed to non-Aboriginal Canadians that her objectives were altruistic, Ravenhill's vision, and that of the BCIAWS, remained paternalistic. While coloured by her own social reformist attitudes, Ravenhill's understanding was further bolstered by her reliance upon a combination of relatively recent ethnological and anthropological theory, albeit from varying streams of thought (e.g., Otis T. Mason, Franz Boas, Ruth Benedict, and Erna Gunther) as well as from pioneer accounts and local figures (e.g., Paul Kane, Captains Cook and Mayne, Father Morice, and C.F. Newcombe).

The main emphasis in much of these texts (i.e., the disappearance and anthropological salvage[22] of First Nations peoples and optimism about the "Changing Indian") led to an acceptance of the possibility of a revival in "modern" terms. "Common sense" solutions to the "Indian problem" entailed economic integration and proper preparatory training. Quality control strategies (such as the provision of museum examples) in combination with the promotion of hand-crafted goods as a "modern" luxury item soon formed the BCIAWS's main arts policy.

The objectives of the BCIAWS, as drafted by Ravenhill and her associates in 1939, were:

1. To promote the welfare of the Indians, particularly those of British Columbia, by supporting all movements directed towards an improvement in Indian Health, Education and Social Welfare.
2. To bring to notice of the public, the innate merits and deep-rooted artistic talents of the Indian people by means of Exhibitions of their Arts and Crafts, Folklore, Music, Drama and Dance; and through Meetings, Conferences, Publications, Radio Broadcasts, Television and the Press.
3. To arouse the Indians themselves to a realization of their true place in the social organization of this country, and to encourage them to work for, and to take advantage of, the opportunities which are offered under the revised Indian Act, and to prepare themselves for community service.
4. To devote particular attention to the needs of the younger generation of Indian people, and to work in their interest to remove the inequalities of opportunity which still present almost insurmountable handicaps to young Indians trying to enter the occupation of their choice.[23]

The executive committee members included Major Bullock-Webster, director of British Columbia School and Community Drama and Ravenhill's successor as BCIAWS president; Alma Russell, formerly of the BC Archives; representatives from the Victoria and Island Arts and Crafts Society; and Madame Sanderson-Maugin, whom Ravenhill thought "invaluable for her ... wide social connections which enabled her to secure for the young Society sufficient funds to publish"[24] its first children's book in 1940. Three influential new members joined the committee in 1941: Willard E. Ireland, provincial archivist; Clifford Carl, director of the BCPM (who immediately offered the museum as the society's official address); and A.E. Pickford, author of *Food Plants Used by the Natives of British Columbia*. By 1942 Lieutenant-Governor W.C. Woodward became the society's honourary patron, and a BCIAWS off-shoot was established in Oliver in 1941.[25] The Reverend J.C.

Goodfellow, formerly with AHSAV and author of the first pamphlet on the Stanley Park poles, became the honourary president in 1942, and, throughout 1943, "a number of B.C. Indians became Honourary Members."[26]

The group typified a social reform ideology popular at that time in British Columbia. It emphasized the use of study groups, cooperation, and citizenship education in an effort to improve impoverished sections of Canadian society.[27] It relied upon models from England and the United States, and it recognized the potential of the popular value of First Nations "art," seeking to gather the various ideological threads and display strategies that had been developing since AHSAV's first attempts in Stanley Park. Following earlier leads, tourism was singled out as important;[28] however, not surprisingly given Ravenhill's background as an educator and the interests of the forming committee in general, the society initially concentrated on educational activities.

The first publication of this organization had no Northwest Coast content; rather, it was a Christmas tale from the Okanagan Valley. *The Tale of the Nativity* was illustrated by children of the Inkameep reserve in Oliver and was based on myths performed by the students at the opening of the BCPM's Thunderbird Park in 1942.[29] Between 1941 and 1943 a second Nativity book (illustrated by François Batiste, who signed his name Sis-hu-lk),[30] and a book entitled *Meet Mr. Coyote* (an illustrated storybook from the Indian residential school at Lytton) were also published by the society.

The image of cooperation and kindly paternalism suggested by the BCIAWS in its promotion of art and literature by First Nations children masked the horrific treatment the children themselves all too often received. The policy of disrupting families by removing First Nations children to either residential schools or to Euro-Canadian foster families is alluded to in Sis-hu-lk's illustrations. In one (see Figure 20), a simple line drawing depicts two of the three Wise Men as First Nations chiefs, thus suggesting Biblical stories as part of a shared heritage. In another, the character of Joseph is transformed into Jesus' foster-father with whom, according to the caption, "The Child" spends a "Happy Boyhood." This goes to the heart of assimilationist educational policy in the 1920s and 1930s, when Christianization, through adapting Euro-Christian traditions to a First Nations context, disintegrating the extended family pattern, and disrupting the relationship between generations, were critical to remoulding First Nations children into "good" members of Canadian society.[31]

Sis-hu-lk's drawings are more a celebration of this policy than they are of his achievements or those of his schoolmates. The emphasis on a "Happy Boyhood" with a "Foster-Father" is typical of the silences of the time. However, "recent reports dealing with the residential schools focus on the horrendous physical and sexual abuse many native children suffered while in these institutions. Abuse of this nature follows its victims throughout their

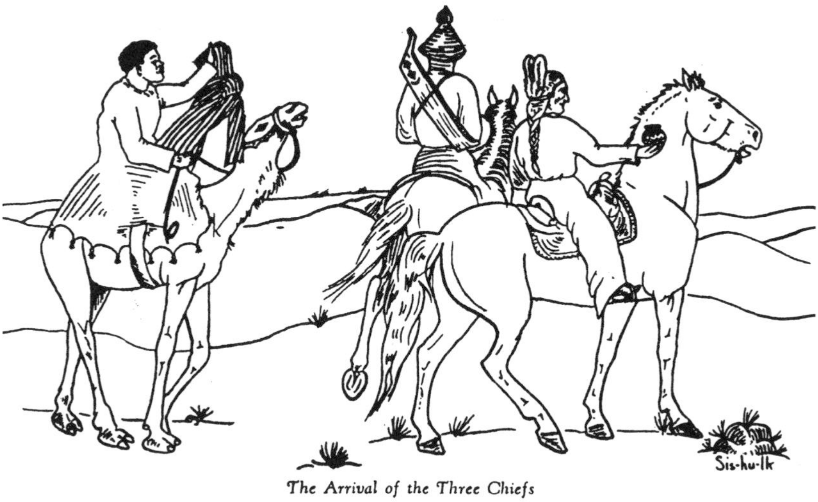

20 One of Sis-hu-lk's (François Batiste) illustrations, from *The Tale of the Nativity*. It depicts two of the three Wise Men as First Nations chiefs on horseback.

lives and colours their relationships with others," writes Ernie Crey. "Those who have written about these institutions emphasize those aspects of the institutions designed to assimilate aboriginal children."[32] Although Walsh was a key instigator in the BCIAWS and was clearly concerned about the welfare of his students, with what is now known about the sometimes tragic consequences of assimilation through education, these publications often seem obscenely ironic.[33]

Following the success of *The Native Tribes of British Columbia*, the BCPM and the BCIAWS cooperated in the publication of Ravenhill's *A Cornerstone of Canadian Culture: An Outline of the Arts and Crafts of the Indian Tribes of British Columbia*. This work was first intended as a selection of wall charts drawn from the BCPM's collection and originally commissioned by the Department of Indian Affairs to show "examples of the arts and crafts formerly practiced by the Indian tribes"[34] of British Columbia. Accompanied by a handbook, these were to circulate among First Nations schools to "provide teachers and students with a record of former tribal decorative arts and crafts which have possibilities of further development and utilization in modern life."[35] The commission fell through, and the result was this smaller book-version published by the BCPM in 1944. Included were designs drawn for Swanton by Charles Edenshaw – designs that later served as a source for Bill Reid's early Haida-style jewellery efforts.[36] Thus, one might argue that, through Reid's earliest Haida work, Ravenhill and the BCIAWS were indeed successful in providing inspirational fodder for the most widely recognized First Nations artist from British Columbia – a feat that surpassed the implicit aspirations of their published objectives.

BCIAWS Exhibits and Promotional Activities

In addition to the publication of texts on First Nations peoples and arts, beginning in 1943 the BCIAWS co-sponsored an annual exhibition of First Nations art at the BCPM. The exhibition was primarily intended to provide exposure for young First Nations artists, like Batiste and Judith Morgan, who were still in school. However, a number of mature artists also gained considerable exposure through the exhibitions, including, most notably, George Clutesi and Ellen Neel.

As museums had extended their contacts to other museums and public institutions, objects and paintings in the annual exhibitions were sometimes selected for loan to institutions outside Victoria. Under the auspices of the BCIAWS, and shipped through the BCPM, in 1943 a number of objects were sent to the Annual Exhibitions of the Royal Canadian Academy

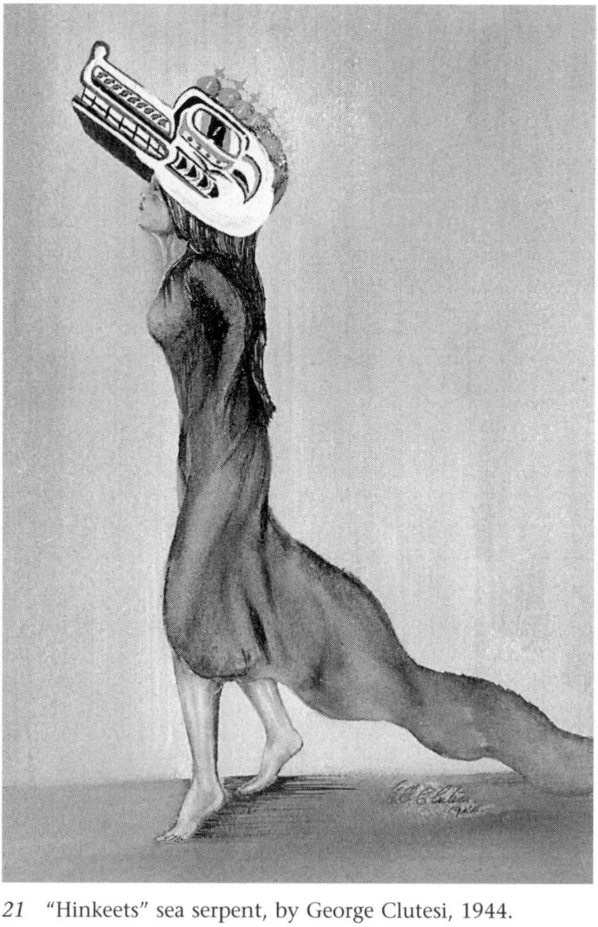

21 "Hinkeets" sea serpent, by George Clutesi, 1944.

of Arts in Quebec and Montreal. This resulted in individual prizes for the basketry work of Mrs. Johnny Johnson of Kakawis, the knitting of Madeline Charlie of St. Catherine's School in Duncan, as well as school prizes for Christie Indian School in Kakawis (for design) and to Inkameep School in Oliver and Christie Indian School (for applied work).[37] In commemoration of the provincial enfranchisement of First Nations peoples in 1949, the provincial government bought five of Judith Morgan's paintings selected from the annual exhibit. The five, *Morning Mist, Hamatcha Dance, Bear from Kitwancul, The Origin of the Wolf Society*, and *The Inheritance Dance*, were then shipped to Ottawa for a solo show, funded by the DIA, at the national museum. Typically, Morgan illustrated Gitxsan myths and ceremonies in an illusionist style, and her work thus sparks comparisons with the Southwestern and Southern Plains painting associated with Indian schools in New Mexico and Oklahoma in the 1920s and 1930s.[38] Rather than adhering to the indigenous conventions of two-dimensional patterns built of flat black and red lines and shapes common to ceremonial painting in the Skeena Valley, Morgan typically illustrated Gitxsan myths with naturalistic compositions heightened through dramatic chiaroscuro – a potent synthesis that could have potentially challenged the use of First Nations themes in the work of Carr and other non-Aboriginal painters who lacked the intimacy that, as a cultural insider, Morgan would have had.

Morgan's paintings and other selected works from the annual exhibitions were also shown at the Philbrook Art Center in Tulsa, Oklahoma, and at the Portland Art Gallery in Portland, Oregon.[39] The annual exhibits began to garner considerable attention for both the BCIAWS and young individual artists. And, as Anthony Walsh pointed out in his introduction to *The Tale of the Nativity*, the artistic activity was all part of a larger agenda. Using First Nations art, it was possible to gain media attention, and "by newspaper publicity and other means, our own citizens are gradually being awakened to their own responsibility to the Indian as an integral unit of Canadian national life."[40]

As well as attracting public attention through the arts, these organizations also submitted briefs directly to the government. In 1943 the Okanagan Society for the Revival of Indian Arts and Crafts submitted a brief to the federal Committee on Reconstruction and Re-establishment entitled *Native Canadians: A Plan for the Rehabilitation of Indians*. The society's two fundamental proposals included a replacement Indian Act modelled on the American Bureau of Indian Affairs New Deal policy and the establishment of a royal commission on Indian affairs.[41] Both the BCIAWS and the Oliver offshoot lobbied for enhanced educational opportunities. In its 1943 brief the Okanagan group argued for postsecondary education, suggesting that "the balance, judgment, and organizing ability of the leaders of the Native Brotherhood of B.C. with five thousand Indian members compare favorably with that of white executives" and that, therefore, "there are apparently no more limits to an Indian's capabilities than there are to those of other races, when adequate educational facilities are provided."[42] In 1942 the BCIAWS also submitted a brief entitled *Suggestions on the Encouragement of Arts and Crafts in the Indian Schools of British Columbia* to the DIA, and Ravenhill prepared a BCIAWS brief to the 1946-8 joint committee on the Indian Act.

By the time the Second World War had ended, patriotic rhetoric aimed against European fascism and the eugenic principles of Nazi nationalism had brought racism into disrepute. "As a result of the atrocities committed during this war, the world community examined its collective conscience," comments Wet'suwet'en/Carrier writer Shirley Joseph, "and in 1948 produced the United Nations Declaration of Human Rights. The government of Canada, in standing with the world community as signator to the Declaration, was forced to examine its treatment of aboriginal people."[43] The BCIAWS and other groups used the new postwar rhetoric of racial tolerance to call for a readjustment in Canada's own domestic, racially based policies. Despite her own adherence to a social evolutionary understanding of so-called "primitive" societies, Ravenhill suggested, in terms particularly meaningful to a population now exposed to the realities of German death camps, that "certain 'out of date' opinions are clung to tenaciously despite 'up to date' science calling for their revision. Of these what is now described as the 'discarded Myth of Racism' is responsible by its persistence for many misunderstandings among otherwise well intentioned Canadians and their enduring misjudgments of a people over whom Canada assumed jurisdiction nearly two centuries ago."[44] In spite of the widespread pre-war acceptance of eugenic theory in Canada, the state was now caught in a conflict between its wartime condemnation of such theory and practice in Europe and its own racist domestic policy. The BCIAWS's most important contribution may have been to represent the Anglo-Celtic middle class while, at the same time, highlighting the aforementioned contradiction.

So while the role of the arts and of promotional organizations like the BCIAWS need to be understood within the context of conversations around the Indian Act and the ongoing "Indian problem," the intersection of various concerns and organizations certainly resulted in greater attention for the arts and the emergence of a new category of *contemporary* Canadian artist; namely, the "Indian" artist. By the late 1940s the so-called "revival" seemed real enough to demand a marketing agency to ensure the equitable treatment of First Nations artists. It was at this point that the BCIAWS began to surpass Ravenhill's founding vision. Ravenhill and some of her contemporaries had primarily advocated the artistic training of younger children alongside the education of the private corporate sector about the commercial potential of First Nations designs, strategies that seem closely aligned to Dorothy Dunn's work in Santa Fe and the emergence of the Santa Fe and "modern" southern Plains easel painting styles.[45] The apparent realization of an emerging, although fragile, market for First Nations objects demanded an institutional infrastructure modelled on the professionalization of the parallel world of non-Aboriginal art, which was also beginning to emerge in Canada. The BCIAWS involvement in institutionalized marketing further coincided with a shift in adult education and other community-support programs from social reform to professionalization, from the use of art as an exercise in self-help to the maintenance of supportive, professional infrastructure for art producers.

A formal BCIAWS marketing strategy was first prepared in November 1948 by Josephine Godman, four years after Ravenhill's retirement to her new position as the society's president emeritus. The biggest impetus for this strategy was the 1948 Conference on Native Indian Affairs held at the University of British Columbia in April 1948 and co-sponsored by the BCIAWS and the BCPM, although Godman had been actively addressing some of the issues considered in the proposal prior to the UBC meeting. At the conference, she cited sales through the association amounting to $3,000 in 1947, and this with neither a shop nor advertising.[46] Out of this emerged one of Godman's biggest concerns, the fluctuation in the quality of the material production available on the market. For example, in 1947 she wrote: "Some of the dye in baskets have not stood up to sunshine very well and have faded. This has brought complaints from buyers ... We must keep the standard high for the best prices."[47] She acquired information on reliable dyes for vegetable fibres from the Technical Information Service in Ottawa and then obtained a selection directly from a specialty dye company, making these available to any interested basket weavers through a small article in the Native Brotherhood's newspaper, *Native Voice*.[48]

The November 1948 marketing proposal was a response to the BCIAWS's call for a coherent strategy to be submitted to the DIA. In this proposal, Godman recommended that the DIA appoint a teacher who "could then visit the likely Reserves with a good exhibit of saleable articles and ... show the difference between those and the poor work, [and] also [be able] to give patterns of saleable articles and a variety of designs."[49] These patterns would be provided by the BCPM. Godman also recommended the establishment of small shops or stalls run by First Nations saleswomen. These shops would be supplied by a central supply depot which would in turn buy from communities with no established market. The combination of high-quality maintenance, buying at low prices, and operating with a low overhead would enable the BCIAWS to undercut the established craft shops, which "often sell rubbish at a high price."[50]

Conference on Native Indian Affairs, UBC

The event that both stands as the climax and summary of the arts-centred social reform path is the BCIAWS/UBC conference held in April 1948 and its *Report of Conference on Native Indian Affairs at Acadia Camp, University of British Columbia*, edited by H.B. (Harry) Hawthorn, professor of anthropology at the University of British Columbia. The conference was divided into four sessions: (1) arts and handicrafts, (2) health and welfare, (3) education, and (4) training of teachers and other professionals. Events accompanying the conference included an exhibition of art works by Emily Carr; an exhibition of the work of such First Nations artists as Judith Morgan, George Clutesi, Leslie John, and Ellen Neel; an exhibition of children's art from the Inkameep School and the Alberni and Christie residential schools; an exhibition of literature; the display of antique pieces from private collections; and a display of Ravenhill's needlework.

This juxtaposition of differing interests and exhibitions demonstrates how art became the rallying point for a patchwork of communities, organizations, views, and approaches. Art was a useful rallying point for a variety of reasons. First, it was perceived as essentially apolitical in nature and, hence, was not threatening. Second, it brought people sympathetically predisposed to First Nations peoples to meetings where the more pressing problems of education and health could then be discussed. Together these attitudes bridged political alignments and lent the cause of "Indian" reform a sense of righteousness. A direct assessment of the role of arts in this varied program came from Walsh, who summarized the fundamental social reformist interest in First Nations arts as follows: "This group wouldn't be meeting today if it weren't for the art of the Indian. It has been the one approach for interpreting the culture of the Indian people to the public."[51]

The session on arts and crafts presented a microcosm of the uncertain status of First Nations peoples in Canadian society, of the division of positions regarding this racial divide, and of the basic economic problems faced by First Nations throughout the province – issues that were at the base of the problems discussed in the other three sessions. The proceedings were opened by the citation of a myriad of telegram greetings from around both the province and the country, including those from W.T. Straith, the provincial minister of education; Byron Johnson, premier of the province; and the deputy ministers of welfare and health. Following Manuel's reference to a growing body of concerned, sophisticated, and primarily urban voters, politicians were being forced to at least pay lip service to issues pertaining to First Nations affairs.

The first and most academic of the speakers was A.E. Pickford, an anthropologist with the BCPM in Victoria. Anthropology had been a university discipline for only a generation, and there was a public debate flaring over the relevance of universities and other cultural institutions to everyday life in Canada. Pickford tied the separate discourses of social work and anthropology together with her assertion that "social service is now a science, and, in common with all other sciences, it cannot be conducted without a proper understanding of the basic material involved."[52]

Pickford implied that institutions like the museum were to take responsibility for providing this understanding. Here, she sought to legitimize the museum as a knowledge-producing institution and, thus, to align the state and the museum in the cause of reform. This legitimacy, however, was associated with state hegemony, which was maintained through the museum and its anthropologists – a fact that it is important to remember about this time, when state officials were seeking to regulate and professionalize the arts in Canada. She suggested that efforts from Andrew Paull and the North American Indian Brotherhood, the Native Brotherhood, and, "more humbly," the BCIAWS, were preparing a new page in Canadian history, one "turned ready for our inscription."[53]

Pickford then followed this call for historical consciousness with a summary of First Nations peoples in British Columbia: "the artistic, and, one time, warlike Haida ... the rich traders and highly cultured Tsimshian ... the dramatic Kwakiutl."[54] While she strove for a sense of variation and difference in conjuring up a complex image of cultural diversity modified by historical contingencies, in the end, much of what she said came out as a shopping list of evolutionary stereotypes. That Pickford and many of the other speakers felt obliged to stress the high standard of intelligence of contemporary First Nations children is indicative of the intransigence of negative stereotypes in both public opinion and public policy. The strategy of many of the conference speakers involved reinforcing positive characteristics, albeit within the framework of reductive evolutionary stereotypes.

This was evident in Mildred Valley Thornton's address. Thornton, a painter and illustrator with the *Vancouver Sun* who also wrote art criticism, directed her comments to the positive role of art in the education of First Nations children. Her opening anecdote covered her experiences painting portraits of Blood school children in southern Alberta. "The children came up and looked. They had been taught not to touch things. One wouldn't dare leave some children with paints. I have never seen them so animated. They are usually shy and quiet, but became just as noisy and interested as any group of white children. We had touched a hidden spring. They were really in their native element and able to express themselves."[55] Here was the miracle key to reaching and, thereby, controlling First Nations school children and to instilling in them a sense of self-worth. "All the children need is the guidance from others to set this spirit, this enthusiasm alight. To create pride, to kindle self-respect, and to present a whole new creative experience in art is the tinder ready, waiting, for someone to apply the torch."[56]

Godman followed Pickford and Thornton's solutions to the "Indian problem" with a summary of BCIAWS marketing activities. She stated that, "if every third person in B.C. bought one small piece of Indian craft a year,

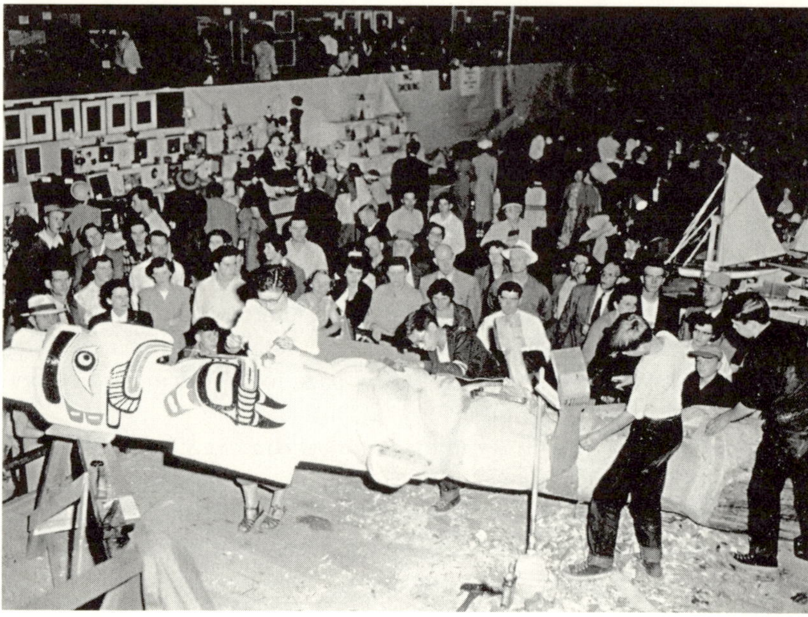

22 Ellen Neel and family carving a totem pole at the Pacific National Exhibition, Vancouver, ca. 1950.

there would not be enough to go around."[57] The craft industry held a viable response to economic dire straits. She then outlined her thoughts on how the industry should be structured. "I feel that that will be the answer to our problem: co-operatives for the Indians, and a general market held once or twice a year."[58]

Kwakwa̲ka̲'wakw carver Ellen Neel (see Figure 22) spoke last. Ellen May Neel (K̲aK̲aso'las), a Kwagiulth Kwakwa̲ka̲'wakw, was born in 1916 at Alert Bay. She attended St. Michael's Residential School in Alert Bay and learned to carve from her grandfather Charlie James; consequently, the use of the art in ceremonial practice was, for her, a living reality. In 1939 she married Ted Neel, and in 1943 she moved to Vancouver. In 1946 Ted Neel suffered a serious stroke and Ellen turned to producing and selling objects for the tourist trade on a full-time basis. She worked at restoring poles at the University of British Columbia in the late 1940s before introducing university curators to her uncle, Mungo Martin, and returning her full-time attention to the tourist business. She continued as a well-known carver throughout the 1950s and died in 1966.[59]

Although, throughout her career, she showed a willingness to experiment with totem pole forms, which included using non-traditional figures and a range of sizes, conceptually her work was much closer to that of her teacher, James, than was the work of either George Clutesi or Judith Morgan to that of previous Nuu-chah-nulth or Gitxsan generations. Neel's painting usually consisted of providing two-dimensional decoration for her carvings, and it followed conventional Kwakwa̱ka̱'wakw colour schemes, relying primarily on black, red, and white. Similarly, her carving typically echoed the shapes and compositions of conventional Kwakwa̱ka̱'wakw monumental pole carving (see Figure 23).

In her address to the 1948 conference, she rebuked the artistic limitations of a temporally located market demand for authenticity and belittled the assumption that First Nations "culture" had died. Her use of Kwakwa̱ka̱'wakw conventions was influenced by the training she received from James and certainly helped contribute to a sense of artistic and social continuity. However, she also clearly accepted the notion of formal and technical innovation in the field of First Nations art:

> To me, this idea is one of the great fallacies where the art of my people is concerned. For if our art is dead, then it is fit only to be mummified, packed into mortuary boxes and tucked away into museums. Whereas to me it is a living symbol of the gaiety, the laughter and love of colour of my people, a day to day reminder to us that even we had something of glory and honour before the white man came.[60]

She then stressed that this matter of "glory and honour before the white man" still held currency. "And our art must *continue* to live, for not only is it part and parcel of us, but it can be a powerful factor in combining the best part of the Indian culture into the fabric of a truly Canadian art form."[61] While establishing her position as seeing a place for First Nations peoples within the Canadian whole, she demanded the right to go beyond the parameters of past production.

> If the art of my people is to take its rightful place alongside other Canadian art, it must be a living medium of expression. We, the Indian artists, must be allowed to create! We must be allowed to use new and modern techniques; new and modern tools; new and modern materials. For in every instance creative capacity has followed the discovery and use of better material. I do not mean that we should discard the old, only that we be allowed to use the new.[62]

The general discussion following the more formal presentations further highlights problems arising from the economic situation of First Nations arts and the discrepancy in attitude between the two ethnic camps. Godman points out that, in order to maintain quality, the BCIAWS had developed a trademark. In order to qualify for this mark, the work had to "have a true Indian design and must be truly Indian. If it comes in with a rose or a

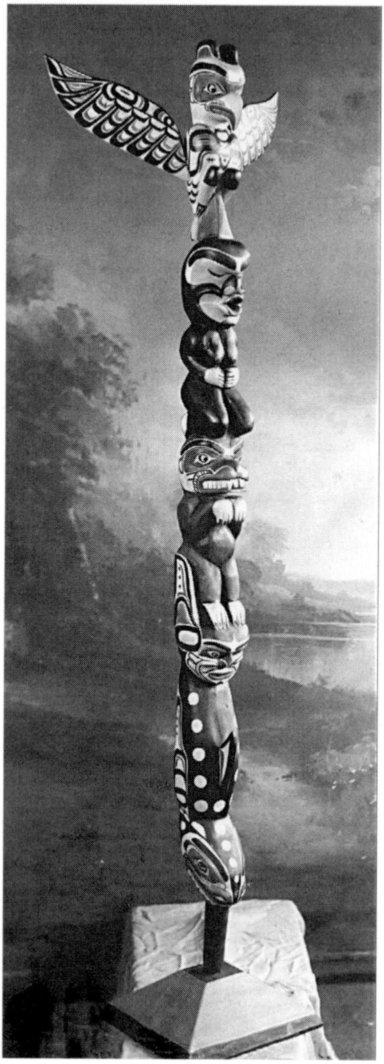

23 Model pole, by Ellen Neel.

butterfly, or some bird I've never seen, I do not put the trade mark on it."[63] In response, Nanaimo carver Leslie John detailed the tough economic situation faced by most First Nations artists:

> The price of totem pole, I make less than $1.00 a day. If lucky make $1.25. The more cheap ones – 35 cents – make $2.50 a day. Fishing on the coast was on three weeks last year. Don't make enough money in fishing ... I am not feeling well, and my mother is in the hospital. My father is not well. My

> older brother has a broken back when small. Just my younger brother – seventeen years – who is in the woods, and me, to make a living. You can't make much on totem poles. On good poles you can't make a living and that is the reason we do not make any for the Welfare Society.[64]

Ruth Smith, editor of *Native Voice,* brought up a second, related point when she noted the lack of protection for First Nations art designs. This was of particular concern among Northwest Coast peoples because of the ownership of social prerogatives relating to the display and performance of crests, objects, songs, stories, and performances. And, within this context, the issue of ownership was doubly significant due to economic competition in the curio trade. While Godman expressed concern over the "authenticity" of designs in the Euro-Canadian field of consumption, Smith expressed concern over the ownership of the designs within the Aboriginal field of production. The two solutions emerging from the brief discussion involved copyrighting (which, in the end, was seen as ineffective since images could be changed slightly, thus negating the legality of the copyright) and trademark. No thought was given to who would establish the criteria for ascertaining authenticity.[65] If this burden were to fall to the BCIAWS, it seems that the criteria would have been set by museums and implemented by craft societies. Control over knowledge, its distribution and application, would necessarily have rested with state officials and public institutions, leaving Aboriginal modes of authority and leadership out of the loop.

7
Mathias Joe, Mungo Martin, and George Clutesi: "Art" as Resistance

While Ravenhill and Raley advocated change through the promotion of First Nations art as Canadian, First Nations individuals and groups cultivated the resulting public interest to promote political change from a First Nations perspective. In this chapter, I discuss the public activities of individual artists Mathias Joe, Mungo Martin, and George Clutesi between 1936 and 1949. Although Clutesi exhibited with the BCIAWS, and although this period overlaps with those presented in the two previous chapters and the one following, I am focusing here on the public uses of First Nations art in developments related but parallel to the campaigns of the non-Aboriginal social reform movement. Joe, Martin, and Clutesi were among the First Nations artists who used their art to assert claims to Aboriginal rights, to gather non-Aboriginal support for legislative reform, and to instill a sense of pride in First Nations youth. The result of these activities was both additional pressure for the restructuring of the Indian Act and a higher public profile for individual First Nations artists. First Nations use of art as a lobbying tool was a contributing factor in the reinvolvement of the government in art-related promotional programs at the end of the 1940s, and it encouraged the 1949 provincial enfranchisement of First Nations peoples.

Mathias Joe and the Thunderbird Dynasty Pole

Ironically, the potlatch ban and the draconian Indian Act amendments that followed the Cranmer prosecutions in the 1920s partially fuelled the political manipulation of First Nations monuments and the commemorative events around them. Even though the Aboriginal ceremonies that conventionally empowered the objects were banned, as I have demonstrated many Euro-Canadians were intent upon constructing these objects as integral to national identity. This opened up possibilities that had been overlooked by Euro-Canadian authorities. There were moments when feasts, speeches, and other ritual activities – "Indian festivities," in the language of the Indian Act – could simultaneously incorporate Euro-Canadians and assert First

Nations identity and political aims. After the 1927 prohibition of organized land claims activities, this further opened the potential for "art" and its accompanying rituals as valuable public vehicles for political self-expression. Robert Paine and Noel Dyck use the term "ethnodrama" to refer to the use of public cultural performances within museums and other institutional sites as a stratagem to push forward Aboriginal political agendas.[1] It was between the conflicting spaces of the potlatch/land claims bans and Euro-Canadian nostalgia for the pomp and colour of First Nations ceremonies/objects that such ethnodrama was born.

The ban's acceptance was uneven in Euro-Canada. For example, when Governor General Thomas Freeman, Earl of Willingdon, visited the Nuu-chah-nulth community of Yuquot (also sometimes referred to as Friendly Cove or Nootka) in 1929, "he was welcomed and feted according to West Coast traditions of hospitality"[2] and was then presented a free-standing crest pole by Captain Jack (see Figure 24) "following a parade of decorated warriors along the beach and a ceremony in the Indian language in one of the many halls in the village."[3] Since Lord Willingdon "engaged" in celebrating an "Indian festival ... of which the giving away ... of money, goods or articles ... is a feature," he was, strictly speaking, "guilty of an offense and ... liable on summary conviction for a term not exceeding six months and not less than two months."[4] Instead, Lord Willingdon immediately returned the pole to the village for safe-keeping but planned for the arrival, two months later, of CNR engineer T.B. Campbell, "known throughout the Dominion as 'Totem Pole' Campbell for his work in connection with the restoring of Canada's valuable and historic Indian relics,"[5] to orchestrate the pole's removal to Ottawa.

Plans had been made for the pole to be shipped to Victoria by way of the Canadian Pacific Railway's steamer *Princess Norah* and then from Victoria to Vancouver and then to Ottawa on the CNR. According to a *Daily Colonist* report dating 19 July 1929, no one had informed the people in Yuquot of this decision. The article's source, S.L. Howe, the provincial secretary, said: "It appears from the story told me that the chief and the tribe did not expect His Excellency to accept the totem pole outright. In fact it was tendered in the old potlatch sense – a gift to be received and returned. I was told His Excellency so understood it and had in mind having a brass plate planted at the base to commemorate his visit and the good spirit shown by the Indians."[6] This was simply a press release. Departmental correspondence indicates that the final costs for the pole's transportation would reach $3,000. There was a further split in the village between Muchalat and Moachat peoples, and, although Captain Jack did not object to the pole's removal, the governor general decided that the dispute provided a suitable excuse for backing out of moving the pole to Rideau Hall in Ottawa and having to deal with the expenses this would have entailed.[7]

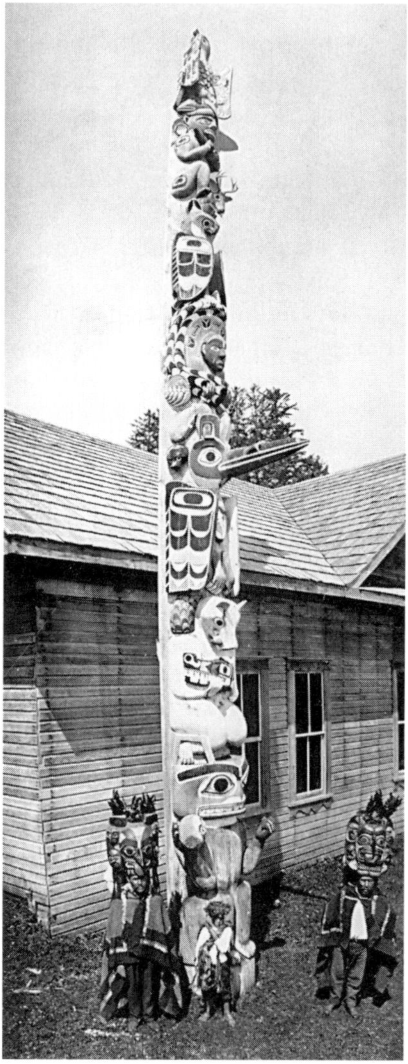

24 Free-standing crest pole presented by Captain Jack to Governor General Thomas Freeman in Yuquot, 1929.

It would not have been unusual for a guest of the governor general's stature to be treated with such respect when visiting Nuu-chah-nulth territory. However, the presentation of a gift to the king's representative in Canada was also a highly potent, politically symbolic event. Part of the case for the enshrinement of Aboriginal rights within BC courts rests upon the Royal Proclamation of 1763. This proclamation, sometimes referred to as the "Indian" Magna Carta, extended British sovereignty and protection over First

Nations west of the British colonies in the eastern part of the continent, but it acknowledged continuing First Nations ownership of land used and occupied by First Nations peoples.[8] For this reason, First Nations political organizations have sought to have their cases brought before the Privy Council in London in the hope that it would enshrine Aboriginal land title, thereby denying the terms of British Columbia's entrance into Canadian Confederation and the jurisdictional authority of both the provincial and federal governments over First Nations affairs.

While correspondence from the Governor General's Office indicates that Lord Willingdon did indeed feel obligated by Captain Jack's gift, a photograph of Lord and Lady Willingdon and a brass plate commemorating their visit was deemed sufficient repayment. When the governor general was informed of Captain Jack's disappointment with this, he threw in a watch for good diplomatic measure.[9] The presentation, however, proved that totem poles and Euro-Canadian leaders together were a matter of public interest and, therefore, newsworthy. The affair attracted both local and national media, setting a precedent for future events. Similar occasions occurred in Vancouver in 1936 and 1946, although each time contemporary artists raised or carved a new totem pole specifically for the event.

The first of these was for a celebratory festival in 1936, the Golden Jubilee, which was aimed primarily at drumming up business: local, Dominion, international, or otherwise. American warships, industrial exhibitions, an aviation week, symphonies, choirs, strolling singers, military tattoos, and the erection of four crest poles went together to highlight Vancouver as a city of exciting financial and cultural opportunity, "to make known to the world the natural beauty and advantages of Vancouver as a great city and a great port in the British Empire."[10] Furthermore, according to the program outline's telling assertion, "the women of the city are not behind in the march of programme progress."[11] Tea shows and tea mugs, beach fashion shows and period costume balls thus jockeyed with professional baseball and box lacrosse for public attention. Despite military pageants, the erection of a pole by a contemporary carver still made headlines in the Vancouver newspapers. Once again, Vancouver's business and "cultural" communities sought to use totem poles in the construction of the city's modernity, a tactic well illustrated in the committee's letterhead: an hourglass, the top of which is dated 1886 and which shows a Northwest Coast village in a pastoral setting; the sand bleeds into the bottom, which is dated 1936 and depicts a modern city (see Figure 25).

Not coincidentally, this event meant that the city parks board and individuals from the Art, Historical, and Scientific Association of Vancouver, in partnership under the banner Indian committee of the Golden Jubilee Committee, could respond to the concerns expressed by Andrew Paull and the Squamish band council in 1925. Although when the committee was first

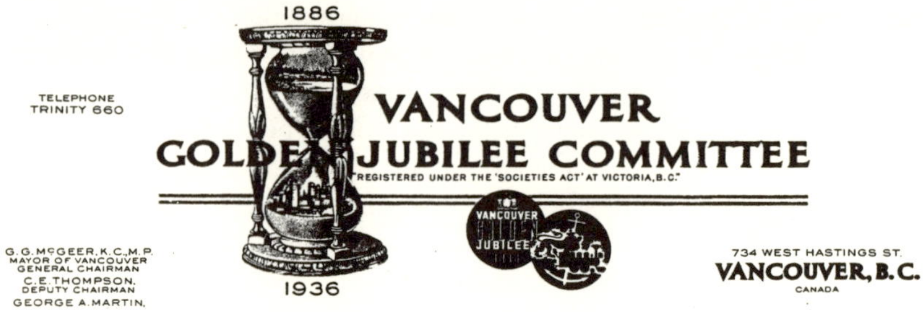

25 Vancouver Golden Jubilee letterhead showing hourglass motif, 1936.

formed in 1934 the proposal again called for the erection of an entire village in Stanley Park, by 1935 it had been scaled down to the erection of a limited number of poles.

Three poles for the 1936 celebration were erected at Lumberman's Arch. Two of the poles were Kwakwa̲ka̲'wakw and one was Haida. The two Kwakwa̲ka̲'wakw poles, obtained by AHSAV from Knight Inlet through Dr. Darby and Indian Agent C.C. Perry,[12] were: the Dsookwa-dse pole (see Figure 26), originally erected at Rivers Inlet in 1893 by Chief Kla-ool-dso-lah and sometimes referred to as the Yahk-dsi pole; and the Nhe-is-bik pole (see Figure 27) carved by See-wit of Blunden Harbour in 1892 and obtained from Wakius. The Haida monument was a mortuary pole from Skedans (see Figure 28) purchased from Ske-dans (Henry Moody) of Skidegate.[13] These three poles, like the AHSAV poles at Lumberman's Arch, were touted as anonymous relics.

In August 1935, although George Raley was on the executive committee, it was another executive, Leander Manley, who approached Squamish chief Mathias Joe and asked him if he would participate in the program. This was an important move for the committee.[14] Mathias Joe (1885-1966) was a Squamish carver from the Capilano reserve on Vancouver's North Shore. He was frequently photographed and featured in the local newspapers, and he used his status as local celebrity to draw attention to First Nations issues, including what he considered to be an unsatisfactory payment ($25,000) by the City of Vancouver for two acres of the Kitsilano reserve lands on the south end of Burrard Bridge. Vancouver newspapers also reported that he was an official guest at two coronations and, along with his wife, Ellen, the first First Nations person to cast a ballot in the 1949 election after provincial enfranchisement.[15] The fourth pole (see Figure 29), intended to symbolize the Squamish's historical significance to the city, was newly carved by Joe and erected separately at Prospect Point, also in Stanley Park.

Moved by Denny Paull, in April 1936 the Squamish band council voted unanimously to accept Joe's pole as "representing the Squamish Tribe, and commemorative of the meeting of the Squamish people with Captain

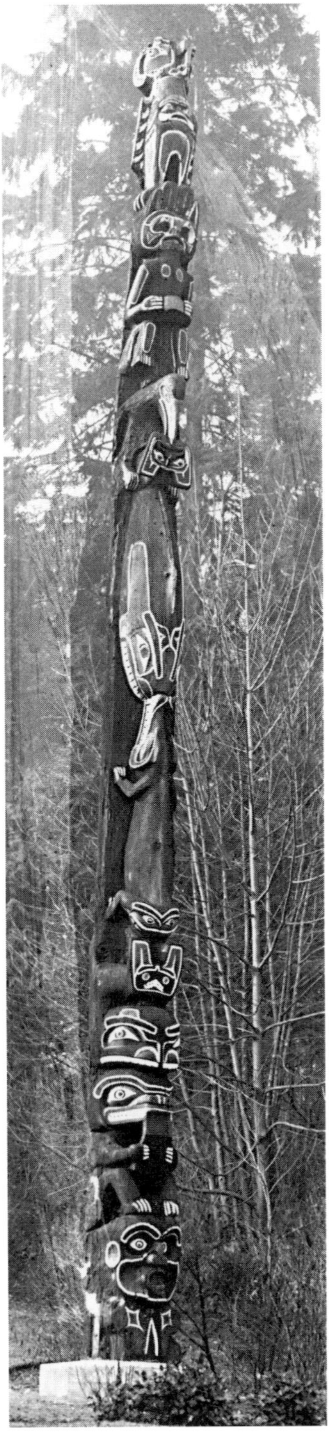

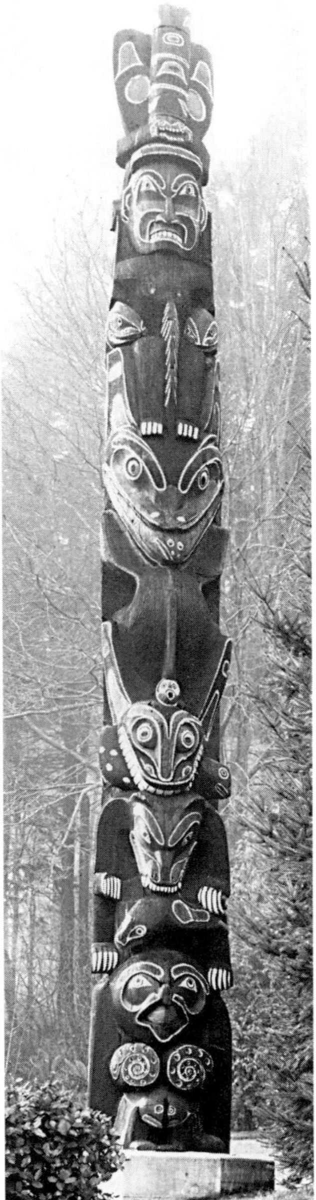

27 The Nhe-is-bik pole, Lumberman's Arch, Stanley Park, 1936.

26 The Dsookwa-dse, or Yahk-dsi, pole.

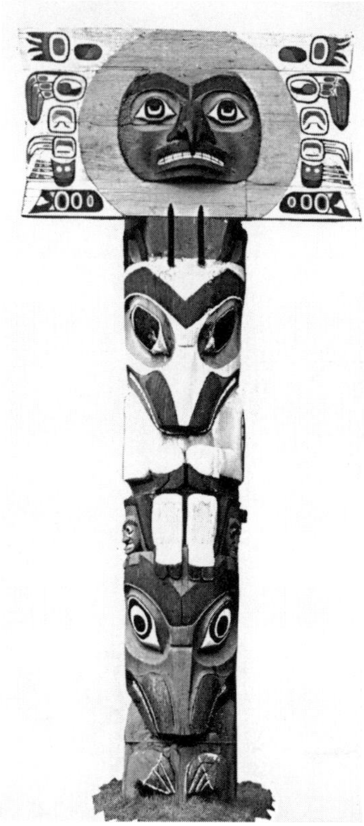

28 The Skedans pole, Lumberman's Arch, Stanley Park, 1936.

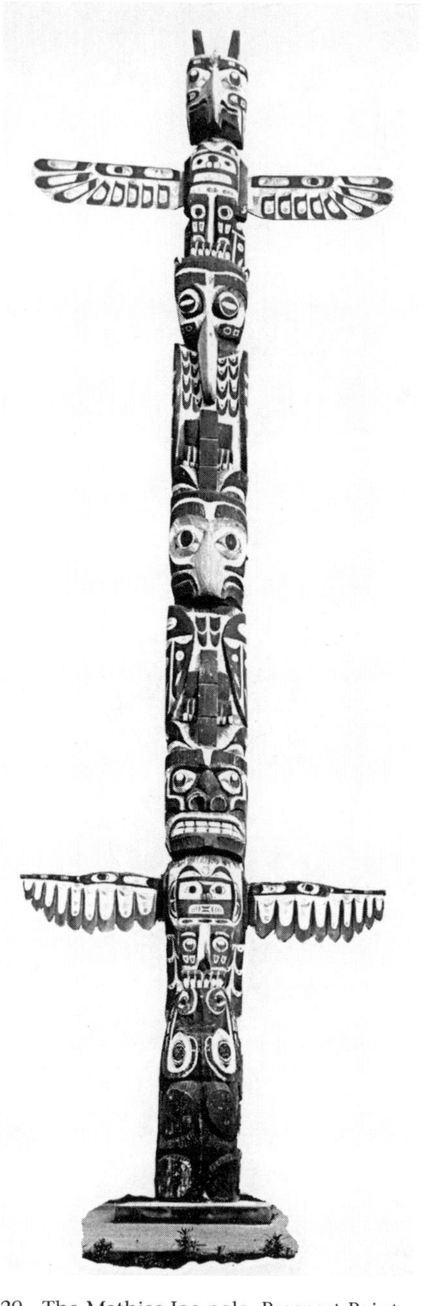

29 The Mathias Joe pole, Prospect Point, Stanley Park, 1936.

Vancouver in Burrard Inlet off the Capilano River on June 13th, 1792."[16] As a number of land claim issues were (and still are) unresolved, including compensation for Stanley Park itself,[17] it was useful to the Squamish to reassert themselves on the city's landscape and to maintain a historical link to it that preceded European presence. It was, perhaps, for this reason that the Golden Jubilee Committee's Managing Board entertained Raley's January 1936 suggestion that the committee request the federal government to officially instruct the officers of the Department of Indian Affairs to cooperate with the committee.[18]

The choice of Joe's pole for Prospect Point was significant to the Squamish for two other, and more immediately tangible, reasons. First, Prospect Point, like XwayXway, had been occupied by Squamish people. It was known as "'Chay-thoos' (the clearing, meaning 'high bank')."[19] According to J.S. Matthews, the city archivist in 1938, Chief Haatsalanogh, "from whom Kitsilano[20] takes its name,"[21] had built a house there, which was shown on Royal Engineer field survey notes made in March 1863. Around 1870 his son, Haytulk, or "Supplejack," demolished it and replaced it with a cottage constructed from milled wood.[22] This house, like those at XwayXway, was demolished when the "Park Road," which encompasses Stanley Park, was built in 1889.[23] Squamish claims to the point were thus asserted through Joe's pole.

Second, the point overlooked Lions Gate, the entrance into Burrard Narrows and the main port facilities and Vancouver harbour. A Squamish pole located there would be a symbolic statement of their historic presence – a statement visible to all passenger and commercial boat traffic in and out of Vancouver. Joe's pole at Prospect Point quickly took on added significance with the construction of the Lions Gate Bridge, which, in 1938, connected Stanley Park and Vancouver through Squamish land to the Guinness-owned British Pacific Properties housing development on the city's North Shore.[24] Once again, any symbolic reminder of the Squamish claims to lands around Burrard Inlet might contribute either to control over valuable real estate or to significant financial compensation.

Despite Squamish interests, the Golden Jubilee was really intended to attract investment to Vancouver. Within this context, it was essential to assert First Nations land ownership, especially since council member Andrew Paull, through his participation with the Allied Tribes and its resistance to the McKenna-McBride Agreement, had intimate knowledge of the potential for land cut-offs. Joe's pole provided the opportunity for just such a cut-off and was, therefore, endorsed by the Squamish band council.

Barbeau, quoting Raley, describes the pole's iconography as follows:

> The topmost figure is Swi-ve-lus, whose highly ornamented body depicts many things. For instance, on his chest is the creator of the world, the wide

open eye signifying daylight and work, – the sightless eye, night, moon, stars, rest and sleep. The wing feathers symbolize rain, snow, hail and wind, while fire is seen under the great beak.

The right leg shows the eye of the sea monster, who is both father and mother of all the sea people, or fish, while the eye on the left is that leg of the land monster, who produces human beings, animals and birds.

The left side of the tail shows the water marks of the high and low tides, while the right side symbolizes the flow and drip of mountain water which makes lakes and rivers.

The second figure, Kah-mi, controls the storms of rain, snow, sleet, hail and wind.

The third figure, Tsa-itch, concerns herself especially with the season's growth of grass, herbs and trees.

The fourth, Great Thunderbird, hiding in the clouds, blinks his eye and shoots forth lightning; a gentle shaking of his feathers produces little disturbance, but when he flaps his wings there is violent thunder and forked lightning. When he is angry with the people of the earth he makes the lightning and sets fire to the forests, and at times warns his own crest people of approaching death.

The fifth figure on the pole is somewhat shrouded in mystery. He is called the great dragon or the giant lizard, Tchain-koo. This amphibian is supposed to be the principal food of the Thunderbird. He is of a bright colour and his fins and scales are of gold. The scales are worn as a charm by anybody who has the good fortune to find them when they are shed.[25]

According to Gunn, the pole, which he calls the "Thunderbird Dynasty Totem,"[26] tells the "story of the Creation by Thunderbird."[27] Gunn, "as explained ... by the carver, Chief Mathias Joe Capilano,"[28] also provides other names for some of the figures: Swivelus becomes "the Son of Thunderbird."[29] Kahmi, "Daughter of Thunderbird, also known as Qolus,"[30] Tza-itch, "Mother Thunderbird,"[31] Sho-yuh-wa, "Thunderbird the Great, Father of the Great Family and Lord of Creation. Kwing-kwankulegyi in the Kwakiutl tongue, El-Anga in Haida."[32] Together "these honoured personalities rule the universe, control the elements and create life. They are supernaturals, but like mortals, they live and eat."[33] In Gunn's version, Tzain-koo, "the Giant Dragon, sea monster and huge lizard in one, is the main food of Thunderbird."[34] Raley characterized the pole in a similarly romantic fashion as illustrating "the striving of the primitive imagination to interpret the universe, to solve the problem of life, and to account for natural phenomena."[35]

Gunn held that "it is appropriate that this totem should tell the story of the Creation. For what it commemorates – the meeting of the Indians and the white man – opened an entirely new world for both."[36] More to the point, "unlike the other totem poles, this is an example of the art of the

Indians in our immediate vicinity ... Crowning Prospect Point, it is the only pole that stands at the original site it was raised and appropriately constitutes one of the most memorable landmarks of the City of Vancouver."[37] It was also the first multi-figured, free-standing Squamish pole and, therefore, an extremely rare example of Salish "art."

Joe's pole immediately recalls the Charlie James houseposts with its avian figures, wings outstretched, and the extensive two-dimensional patterns of repeated u-shapes over the flat surfaces. Thus, Joe seems to have been influenced by Kwakwa̱ka̱'wakw carving generally and, when one compares the patterns on the wings, by James's carving specifically. However, Joe's pole is taller and has more figures on it than do James's houseposts, and this is uncommon in Coast Salish monumental sculpture. The painting was not executed as carefully as was James's, and Joe did not adhere too rigidly to bilateral symmetry.

Uncommon with regard to form, the pole appeared to be unconventional as well. While origin myths pertaining to local kin groups or to secret societies frequently referred to ancestral encounters with spirit beings, the depiction of multiple figures (presumably references to the different villages amalgamated after contact and settled on the Squamish reserve) did not occur within one composition for the simple reason that they represented distinct social groups. The idea of representing the various origins of the Squamish peoples in one object, like the concept of the Squamish as a united nation, was an innovation that was at least partly the result of the external pressures of European and Euro-Canadian assimilationist colonialism.

Wayne Suttles argues that, "while some Central Coast Salish art may have been purely decorative, much of it can be related to four sources of power and prestige – the vision, the ritual word, the ancestors and wealth."[38] In response to Bill Reid's suggestion that the aesthetic accomplishments of the Coast Salish were uneven,[39] Suttles points out that the representations of visions or guardian spirits were constrained by the notion that "it was dangerous to reveal too much about it,"[40] that with "art related to the power of the ritual word ... its efficacy depends not on the private experience of a vision but the private knowledge of ritual words that have inherent power."[41] He believes that ambiguity in "the portrayal of ancestors"[42] may have been motivated by "fear of ridicule."[43]

Suttles's notion that the Central Coast Salish may have been cautious in their approach to representation might explain the vagueness of the iconography of Joe's pole. Joe, and, through him, the Squamish, implied a historical legitimacy to their claims to Stanley Park by referencing a body of stories that were never explicitly explained in the public press. How these "origin" myths may have delineated Squamish history was perhaps tangential to the pole's role as a reminder to visitors and residents alike of the historical Squamish presence in Vancouver and, thus, to their claims to land, water, and other resources. Joe's pole is not a reconfigured ceremonial object, like the Kwakwaka'wakw poles at Lumberman's Arch, but rather, a monument intended to say something about the Squamish directly and specifically to Vancouver's non-Aboriginal population. Although the thunderbird is indeed a personage appearing in Salish mythology, the fact that Joe chose it for the subject of his pole may be a reference to Charlie James's popular houseposts, which he carved in order to reinforce, through formal familiarity, the Euro-Canadian acceptance of the pole at Prospect Point.

The press releases were predictably filled with fictional references to the erection of the pole as "ancient tribal custom" with Joe only using "primitive tools."[44] "The mighty thunderbird totem whose outstretched wings welcome shipping through the Lions Gate,"[45] went the dramatic description in one of the local papers, which referred to the pole as "this famous symbolic emblem of the Squamish nation, forerunners of the white man on Burrard Inlet."[46] Andrew Paull, speaking again for the Squamish nation, used this historicist reference to counter the notion that the land was surrendered and to specifically justify the Squamish possession of reserve land on the city's North Shore: "In the early days the Indians and British made a joint agreement to defend Burrard Inlet. The British were to defend the south side of the Narrows, which later became Stanley Park. The Indians promised to defend the north side, which became the Capilano Reserve."[47] As for Joe, sometimes referred to in the local press as Joe Capilano or Mathias Capilano, he declared, "I believe that when my totem pole is standing there, I'll be standing with it all the time."[48]

The commission partly accomplished for Joe many of the things that Raley, in his revival scheme, had envisioned for other unnamed artists. The pole commanded attention by virtue of its location in the city's most important tourist site and was almost immediately seen as a significant city landmark, further identifying totem poles as an aspect of Vancouver's cultural identity. A thunderbird pole in combination with Joe's colourful tendency to dress up for public events in full feather bonnet and buckskin captured the local public imagination. And although, as early as 1932, he made it into the local newspapers as an expert in "Indian lore" and a carver of model poles, Joe received a number of significant commissions through the 1940s and early 1950s in direct response to the Stanley Park pole. Many of these commissions were from companies cashing in on the postwar natural resource boom that sought publicity that would evoke their connection to the natural environment. Joe carved a thirty-foot pole for a resort in Princess Louise Inlet at the head of Jervis Inlet in 1941; a thirty-foot copy of the Stanley Park pole for presentation to the governor of Texas (plus several more during a six-week carving demonstration tour of the state in 1948); twenty poles at $200 each for Maurice Anly, the distributor of British Columbia shingles in Texas and the sponsor of his demonstration tour; a twenty-foot pole for Dr. Gerhard Fisher in West Vancouver in 1954; a thirty-foot pole for Davis Lumber Company in St. Catharines, Ontario, in 1955; and an assortment of model poles for various visiting luminaries, including one in 1951 for Princess Elizabeth.[49]

Furthermore, Joe used the spotlight created, in part, by the Stanley Park pole (and, in part, by his own performances for the media) in a way probably not envisioned by Raley.[50] In 1953 he announced that he was setting up a teepee on Marine Drive in North Vancouver to protest the city's offer to purchase more Squamish land for the construction of a second bridge connecting the city centre to its North Vancouver suburb. "I'll build a fire there, do my cooking and the traffic will flow past on either side of me,"[51] he was reported to have said in an article accompanied by a photograph of him and his teepee with the Lions Gate Bridge in the background. "From my teepee headquarters I shall pass out leaflets telling all about the big steal. We are offered the ridiculous price of $750 an acre when we should be getting at least $5000."[52]

Raley's ideas about the promotion of First Nations art were intended as a way of further integrating First Nations peoples into the Euro-Canadian socio-economic system. Joe's public protests added an extra dimension, demonstrating that object producers from within First Nations communities were not always simply seeking economic independence. Both written and oral First Nations discourses around the objects were often related to more controversial issues, specifically land, its value, and its ownership. While Raley did recognize the political imbalance inherent in the Indian Act and the DIA, he was careful not to directly criticize the founding ideals of state policy. From Raley's point of view, the "assimilation" and, therefore, "modernization" of the First Nations had to be a priority for members of both church and state; indeed, he saw this as part of their moral obligation. His solution for the political displacement of First Nations peoples was their absorption into the displacing system. Art, his own passion, would be the absorbing agent.

On the other hand, it was clear that Euro-Canadians were interested in the imagined poetic progress from the precontact world of First Nations peoples to the world of the modern state. It was from this vantage point that Euro-Canadians might be addressed. Paull, Joe, and others participated in the discourse about art because it opened up the possibility of asserting a historically recognized presence that might partially counter the overt racism of everyday life in Canada and that would certainly develop into a useful public relations outlet.

The Native Brotherhood of BC: "Indian" Culture, "Indian" Rights

The use of the media to press for reform accelerated after the Second World

War, especially in conjunction with the Native Brotherhood of British Columbia, which followed Captain Jack's example and presented a pole to the new governor general, Viscount Alexander, in Vancouver's Diamond Jubilee celebrations, ten years after the raising of Mathias Joe's pole. This presentation was part of a larger lobbying campaign whose attention-grabbing tactics were well illustrated in January 1947, when Chief William Scow, president of the Brotherhood, issued the following proclamation to John Hart, premier of British Columbia:

> Whereas the present government of the coast has been established by voting white settlers resident in Indian territory; and
>
> Whereas legal title of the Indian lands has never passed from our hand; and
>
> Whereas the present white chiefs in the village of Victoria have seen fit to deny residents of thousands of years ancestry the right to take part in governing their lands;
>
> We, in the name of all Pacific Coast bands, do hereby declare the white chieftains to immediately surrender their false authority to an all-Indian committee which we will form shortly.
>
> This proclamation will inform you that your government which has not seen fit to permit the owners of Pacific Coast lands a voice in their control, namely by voting, has no longer any standing.[53]

The Native Brotherhood had been formed in 1931 shortly after the collapse of the Allied Tribes of British Columbia and the implementation of the federal ban on land claims. The Brotherhood was modelled after the Native Brotherhood of Alaska. It was essentially a "pan-Indian" political organization, although in the beginning its constituency was primarily Haida and Tsimshian. Organized along the same lines as Euro-Canadian unions and political parties, with a paying membership and an executive leadership committee, it sought to address the whole range of inequalities enshrined in the Indian Act. During the Second World War the Brotherhood began to forge close ties with labour unions, which were enjoying a major expansion.[54] The Brotherhood amalgamated in 1942 with the Pacific Coast Native Fishermen's Association (PCNFA), appointed Andrew Paull (formerly of the Allied Tribes) as business agent, and presented a petition to the federal government in Ottawa opposing the implementation of an income tax on First Nations people. "No taxation without representation," it asserted, noting that BC First Nations individuals were still denied the right to vote either provincially or federally.[55]

In 1945 the Brotherhood incorporated itself under the British Columbia Societies Act, a move that established it as a legally chartered organization with specific rights and obligations.[56] Jacqueline O'Donnell suggests that "the organization was utilizing the methods of the majority society for good public relations and to attain recognition as well as respect for its aims and goals from industry and Government officials."[57] From the mid-1940s on, both government and industry officials had indeed moved to recognize the Native Brotherhood as a legitimate and powerful bargaining agent. Cannery officials acknowledged it as a stabilizing force in the industry, an important consideration during the Second World War.[58] Dianne Newell points out that the First Nations fishing fleet was more unionized than was its Euro-Canadian counterpart at the outbreak of the war and that it then gained further prominence after 1942, when Japanese-Canadian fishers and cannery workers were interned away from the Coast.[59]

After the formation of the Special Joint Committee on the Indian Act in 1946, which sat until 1949 and ultimately led to the passing of a new Indian Act in 1951, the Brotherhood was selected by the federal government as the sole representative of BC First Nations, and it presented its brief before the committee on 1 May 1947. A second BC political organization, the Confederacy of Interior Tribes, quickly wrote a petition protesting the preference the commission showed the Brotherhood as well as its apparent ignorance of the political diversity within First Nations communities and the differing social circumstances of the Coastal and Interior peoples.[60] Nonetheless, in the eyes of Euro-Canadians, the privileging of the Brotherhood at the expense of other First Nations associations was a measure of its political ascendancy.

George Manuel and Michael Postuns state that the three years in which the joint committee sat saw a severe and multipronged attack on the DIA.

> Local and provincial organizations were beginning to find their feet. The Canadian Association for Adult Education had given rise some years before to the Indian-Eskimo association as an urban-based, non-Indian support group. The anti-poverty craze produced spokesmen of every political stripe within the non-Indian community who were labelling Indian reserves, based on last summer's visit or a canoe trip in their camping days, as Canada's Apartheid Policy. Indians had always been complaining. Now there were sophisticated, organized urban voters, whose view of the matter may have been entirely different from ours, but who were, nonetheless, pointing at the same problems and the same administration.[61]

This was important to the cause of First Nations reform because, as sociologist Nancy Fraser argues, change in state policy hinges on the pressure created through the discursive resources recognized by members of government; these resources include officially recognized idioms, vocabularies, narrative conventions, paradigms of argumentation, and modes of subjectification.[62] In addition, because of social stratification and its extension to political groups and associations, it was clear that First Nations voices alone were not going to be enough to sway bureaucratic and political opinion. Despite the efforts of the Native Brotherhood and other organizations to legitimize themselves within the Canadian political system, First Nations issues were all too frequently greeted by the state bureaucracy with inertia and indifference.[63] The questions facing organizations like the Brotherhood concerned not only how to affect change in state policy, but also, and first, how to galvanize public attention so as to focus it intently enough on the government to stimulate any sort of movement at all (particularly during this time of commissions).[64]

What the activities of the Native Brotherhood and other organizations ultimately did was to encourage, in the late 1940s and early 1950s, the increased recognition of First Nations citizenship rights and the promotion of First Nations arts. This was essential to maintaining public confidence in state policy and to promoting a positive investment atmosphere, both of which were important for a province that hinged its economic development on natural resource exploitation and resource-based industries in the Coastal and northern regions (which were dependent upon First Nations labour).[65]

The lesson that First Nations political organizations learned from Ravenhill and the BCIAWS was that pressure groups had to attach themselves to the most powerful of the informal and constantly shifting circles of the social elite in that network of voluntary organizations that made up Canadian community (and therefore political) life. It was not enough to rail against the system from the outside, as had the Allied Tribes, despite the pretension that the committees in Ottawa and/or Victoria were extending a sympathetic ear. Wartime and postwar economic circumstances raised the value of First Nations labour. The rise in the importance of the First Nations commercial fishery during the war, including an increase in First Nations-owned boats, and the amalgamation of the two strongest First Nations organizations provided the Native Brotherhood with enough resources and economic clout to lobby resource industry officials.[66] Furthermore, Harney reports that, in 1947, representatives from industries such as mining, agriculture, and forestry had approached the government for help in finding new sources of cheap and pliable workers. That same year, King announced a renewal of Canadian growth through mass immigration, declaring "it would be dangerous for a small population to hold so great a heritage as ours."[67] All this added to the value of First Nations labour, which was already settled and, in many cases, trained.

In a postwar British Columbia set for a natural resources-based economic boom, many in First Nations communities felt that the time was ripe for sustained economic growth on the reserves. This growth was to be fuelled by high labour wages, political enfranchisement for all First Nations people, and perhaps even the complete abolition of the Indian Act, which would lead to the entrenchment of Aboriginal rights as well as to greater control over educational curriculum and other matters. In the end, industry and state officials accepted limited reform as a means of placating one of their important labour pools, but the Indian Act revisions fell far short of realizing their initial promise.

In the late 1940s the legitimizing role of the Indian Act committee and of an increasingly vocal discourse from a multicultural and inclusive Canada became important to the federal government. The parliamentary committees and royal commissions addressed crucial issues about both the business of government and the constitution of Canadian society at a time when people were particularly sensitive about the issue of a *moral* state. Canada, fully engaged in the postwar United Nations rhetoric of universal human rights and the humanitarian obligation of those nations left relatively unscathed by the war itself, was under international pressure to accept waves of non-Anglo-Celtic refugees, termed displaced persons (DPs).[68] The acceptance of DPs was matched by domestic pressure for "humanitarian" solutions to the existing problem of Canada's impoverished and marginalized communities.

In 1946 the government passed the Canadian Citizenship Act, which, for the first time, created a Canadian citizenship that was distinct from British subject status. In addition to Canada's issuing of its first passports, its awareness of its independence from the Empire was heightened both privately (due to the fact that government members realized the extent of Britain's financial bankruptcy) and publicly (due to the efforts to construct a unique international identity).[69] The shifting postwar political alignments and the need for massive reconstruction in both Europe and Asia created new markets for Canadian resource products.[70] The pressures brought on Canada by this new international image as well as by the now burgeoning export markets created a demand for adjustments in domestic policies, particularly with regard to race, national "culture," and a common, lingering national self-image as a British derivative.

In 1947 Canada did indeed overturn laws prohibiting Asian immigration as well as the ban on the Asian-Canadian vote, although, due to the ongoing dispute over the extinguishment of Aboriginal rights through enfranchisement,[71] the vote was not extended to First Nations peoples. However, the social reform movement aided the cause of First Nations emancipation by working the accepted network of pressure groups and voluntary organizations and through the early use of media. By the end of the Second World War social reformers had managed to form cross-discipline relationships through meetings and conferences (like the 1948 BCIAWS conference at the University of British Columbia). The ongoing professionalization of the social welfare movement had given it a sense of legitimacy in the eyes of state officials, and associations such as the BCIAWS, whose interests cut across a number of professional boundaries, sought to extend their organizational contacts. Thus the Native Brotherhood was no longer a voice in the wilderness.

Although it had forged contacts within First Nations communities and organizations, the social reform movement was still primarily Euro-Canadian. Individuals within the movement were limited by continuing to subscribe to the idea of First Nations helplessness as delineated in the mythology of the "Vanishing American." This led to the continued entrenchment of Euro-Canadian paternalism. Even when it was seen and accepted that First Nations-based associations like the Native Brotherhood had the skills, resources, and organization to attain its goals, the news media and, therefore, the public in general had trouble accepting an updated vision of the place of First Nations peoples in Canadian society.

The Native Brotherhood saw this and sought to correct the situation. The proclamation against Hart and his provincial government was symbolic, but it nonetheless jolted the media, confused and panicked the premier's office, and raised the public profile of Scow and the Brotherhood. Furthermore, it provoked crucial public debate at a time when the more serious business of letters and petitions was failing to sway the government on the issue of provincial enfranchisement. During the era of postwar reconstruction, any number of causes competed for public attention. The Brotherhood sought to attract that attention by manipulating the media.

This was by and large a successful strategy, at least at the provincial level, where the Brotherhood's influence was strongest. From 1947 on, enough pressure was brought to bear on the provincial government by both social reform and First Nations political activists to force it to acknowledge the importance of First Nations. UBC hired Harry Hawthorn "with the understanding that the progress of the Native people would be one of his concerns."[72] Two years later, in 1949, the First Nations of British Columbia were granted the provincial vote. Nisga'a chief Frank Calder, formerly secretary of the Greenville branch of the Native Brotherhood and president of the Nishga Tribal Council, was elected as the Co-operative Commonwealth Federation (CCF) Member of the Legislative Assembly for Atlin in the 1949 election.[73] The provincial government celebrated the provincial enfranchisement by buying six paintings by the young Gitxsan artist Judith Morgan.[74] From this time on, government patronage of First Nations arts, along with the restructuring of the DIA and the revision of the Indian Act, became part of a strategy to legitimize a new direction in Indian policy.

The purchase of Morgan's paintings was a fitting acknowledgment of the social reform movement's emphasis on youth, education, and art as the vehicles through which First Nations might be included in contemporary Canadian society. Youth, education, and art were also emphasized by the Brotherhood, especially through its newspaper, *Native Voice*. In addition to

George Clutesi's editorials extolling the virtues of formal education, students from residential and day schools were regular contributors. The *Native Voice* tracked Morgan's early career, several times publishing her works on its front cover.[75] It regularly reported on the activities of George Clutesi, who painted in a more "westernized," illusionistic style, and the BCIAWS; but the Brotherhood was also aware of the hold that more "traditional" art forms had on the public imagination, and it sought ways of establishing a sense of continuity with tradition while, at the same time, stressing the participation of its membership in contemporary industry and politics. The best example of this occurred three years before provincial enfranchisement, during Vancouver's Diamond Jubilee of 1946.

For this event, Scow and Ralph Hiltz, a Vancouver show producer and former reserve teacher, created a temporary "Indian village" in Kitsilano. During the two-week Diamond Jubilee celebrations, which began in July, the Kitsilano Indian Village featured Kwakwa̱ka̱'wakw dance performances and an arts and crafts fair. The local media appeared ready to follow a predictable pattern in promoting the village, but Scow and others led them in another direction. Thus, while Scow tantalized the public with the statement, "I can assure you the things our people will be bringing down with them have never been seen by white people,"[76] he also made certain that band names such as Owakalagalis, Pilnaquwilwakwas, Humchitt, Owad, and Nagaeselaq received top print billing. Scow, as a member of the Native Brotherhood leadership, was determined to make and control the First Nations presence at the jubilee.

References to contemporary First Nations reality tempered by the rather colourful language of the newspapers indicated a change in journalistic attitude – a change that, in part, was stimulated by the Brotherhood's activities as well as by a growing awareness of First Nations issues brought on by the federal joint committee. No longer were non-Aboriginals described as the rightful successors to a First Nations past. "At the Indian village now being prepared for them at Kitsilano,"[77] the *New Herald* reporter wrote of the Kwakwa̱ka̱'wakw performers, "they will spend two weeks under the scrutiny of the pale-face race that jockeyed them off Kitsilano lands."[78] The *Vancouver Sun*, reporting on their arrival, described the performers as an "urbane, well-mannered fraternity."[79] Scow, waiting to brief them on their arrival from Alert Bay, was "wearing a fedora at a rakish angle and a natty herringbone suit."[80] The resulting impression, the *Sun* reporter remarked dryly, was that "their only acquaintanceship with a tomahawk or pipe of peace is what they've seen in a movie horse opera."[81] This ironic newspaper play between Hollywood stereotype and apparent contemporary reality, in conjunction with the suggestion that Vancouver's acquisition of Kitsilano lands was less than rightful, marked a promising beginning to the Kwakwa̱ka̱'wakw entourage's stay. The 1946 federal policy shift that was engendered in the Canadian Citizenship bill and that conceived of Canada as a multiethnic state was alluded to by the head of the Vancouver branch president of the Canadian Folk Society, L.H. Thorlaksson, when he spoke of the significance of the celebrations' multicultural components: "We are all Canadians," said Thorlaksson, reciting a now familiar refrain, "but should still foster and preserve the great cultures of our homelands."[82]

Mungo Martin accompanied the entourage, and Hiltz billed him as "one of the province's last great totem pole carvers,"[83] someone who was demonstrating "his vanishing art"[84] in the village's arts and crafts section. Scow and the others then invited Viscount Alexander, British war hero and governor general of Canada (who was to visit the celebrations as part of his first tour of western Canada), to receive an honourary chieftainship and an eleven-foot pole carved by Martin at the Kitsilano site.[85]

However, Kwakwa̱ka̱'wakw dissatisfaction almost shut down the village immediately after their arrival, much to the embarrassment of the city and, most particularly, the organizing committee. Kwakwa̱ka̱'wakw complained "that the Indians were taken to Vancouver from coastal points in second class accommodation, that no arrangements were made in advance for their transportation in the city, that a private citizen had to provide a truck for them to take part in Monday's Jubilee parade ... They also charged that totem poles decorating Vancouver streets are what they term 'cheap caricatures' and 'an insult to our people.'"[86] Other newspapers reported that all thirty-seven performers were stranded without pay.[87]

The group threatened to withdraw from the Jubilee celebrations, and by 9 July, the story was picked up nationally. Within a day an agreement had been reached and, although no specific details were made public, it included the paid return north of seventeen of the dancers in time for the fishing season, some variation on the city's previous offer of room and board, an allowance of one dollar a day for incidental expenses, and the sharing of some $2,000 in profits earned through the village show.[88]

With the settlement, all returned to the next task at hand; namely, preparations for the presentations to Viscount Alexander. According to the inaugural issue of the *Native Voice*, at the July ceremony Alexander was greeted by Coast Salish representative Chief August Jack Khatsolano and then made honourary president of the Native Brotherhood of British Columbia.[89] In addition to accepting the governor general as a chief, the Native Brotherhood also conferred upon him the name Chief Napapunkim. The name was traced back "about 150 years ... when the original Napapunkim was an outstanding leader of the coast Indians, not only for his ability as a warrior but as a serious thinker of his time that made him the jealous guardian of the rights of the Native people in a day when the early white companies and settlers were aggressively encroaching upon the lands of the original inhabitants."[90] The physical reminder of the chieftainship and the name was a

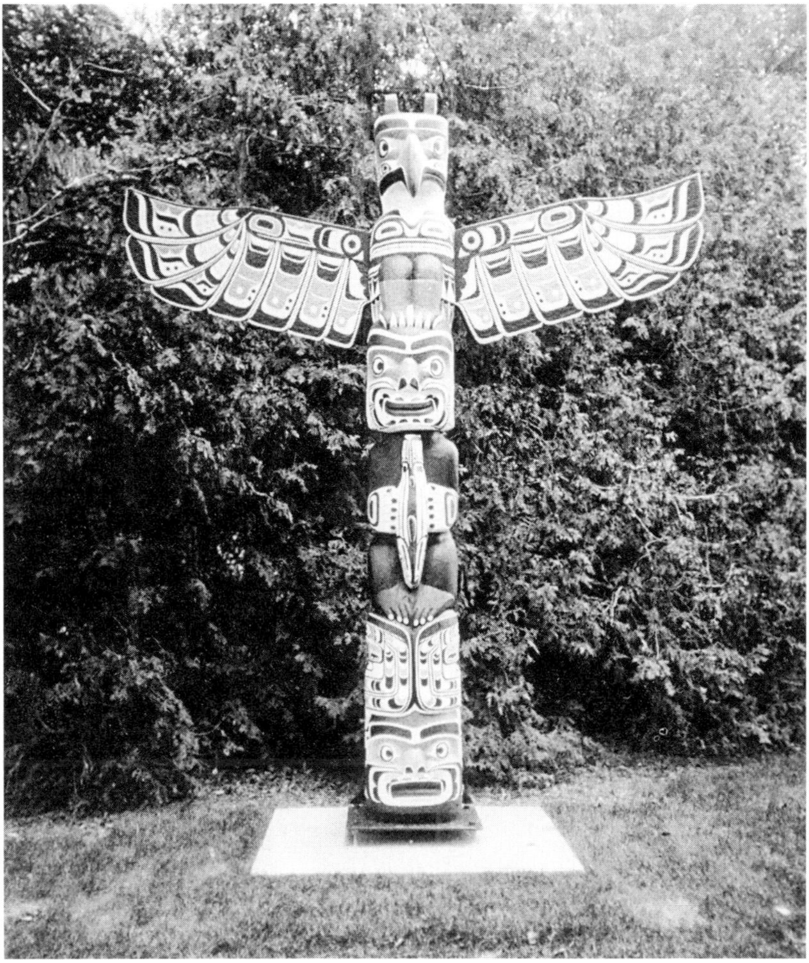

30 Mungo Martin pole presented to Governor General Viscount Alexander, 1946, and now standing at Rideau Hall, Ottawa.

pole carved by Martin and presented at the ceremony (see Figure 30). The name itself was Martin's own prerogative.[91]

Like Joe's pole, Martin's pole was immediately visually reminiscent of James's houseposts. Formally, it is even closer to James's than is Joe's (which is not surprising given that Martin was trained by James). Similar in size and proportion to James's posts, the general composition of Martin's pole consists of three main figures. Although the figures were not explained in the press, the top figure is a thunderbird with outstretched wings covered in crisply painted ornate formline patterning. Under the thunderbird, a human-like figure clutches a smaller figure – apparently a fish. Both these figures are composed in a way similar to those on James's houseposts, perhaps intentionally making a connection to the older carvings and thus implying a sense of artistic and social continuity. However, Martin's work was far from being a slavish imitation of James's. The wings of his thunderbird are more gracefully angled up than are James's, and his two-dimensional painting, especially on the wings, is more sophisticated.

The dance performances utilized what non-Aboriginal Canadians were increasingly terming art. This in itself was an expression of Kwakwaka'wakw power, particularly since the Indian Act still maintained the potlatch ban and, in theory, prohibited First Nations people from dancing off their own reserves. Ethnodrama, as an activity in itself, was a direct reaction, at least in the case of Northwest Coast dancing, to the shackles of the Indian Act. Second, along with the newspaper reports on the dancers' "modern" and "urbane" apparel, the performances pointedly asserted both continuity with the traditions of the past and the full participation of First Nations people in "modern" BC life. Through their presence, the dancers suggested that modernity and First Nations integrity were not mutually exclusive and that First Nations identities were more than touristic.

The Native Brotherhood's commission of Martin's pole as part of the presentation ceremony seems to be Martin's first commission outside of the Kwakwaka'wakw communities. While not the central focus of the presentation, the pole was nonetheless part of a carefully manipulated event intended to raise public awareness and, at least at a symbolic level, oblige the king's representative in Canada (in the same year as the instigation of the federal joint committee on Indian affairs) to live up to a name historically associated with the defence of First Nations rights. The pole also commanded media attention. Newspapers speculated on whether this might be Martin's last pole, perhaps even the last "authentic" pole on the Coast.

For most Vancouverites the political subtlety of the celebrations may have been outshone by the pageantry. It was not missed, however, by the *Native Voice*'s target audience, and it illustrates the use of First Nations "culture" for the promotion of First Nations politics. The call for the preservation of the totem pole, as presented in the Brotherhood's press releases, was an implicit call for the preservation of First Nations arts, perhaps including traditional leadership structures. Certainly, the local media seemed to position Martin as an adjunct of the Native Brotherhood and its leaders.[92]

The Brotherhood repeatedly demonstrated that First Nations arts were not the sole property of the BCIAWS and other non-Aboriginal interest groups. In fact, in 1947 Scow commissioned one of the BCIAWS's emerging stars, Ellen Neel, to carve a large pole to be presented to the University of British Columbia, where Scow's son was attending classes.[93] Intended in part to sanction the university athletic program's use of the thunderbird moniker, Scow's ceremony and its targeting of a large body of non-Aboriginal youth at a university that was intensifying its role in First Nations social issues was also intended to dispel stereotypes and to allow access to "real" First Nations "culture."

In an editorial in the first issue of the *Native Voice,* the Native Brotherhood had implied that this kind of activity was part of a general strategy aimed at the media: "We are prisoners of a controlling power in our own country – a country that has stood under the chaos of two world wars, beneath the guise of democracy and freedom, yet keeping enslaved a Native people in their own home land ... *The Native Voice,* while invading the privileged sanction of the press, heretofore not occupied by our people, does not find it necessary to apologize for its efforts, which will be a long awaited stimulant leading toward a better way of life for all the Native people in Canada."[94] The Native Brotherhood's own newspaper was not the only vehicle that it used in order to manipulate public opinion. The disastrous conditions at the Vancouver jubilee led to the communication of a range of significant issues, including, at a fundamental level, the second-class status of First Nations peoples. The Native Brotherhood, through its focusing of media attention, was also able to address the liberties that non-Aboriginals took with First Nations peoples as well as the city's disempowering use of totem poles that Scow and others characterized as crude and insulting caricatures.

The disagreement at the Vancouver Jubilee further resulted in sympathetic, albeit at times condescending, editorials in the mainstream press. An unidentified editorial on the 1946 Jubilee found in the AHSAV files states:

> The time has come, indeed it is long overdue, to deal with our Indian population justly and intelligently. They should no longer be regarded as wards of the state and kept in a condition of dependence. They should be given the best education facilities, the best economic opportunities, and the fullest rights to citizenship.
>
> The Indians cannot fail to see the advantages of our way of life as demonstrated at the Jubilee celebrations. The accomplishments of sixty years are truly astonishing. What the Indians need is unmistakable evidence that we are prepared to take them into full partnership.[95]

Through both the Kitsilano village and *Native Voice,* First Nations art became attached to the Native Brotherhood's attempt to present First Nations individuals to the non-Aboriginal public as dignified, organized, and professional people. The Brotherhood's use of traditional arts and ceremony complemented the pressures brought to bear by the BCIAWS and other reformers. Their efforts seemed to have some success. Editorials from the mainstream press indicated that, in the course of a generation, there had been a considerable change in the attitudes of the general non-Aboriginal public.

George Clutesi and *Native Voice*

Peter Macnair argues that, after 1920, with the exception of that of the Kwakwa̱ka̱'wakw, traditional Northwest Coast art was in decline.[96] His aesthetic judgment of twentieth-century Northwest Coast objects, which is based on comparing them with objects from the last half of the nineteenth century, overlooks the fact that a growing diversity of forms is a response to the changing social conditions concomitant with intensive non-Aboriginal immigration and Euro-Canadian socio-economic control. A variety of artistic expressions were continuing in and emerging from First Nations communities, and they served different functions, not the least of which was to contribute to the fight for land and the entrenchment of Aboriginal rights. These different genres of art were informed by different social practices. Some sought to reinforce the social positions validated in the underground potlatches; others reinforced the validity of First Nations identities outside the reserves; still others were intended to speak directly to a dislocated sense of pride among the young.

George Clutesi[97] used the postwar access to mass media (afforded by *Native Voice* and by a growing public interest in First Nations affairs) to speak specifically to young First Nations people. While stressing the importance of tradition, he also advocated the importance of the opportunities potentially available to build towards the future. Acknowledging the new pan-Indian political leadership, in January 1947 he wrote:

> The ashes of his past have been gathered together, rekindled and they have begun to burn anew. Keep up the fight you brave leaders. In this young hour you have shown your wisdom. With your guidance have we broken the surface of the tide that so nearly engulfed us to its entirety. The undertow is weakening. The straw that you grabbed proved to be a strong helping and understanding hand. Hang on, fight, your job has just begun.[98]

His choice of words, that "we have broken the surface of the tide that so nearly engulfed us," reflects a general feeling of optimism that was sweeping First Nations communities, who were hopeful that the Special Joint Committee would scrap the Indian Act and finally address issues around land, self-government, and the reserve system.

Clutesi's work complicates the restrictive modern/traditional (primitive) paradigm of First Nations art history that emerged after 1950. Clutesi was widely known in British Columbia in the late 1940s, yet his paintings, like the carvings of Mathias Joe, rarely, if ever, show up in contemporary catalogues on Northwest Coast art. His founding of a travelling Nuu-chah-nulth

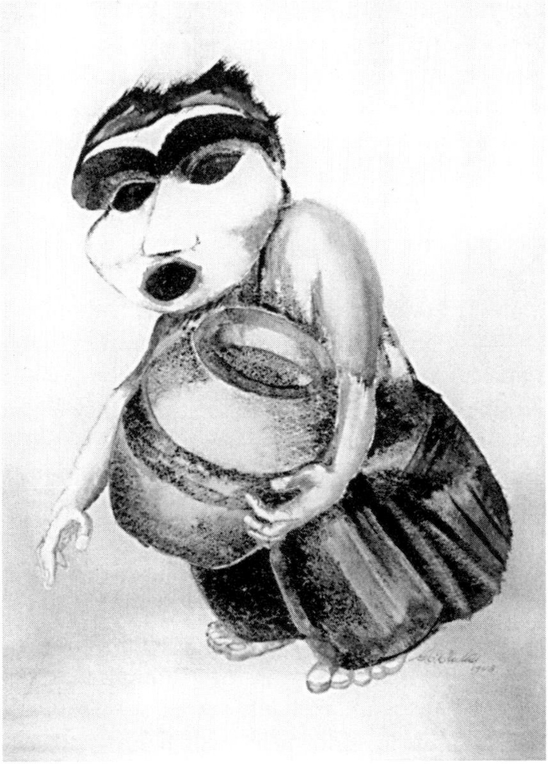

31 Painting of a traditional Nuu-chah-nulth dance, by George Clutesi, 1948.

exhibition dance group in the 1940s broke the terms of the Indian Act as First Nations people were not to dance off their own reserves. Like his dance group, Clutesi's articles and radio broadcasts had a dual intention: first, to make First Nations youth proud of their heritage and history; second, to make White people respect First Nations accomplishments.

His paintings were distinctly "westernized," with their implied narrative and their use of three-dimensional space. In the painting shown in Figure 31, Clutesi focuses upon a single subject: a masked dancer crouches, grasping a bowl-like drum in one hand and beating the bottom of it with the other. The drum is painted with light and shadow, dramatically emphasizing, as does the use of light and dark in Morgan's painting, the object's three-dimensionality. Clutesi foreshortened the figure of the dancer to create the sense that it occupies a real space. Neither Morgan nor Clutesi veered from the essentially traditional practice of using two-dimensional painting to refer to the corpus of stories, songs, dances, and ceremonies of their respective peoples. They both appropriated European illusionism in order to update their manner of depicting this corpus. With Clutesi, especially, this may have been a conscious decision to make his art seem relevant in the increasingly European world in which First Nations peoples found themselves during the middle third of the twentieth century. It is equally possible, however, that Clutesi and Morgan were simply products of their time and that their work exemplifies the coalescence of two visual traditions. From this standpoint, their art may be seen as a visual interpretation for which they simply used the techniques and subjects that seemed most meaningful.

Much of Clutesi's work illustrates various Nuu-chah-nulth Tse-shaht stories and ceremonies. In 1949 he said: "I've been interested all my life in reviving the past life of my own people on Vancouver Island. I have tried to put on canvas what my people lived for, what they accomplished, the dances they created."[99] In short, Clutesi's work complemented the efforts of bands like the Squamish and of political organizations like the Native Brotherhood.

"To live and to survive in this new era," wrote Clutesi, "we must store up for the future."[100] It was for this reason that Clutesi's target audience tended to be children or young adults. In 1947-48 he wrote a number of inspirational articles for the *Native Voice* in which he outlined his personal idea of what it would take for First Nations to survive in postwar Canada. On the surface, many of his ideas, and certainly his art, seem to belong to the progressive era of American pan-Indianism, which advocated education, hard work, and adapting Aboriginal attitudes, values, and habits of life to those of the larger American society.[101] However, as Tennant points out, "the pattern of politics which emerged among British Columbia Indians was the opposite of the early assimilationist pan-Indianism of the United States. British Columbia Indian leaders dedicated themselves to ensuring a distinct and continuing Indian existence."[102]

> Civilization is an awe-inspiring and soul-tearing culture. It brings wonderful miraculous wonders ... but in its very wake, it also brings destruction! ... The sooner we realize this the better we shall be prepared to cope with what has engulfed us so efficiently and so completely, the sooner we realize that we must as individuals prepare ourselves to do our bit to meet this overwhelming onslaught of civilization. The only logical solution, I believe, is to learn as quickly and as efficiently as possible the concepts of this new culture. Reach for and acquire higher education. Without it we are lost, we are like chattels. As long as we are useful we are tolerated; become weak, then we are cast aside.
>
> Therefore thirst after wisdom. Reawaken the desire to administer unto your own in this new culture, prepare yourselves to become doctors, nurses,

> nurses' aids, teachers, ministers of the Gospel, etc. and when you have accomplished these come back to us. We are in need of you most urgently ...
>
> Yes, it is good to adopt our white brothers' mode of life, but I repeat, remain the Native North American Indian that you are, the Great Spirit made you. Be proud of his creation.[103]

Of course, much of the concern of the BCIAWS centred on the promotion and acceptance of "Indianness." Their objectives in this respect were, arguably, part good intentions and part imperialist nostalgia. Although BCIAWS members were often outspoken in their call for pride in First Nations societies, the primary (albeit unspoken) objective of the association was the *integration* of First Nations peoples into the Canadian mainstream. And their insistence on what constituted Aboriginal societies was often affected by the persistence of the modern/primitive paradigm. Clutesi would later write, in a not-so-veiled reference to the kind of social reformist spirit at the heart of the BCIAWS: "What can be done to really help the Indian at this time? One way would be to look for his better qualities. He has some. Meet him halfway. Try harder to become a sincere friend. You cannot fool an Indian with the gushing displays of hypocritical prying of a would-be do-gooder."[104]

Although Clutesi may have objected to the Eurocentric perspective of some of the BCIAWS members, there is no doubt that the association's promotion of his work furthered both his artistic career and his political agenda. Through its exhibitions, conferences, publications, and marketing, it opened doors that gave him a wider audience. In 1947, just after UBC hired him, anthropologist and curator Harry Hawthorn purchased seven of Clutesi's paintings for the newly opened university museum. This signalled the progress that had been achieved by the dual paths of Aboriginal and non-Aboriginal reform efforts. A major public institution had acknowledged a contemporary Northwest Coast artist, an illusionist *painter* no less. The university, if only briefly, recognized both the existence of contemporary First Nations art and a multitude of creative expressions beyond the so-called authentic carvings and paintings of the nineteenth century. Along with such recognition went provincial enfranchisement and the potential, under the joint commission, for a major overhaul of "Indian" policy. In the last years of the 1940s, paternalism seemed to be weakening.

8
UBC, the BCPM, and the Totem Pole Carver Training Program

As the Great Depression had interrupted the institutionalization of national "culture" in Canada in the 1920s, it had been two decades since Canadian public museums made any major attempts to represent Northwest Coast objects as part of the national fabric. Reform groups like the British Columbia Indian Arts and Welfare Society had tried to bridge the gap, but they lacked the funding to do anything on a large scale. The partnership between the BCIAWS and the British Columbia Provincial Museum had been productive in some respects, but the postwar management trend was towards professionalization and away from a reliance upon voluntary arts organizations. Wartime commissions stressed the need for training and the growth of a supportive government infrastructure in order to transform the underdeveloped arts into a viable component of the national economy.[1] This trend translated into a lessening role for the BCIAWS and a growth in state institutions like the BCPM and the University of British Columbia.

The federal government founded the Massey Commission in 1949 to chart the transformation of the arts into a professional industry. This chapter reviews the motivation for the Massey Commission and its effect on institutions in British Columbia. Central to British Columbia's regional contribution to national "culture," the objects of the Northwest Coast would, in the late 1940s, once again receive institutional attention. On the one hand, the resulting programs appeared to answer the calls for change along with the recognition of the contemporary contributions of living First Nations artists. On the other hand, the privileging of professionally trained museum and university authorities over Aboriginals with regard to determining the meanings of Northwest Coast objects created a discursive tension that was played out in the promotional programs. While the catchword for postwar Canadian society was integration, which, in theory, allowed for the maintenance of the traditions of non-British Canadians, in practice this amounted to a role for First Nations objects as touristic commodities within national and provincial economies. This failed to allow for the symbolic role these objects played within the potlatch system, and it represented a shift towards what Halliday had suggested in his 1922 Cranmer post-trial display.

The Massey Commission: "Indian Culture," "Canadian Culture"

In response to the ongoing postwar debate over Canadian identity and the role of public institutions in its promotion, the Royal Commission on National Development in the Arts, Letters and Sciences (the Massey Commission) was formed in 1949,[2] the same year the commission's BC representative, Norman MacKenzie, opened the University of British Columbia's Museum of Anthropology in his capacity as university president.[3]

Paul Schafer and André Fortier report that the roots of the Massey Commission lay in the 1945 Canadian Arts Council (CAC) brief to the House of Commons Special Committee on Reconstruction and Re-establishment (sometimes referred to as the Turgeon Committee), which sat during the later stages of the Second World War, "to uncover the trouble spots in the Canadian economy and prescribe remedies that the government should adopt."[4] The CAC, itself a national umbrella organization hastily made up of a number of community arts groups, called for state patronage in the arts. This call, in conjunction with the national perception of a crisis in the universities (what would be their postwar role and direction?), became extremely influential. Emotions of patriotism stimulated both by the war itself and by the ongoing concern with a Canadian identity independent from both Britain and the United States sensitized the Canadian public to the question of public arts funding.[5]

Paul Litt traces the commission's development to the ruling Liberal party's emerging embarrassment over Canada's shoddy reputation abroad. Liberal Cabinet members like Lester Pearson and Brooke Claxton argued that, if Canada was to fulfill its new international political role, then it was in the government's interest to promote Canadian identity both domestically and internationally. This fit conveniently with the popular belief that the war and the postwar reconstruction constituted a postcolonial climax in Canadian history. As Litt writes:

> National confidence was expressed and reinforced by developments ranging from the admission of Newfoundland to Confederation to legislation making the Supreme Court of Canada the court of final appeal in the land. For a generation weaned on the "colony to nation" theme of progressive national independence, it seemed that Canada had come of age constitutionally, diplomatically, and militarily. A cultural nationalism that cultivated a unique cultural identity was an appropriate capstone for the nation-building process ... Postwar nationalism gave government cultural initiatives a broader base of popular support and a new political relevance.[6]

The commission's final report was made public in June 1951. It issued 146 recommendations on a broad range of interrelated issues, including radio broadcasting, television, the National Film Board, galleries, museums, libraries, archives, historic sites and monuments, universities, the Canadian image abroad, and an arm's-length granting agency named the Canada Council (which was not realized until 1957). While it emphasized a federal structure for the arts, it qualified this in its recognition of provincial authority, particularly in the field of education. Education, defined in the report as "the progressive development of the individual in all his [sic] faculties, physical and intellectual, aesthetic and moral,"[7] was central to its vision of Canadian "culture," further defined as "that part of education which enriches the mind and refines the taste. It is the development of the intelligence through the arts, letters, and sciences."[8] While it suggested that formal education "is definitely a provincial matter"[9] and that "the life-long process of education which the culture of a society is a matter of national and international interest,"[10] any formal promotion was guaranteed as provincial jurisdiction if it was generated through the provincial ministries of education. Since the BCPM had been shuffled into the Ministry of Education, Northwest Coast art became a provincial matter.

Following the release of the 1928 *Meriam Report* during the Hoover administration in the United States, the Roosevelt Indian New Deal hinged much of its reform on overhauling the Native American educational system. In his 1946 opening presentation to Canada's Joint Committee on the Indian Act, Canadian Department of Indian Affairs director Robert Hoey's citation of the *Meriam Report* as the "most comprehensive and one of the most informative available on the question"[11] of "Indian" administration foreshadowed the division of wardship responsibility between federal and provincial states through education. In British Columbia, for example, the most important programs on First Nations arts in the 1950s were instigated by the Massey Commission's own Norman MacKenzie at UBC and at the BCPM under the auspices of the Ministry of Education. The central objective of their cooperative efforts was to promote the reception of First Nations arts and, thus, the recognition of their contribution to Canadian society. An important secondary goal was the stimulation of the contemporary arts market and the strengthening of the arts as a form of employment. These desires had also been at the heart of Collier's efforts in the United States, and they conveniently intersected with the interests of the Massey Commission. They were both part of a general North American trend towards state regulation and management and the professionalization of the arts.

Despite its initially limited implementation, the Massey Commission's report provided a blueprint for solving the problems faced by the individuals and groups involved with various aspects of the arts in Canada. It garnered positive attention through popular media and had a broad impact on

Canadian identity. Although it stressed expanding museum facilities as a hedge against the ongoing loss of national heritage, it also had a separate section devoted to "Indian arts and crafts."[12] Noting that indifference on behalf of both First Nations and non-Aboriginal Canadians was resulting in the loss of the "traditional skills and arts of the Indians,"[13] the commission went as far as to suggest establishing a council for First Nations art that would be parallel to the Canada Council. But the popular hierarchy of the arts, which privileged the primarily male, Euro-Canadian pursuits of painting and sculpture as art and other forms of production as folklore or handicrafts, meant that the promotion of these other forms would remain a local rather than a national matter.

First Nations art was an issue that the commission had to grapple with for a number of reasons. First, First Nations art, particularly that of the Northwest Coast, was perceived as a powerful Canadian symbol and was deeply associated with BC tourism. This association was made more formal through its promotion by the national museum and the national gallery in the 1920s, and by its being paraphrased, so to speak, in the paintings of major BC modernist painters, notably Emily Carr and, beginning in the 1940s, Jack Shadbolt.[14]

Second, during the commission's hearings in western Canada both solicited and unsolicited briefs sought to bring art to the forefront. In 1950 the Massey Commission called on newly appointed professor Harry Hawthorn to complete a report "on whatever measures could be taken to increase a wide Canadian knowledge of Indian Arts and Crafts, and to make more effective the present somewhat casual arrangements for the marketing of these native products."[15] As Litt suggests, the "Massey Commission's hearings ... showed that Canadian cultural development would have to come to terms not just with biculturalism, but multiculturalism as well."[16] This is what Crosby identifies as the recognition of First Nations arts as "part of a larger strategy to focus on culture as the means for creating a federalist ideology that both contain[s] and encourage[s] regional diversity."[17] In this sense, Northwest Coast art, as a symbol of British Columbia, had become a regionalist voice within the fabric of Canadian nationalism.[18]

Third, there was the perennial problem of extending the logic of the concept of two founding nations in order to somehow acknowledge the historical presence of First Nations peoples. In British Columbia, where treaties were non-existent and where the postwar economy centred on natural resources, this historical presence was potentially disruptive.

UBC and the Institutionalization of Contemporary Northwest Coast Art, Vancouver

The war years saw a more integrated, state-managed economy, paralleling the American move away from more liberal, or laissez-faire, capitalism to the Keynesian collectivism favoured by Roosevelt earlier in the 1930s. In this Canadian "New Deal," Mackenzie King and the federal Liberal government introduced their vision of a postwar "welfare" state, beginning with national unemployment insurance in 1940 and including an extended old age pension plan, plans for veteran housing, education grants, farm assistance programs, and retraining programs.[19] Government members were keen to maintain controlled economic growth and to avoid the problems of resettlement suffered after the First World War. Money was therefore funnelled towards giving veterans affordable housing and either employment or professional, career-path education.[20]

Hand in hand with this vision came a concern for professionalization, not only with regard to those producing arts, but also with regard to those producing knowledge about the arts. This meant that the universities were to be in charge of training "cultural" professionals for the museums, and it led directly to the hiring of Harry Hawthorn at UBC in 1947[21] and the hiring of his student, Wilson Duff, at the BCPM in 1949.[22] With the creation of a cadre of professionals responsible for the management of provincial "culture," Northwest Coast art was institutionalized within the structure of the state, thereby reinforcing the authority of institutional officials. Thus control over the distribution of knowledge about First Nations objects came to rest with this professional cadre rather than with the potlatch system. Thus the BCPM became the centre for the preservation and management of First Nations material and UBC became the centre for its study. With the preservation, study, and, eventually, replication of First Nations objects – all of which was handled by this growing state bureaucracy – the 1920s assimilationist project of exerting authority over the construction of meaning for First Nations objects was continued. It was within this context that UBC took on a larger role as the promoter of British Columbian "culture." Between 1947 and 1950, university officials submitted a brief to the Massey Commission concerning the marketing of First Nations arts, funded a totem pole salvage project, and hired Mungo Martin to renovate old poles and to carve new poles for UBC's collection.

This must have been a difficult position for the individuals hired by the institutions to oversee these projects. On the one hand, much of the literature that they had access to explicitly stated that Aboriginal institutions had died out. On the other hand, they were faced with a contradiction. Any attempt at an artistic revival would likely have been motivated by good intentions – the desire to salvage this disappearing tradition. Nonetheless, in order to make the objects relevant to a wider audience, it was necessary to create new meanings for them – as commodities or as historical monuments – and this ultimately continued the process of asserting a European set of meanings over an Aboriginal set, a European conception of authority over an Aboriginal conception. In this sense, it was a no-win situation.

Harry Hawthorn had enlisted the help of his wife, Audrey Hawthorn, the museum's honourary curator, to complete the Massey brief.[23] Ironically, both Hawthorns were recent immigrants to Canada, and their connections to First Nations communities were still developing. "We knew of the peoples of the Northwest Coast, whose great creativity and outstanding arts had been extensively reported," writes Audrey Hawthorn. "We looked forward to further acquaintance with them in their daily lives."[24] She further reports her initial impression that there were strong markets for craft products from the Great Plains and Eastern Woodlands areas. She then developed an acquisition agenda for assembling "as representative a Canadian collection."[25] Both Hawthorns became increasingly interested in using the museum to stimulate what they saw as an unsatisfactory contemporary arts market in British Columbia.

In 1947 English professor Hunter Lewis completed a six-week survey of village sites on the central coast as part of his work at UBC, reporting, upon his return, about a number of salvageable, albeit decomposing, poles. Lewis was president of the Canadian Federation of Artists and likely contributed the section on First Nations art to the federation's Massey brief.[26] He also chaired the Committee on Indian Citizenship of the Vancouver Civil Liberties Union during the years of the Special Joint Committee on the Indian Act.[27] His survey ultimately led MacKenzie to appoint the UBC President's Committee on Totem Pole Preservation. In 1947 the committee decided to purchase poles for UBC and then to create a "Totem Pole Park" on the Point Grey campus.

No one at UBC at that time had the expertise to actually retrieve the poles, and so Lewis and the university administration turned to the most experienced person in the field – Marius Barbeau of the national museum. Barbeau, of course, had been instrumental in the acquisition of poles by foreign and domestic museums throughout the Great Depression. As Cole notes, the national museum had granted Barbeau permission to collect in a personal capacity, and he had frequently taken advantage of his position to improve his own financial standing by dealing in Northwest Coast objects as well as in Quebec church silver and sculpture.[28] He was also careful to shield price discrepancies from the institutions that were paying his way.

Barbeau contracted an in-law, Arthur Price, to purchase the poles for UBC while both he and Price travelled at national museum expense. In addition, Price received expenses from UBC through Hunter Lewis. In return, Price and Barbeau provided the university with eight poles, two carved thunderbirds, a housepost (originally owned by Spruce Martin), and a food bowl – all for a total of $3,200.[29] Price collected the objects from the Nass Valley and Alert Bay between 8 September and 14 October 1947, keeping a detailed record of who the objects were bought from as well as the cost of each object.[30] Price also detailed how much the two charged UBC for each of the objects, conveniently totalling the difference in a separate column labelled "total profit." The final profit was just over $1,700, with the gouging being up to $300 per object.[31] If Price and Barbeau had not overcharged the university, they could have purchased an additional sixty-foot pole that was deemed too expensive for the project's budget.[32]

Price's correspondence to Barbeau indicates a high level of self-consciousness. "My conscience bothers me a bit," he writes on 14 October 1947.[33] Writing three days later from Vancouver, Price reports to Barbeau on his meeting with the university administration: "Yesterday I was very worried that I might run into serious difficulty with the committee here as one of the Publicity made the crack about the fact that U.B.C. might be considered robbed or jipped [sic] – this particular fellow was afraid that one of the newspapers might take up the matter. I kept my mouth shut and all smoothed over."[34] Price's worry seemed to be more a product of his own conscience than any real suspicion on behalf of the university. MacKenzie approached Price after the meeting, asking "if there was much more good enough to buy and restore and wondered if they were sorta [sic] at the bottom of the barrel."[35] Although surprised, Price writes, "this suggestion I jumped on as a solid sinch [sic] for us. Yes – I said, we are unfortunately (being Canadian) the last to appreciate Indian art and had to be satisfied and feel fortunate that there is anything left for Canada."[36]

On Barbeau's return to Vancouver, he contacted Ellen Neel while seeking information on Charlie James.[37] Barbeau's attention gave their work academic validation and their reputation quickly spread. Ellen Neel's keynote address at the 1948 UBC conference secured further attention, and she was approached the same summer, by Lewis and the university, to help with the restoration of the poles purchased through Barbeau.[38] This was part of a growing plan to make UBC a centre for the study of First Nations culture, and it complemented Hawthorn's appointment, the Barbeau purchases, the purchase of Clutesi's paintings, and the 1948 conference. It appears to foreshadow the Massey Commission's suggestion that universities serve as centres for local culture.

Ellen Neel worked part time on the restoration project during the summer of 1948. Nuytten reports that the objectives of the restoration program expanded under the influence of Hawthorn. He suggests that it was Hawthorn's idea to address the perennial problem of the owners' reluctance to sell, given the "ever-growing awareness of the fragility of their heritage,"[39] through commissioning contemporary artists to replicate the poles instead of continuing with the patchwork repair of the older poles begun under Neel. The pay was unfortunately even poorer than it was in the curio business, so the following summer, when she was again approached, Neel introduced the university committee to her uncle, Mungo Martin. Martin worked for UBC over the next two years.

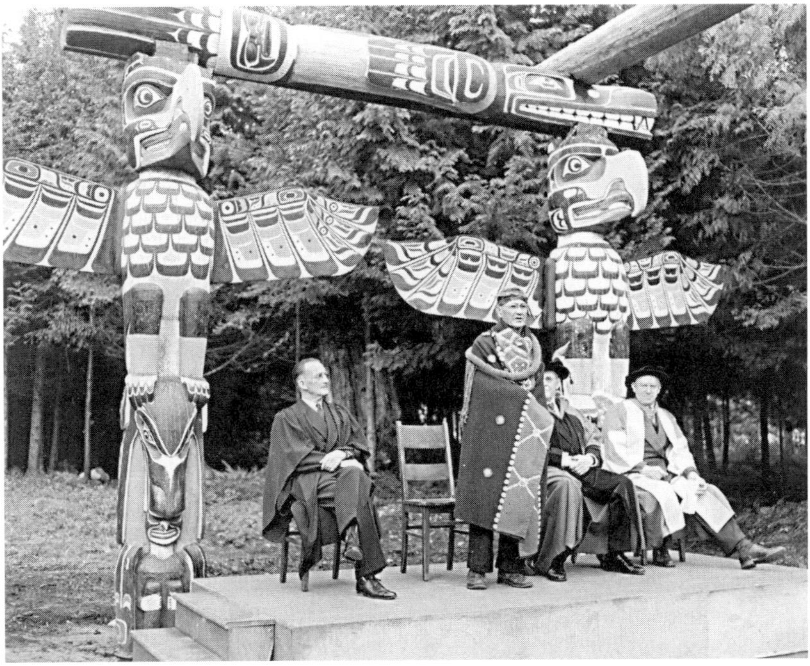

32 Mungo Martin, standing, with Norman MacKenzie, seated at right, at the opening of the University of British Columbia's Totem Pole Park.

Although Martin and Neel were both trained by Charlie James, Martin turned out to be both a public relations bonanza and an academic dream for the university (see Figure 32). Mungo Martin (Na<u>k</u>a'p<u>a</u>nk<u>a</u>m) was born in Fort Rupert in the early 1880s. His step-father was Charlie James, with whom he carved during the first three decades of the twentieth century. He married Sarah Constance (<u>A</u>baya'a), who accompanied him to Vancouver when he took over as carver for UBC's early totem pole restoration program in 1948-49. He became chief carver at the BCPM in 1952, where he worked with his son, David Martin, and his son-in-law, Henry Hunt, until shortly after David died in a boating accident in 1959.[40] He would eclipse all other contemporary Northwest Coast artists until Bill Reid. In 1980 Peter Macnair described him as "almost singularly responsible for the revival of Northwest Coast Indian art."[41] According to the museum officials with whom he worked, Martin was keen on using the university and the museums as storehouses of knowledge pertaining to Kwakw<u>a</u>k<u>a</u>'wakw culture – a kind of resource that both educated non-Aboriginals and safeguarded information for the Kwakw<u>a</u>k<u>a</u>'wakw themselves.[42] Harry and Audrey Hawthorn both relied heavily upon Martin for ethnographic information relevant to their collection. Audrey Hawthorn's two important books on Kwakw<u>a</u>k<u>a</u>'wakw art, published in 1967 and 1979, respectively, are based in part on information provided by Martin and A̲baya'a.[43]

Martin was, in addition, an older man, which fit well with the public image of the "last of the old-time totem pole carvers." The university needed such a figure to attract public attention and to justify the necessary funding allocations. While Martin was interested in recording First Nations tradition and promoting it widely through the museum, Neel thought of her work in more modernist terms, seeing herself as an artist creating unique works for sale and circulation outside of the First Nations communities. Martin recorded songs, transcribed stories, explained the meaning of UBC's collections within the context of the potlatch, and demonstrated carving and construction techniques on film and in person. Neel took great liberties with the forms she incorporated in her work. She would include portraits of Hollywood stars in her model poles or incorporate imagery outside of Kwakwa̲ka̲'wakw culture. Because of this, her work was not allotted the same respect as was Martin's, and she became more associated with tourist than "traditional" art (although during the summer of 1949 she did assist Martin with his restoration of the poles at UBC). Martin recarved sections of two poles. One of these poles had been carved by himself almost forty years earlier, and the other had been carved by Charlie James[44] in preparation for the erection of the Barbeau-purchased poles, which were to go towards simulating an "authentic" village on the UBC campus. The university planned the village park to showcase the different regional artistic styles of the Coastal peoples.

In addition to the historical legacy of tourism and Northwest Coast art, by the time of the Massey Commission, First Nations art seemed increasingly important as a physical part of Vancouver and of British Columbia. The Native Brotherhood's Kitsilano Indian Village had garnered local and national attention through both its problems and the presentation of Mungo Martin's pole to the governor general. The Totem Pole Park at UBC was well under way and was supplementing the poles standing in Stanley Park. The Scow-sponsored Ellen Neel pole presented to the UBC students' society was now standing outside Brock Hall in the centre of the university, and Neel was visible both in the workshop at Stanley Park and, during the summer tourist months, at the Pacific National Exhibition grounds in east Vancouver's Hastings Park.[45] Within a year, the premier himself was appointed honourary president of the Totemland Society (a non-governmental organization for the promotion of tourism).[46] This, to be sure, was a public relations ploy on the part of the society, but it was one that indicated the widespread acceptance of the importance of First Nations art to British Columbia's identity and touristic economy. Also, in Victoria, the BCPM's Thunderbird Park had become a major tourist destination, located barely a block from the city's inner harbour and across the street from the Canadian

Pacific Railway's massive Empress Hotel. Victoria was the main port of call for American and other tourists heading north on the inside passage route to Alaska. The CNR had opened its own totem pole park in Prince Rupert, another port on the way to Alaska, in the mid-1930s.[47] New poles were also beginning to filter out through North America through Neel's series of Totemland poles as well as through Mathias Joe's corporate commissions in Texas and eastern Canada. A major canning company, BC Packers, had begun making enquiries into the possibility of purchasing and removing old poles to their canneries.[48] The poles represented a unique and memorable evocation of the province, its geography, its history, and, through the oppositional paradigm of primitivism giving way to urban modernity, its current industrial success.

The BCPM and the Institutionalization of Contemporary Northwest Coast Art, Victoria

In 1949, the same year as provincial enfranchisement, the provincial government responded to growing public, institutional, and commercial interest in totem poles. Minister of Education W.T. Straith announced that "both the Provincial and Federal governments were interested in the advancement of Indian crafts, not only to preserve their culture, but also to help the natives make a livelihood."[49] The first step was to hire Wilson Duff, who immediately joined with Hawthorn to complete an ethnographic survey of the Nass and Skeena Rivers. The same year, the BCPM launched its "Anthropology in B.C." series.[50] In 1951 Duff prepared an influential report for Straith on the possibility of the "permanent preservation" of poles in British Columbia.[51]

When Thunderbird Park was opened in Victoria in 1940, one of the project's goals was to preserve the poles in the museum's collection. A decade of exposure had not achieved this goal, and although efforts had been made in the early 1950s to slow the decay, it was clear that their storage outside was not conducive to preservation. Taking advantage of the politicians' interest in the Totemland Society and its efforts, Duff warned, "unless vigorous steps are taken soon, we'll have a 'Totem Land' with no totem poles."[52] Duff then proposed to follow and expand upon Hawthorn's example at UBC and have the old poles stored inside and to have copies of them placed in the park. "Newly-carved wooden poles," wrote Duff, "could last at least a century outdoors if given the proper care."[53] The choice that Duff offered Straith was preservation (1) through having copies made from concrete casts and plastic moulds or (2) through "having the poles copied by an Indian who is without a doubt the finest carver still alive on the coast"; namely, Mungo Martin. Duff, unable to hide his enthusiasm for his second option, wrote "what an unparalleled tourist attraction it would be to have him working in Thunderbird Park!"[54]

Of course, Duff's Martin option fulfilled the provincial government's professed desire for "the advancement of Indian crafts ... to help the natives make a livelihood."[55] It was with this interest in promoting First Nations-specific employment and in professionalizing the production end of the market in mind that, the following year, the museum announced a three-year totem pole restoration program and appointed Mungo Martin head carver. "The primary purpose of the programme," announced the museum, "is to replace the present badly decaying exhibits in the park with a permanent and more representative collection – in part new poles, in part exact replicas of old ones – so that the fine original carvings can be preserved indefinitely indoors. By employing native carvers and having its operations in the park itself, the programme accomplishes two important secondary aims: to preserve the art of totem-carving and to serve as a unique tourist and educational attraction."[56] The museum also hired Martin's son, David Martin, as his assistant, and his granddaughter, Mildred Hunt, as an apprentice carver.[57] The inaugural projects included a memorial figure, two poles, and, most important, the construction of a Kwakwa̱ka̱'wakw house that would be completed and dedicated the following year, 1953.[58]

The museum built a workshop with construction materials donated by British Columbia Forest Products (see Figure 33). MacMillan-Bloedel donated and delivered cedar logs for the poles. One of the significant suggestions

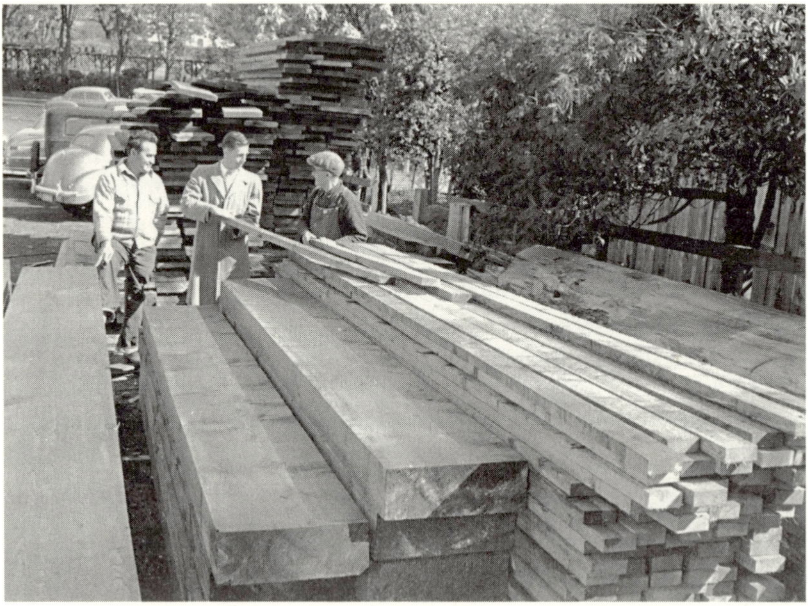

33 Mungo and David Martin receive wood donated by MacMillan-Bloedel, ca. 1952.

made by the Massey Commission in the 1951 publication of its findings was that industry and government cooperate in supporting Canadian "culture," a suggestion that was apparently well received in British Columbia. The promotional benefits of such projects were not lost on either MacMillan-Bloedel or BC Forest Products. Indeed, the museum almost gleefully reported that, in "two eight-hour days during the tourist season ... 2,375 persons watched the carvers at work. Nine hundred and sixty-two of them took pictures, including 196 with movie cameras."[59] These were numbers that advertised the museum, its programs, its sponsors, its employee-artists, and the art itself. The museum's functionalist approach equated community good with economic promotion.

Wa'waditla: Reappropriation and Resistance

Within less than a decade, First Nations art in British Columbia had gone from the publication of *The Tale of the Nativity* to the Native Brotherhood's gift of Martin's pole to Viscount Alexander, to an integrated salvage program that included both restoration and carver training. No longer was this art the preserve of a fractured and obscure social reform movement, destined (by the reformers' own estimations) to slowly suffocate from lack of interest. Nor was the art seen as the exclusive property of the Northwest Coast peoples. Government officials had gathered corporate support and invested in the institutional promotion of Aboriginal art through UBC and the BCPM. The carver training program was designed to ensure the continued manufacture of a quality, monumental product – an objective that, at least on the surface, contradicted the thrust of seventy years of assimilationist policy. In these new programs, the contemporary resurgence of the totem pole was projected as something of which the whole province could be proud. Thus provincial authorities simultaneously attempted (1) to depoliticize the meaning behind the poles as used by First Nations at contemporary political events and (2) to use the poles as a symbol for British Columbia and its businesses, products, and investment opportunities.

And yet, for all the discussion of First Nations affairs and the emergent programs aimed at both restoring museum collections and revitalizing First Nations arts as an employment option, the various levels of government failed to address, let alone settle, the problems of land claims and Aboriginal rights. The findings and proposals of the joint committee on the Indian Act were released in 1950, and the government tried to push the new act through immediately. While promising to consult with First Nations leaders and political organizations, the government was soundly criticized for not providing enough time for consultation, and the passing of the act was delayed a year.[60]

The Indian Act, when it was finally passed, was a bitter disappointment to First Nations peoples and many others. Apart from some administrative restructuring, including the reassignment of DIA to the Department of Citizenship and Immigration, essentially nothing changed. During the preliminary parliamentary debates on the act, the *Vancouver News Herald* announced that "the mountain has laboured and brought forth a mouse. What was to have been the 'Magna Carta' of the Indians turns out to be little more than a revamping of administrative regulations. The committee's long hours of work have been a waste of time."[61] Aboriginal rights were not guaranteed; enfranchisement was not granted. The bans on land claims, dancing off the reserve, and the potlatch were quietly dropped, but they were not repealed.

In terms of First Nations "handicrafts," a small subsection was devised within the department's welfare section, which had been created by the administrative restructuring of the DIA. It was given a small annual budget of about $750, most of which went to encouraging basketry in eastern Canada in the Pierreville, St. Regis, Manitoulin, Lorette, and Maniwaki agencies.[62] The BC provincial government emerged from the years following the war looking much more progressive than its federal counterpart. It had granted enfranchisement in 1949, appointed the Indian Inquiry Committee within the Department of Labour in 1951, and by 1952 had begun its totem pole restoration and carver training program.

The provincial right to vote, a token committee, and a refurbishing program for historic objects did not buy favour, nor did it erase the last 100 years of state policy. First Nations groups and individuals continued to press for recognition of Aboriginal rights and claims to land and to assert themselves, their identities, and their histories in defiant and celebratory terms. The dropping of the potlatch ban from the Indian Act, however, did provide for the "legal" return of public celebrations of First Nations ethnicity.

Almost thirty years after the Cranmer potlatch, and with a new wave of efforts by state officials to control the production and marketing of First Nations art, the first public potlatch since the imprisonment of the Cranmer potlatch participants was held in, of all places, a state institution. Gloria Cranmer Webster writes that, although "clandestine potlatches were held before the revision of the Indian Act, it was not until 1953 that the first public 'legal' potlatch was held. It was held in Coast Salish territory, a long way from the homes of the Kwakwa̱ka̱'wakw."[63] It took place in Victoria in celebration of the opening and naming of Mungo Martin's BCPM house in Thunderbird Park (see Figure 34).

Martin imposed demands on the museum that were intended, as much as possible, to keep the event within the traditional rules of potlatching and, therefore, that limited the input of museum officials. The potlatch was held on three consecutive days: one for family and friends only, one for the museum and other officials, and one for the general public. Helen Hunt translated and Duff was responsible for recording and transcribing both the rehearsal and the first day of potlatching. That all three days were important events

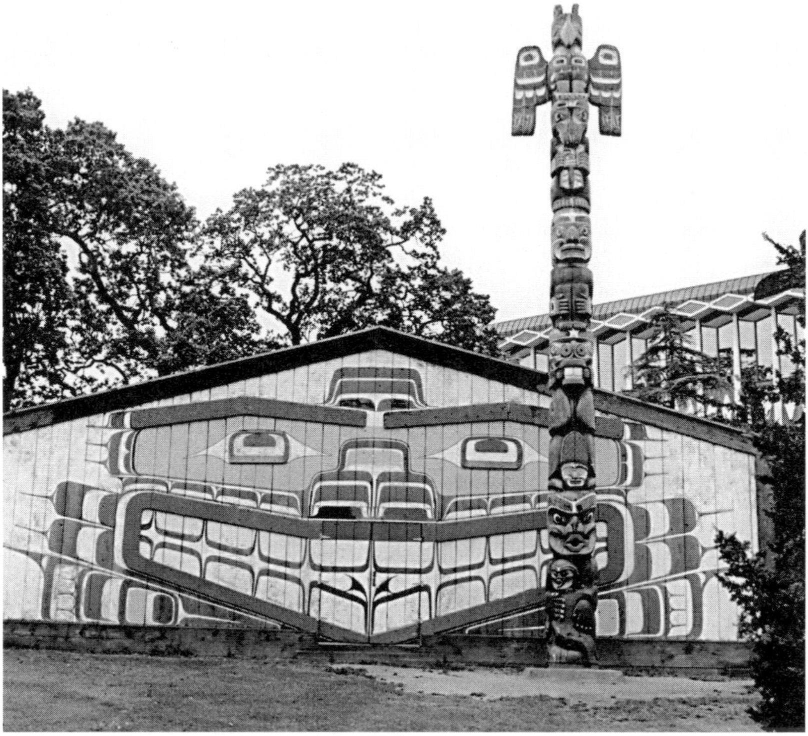

34 Wa'waditla, Thunderbird Park, Victoria.

for the Kwakwaka'wakw participants caught the curatorial staff off-guard, and it indicates just how little was understood about the Kwakwaka'wakw in 1953 – about their relationship to the museum and the power the museum had to represent First Nations peoples. Up until that point, it seems that Wilson Duff believed his (and the museum's) own rhetoric; that is, that they were resuscitating something that had already died. Diane MacEachern Barwick recalls that the "formal presentation ceremony" was "one of the few occasions on which Wilson [Duff] failed his own exacting standards as historian and ethnographer. He told me not to bother arranging for a recording and was chagrined when Mungo's magnificent oratory, ably translated by Helen Hunt, transformed the gathering into a kind of Kwakiutl potlatch ... Wilson ruefully admitted that he had expected a perfunctory handing-over to the Minister; 'but I ought to have known that Mungo would make it real, would make it history.'"[64] The presentation ceremony, occurring on the second day, was important with regard to transferring the maintenance of the house to the museum; for the Kwakwaka'wakw it was not simply a photo opportunity, as, according to Barwick's description, it was for the various non-Aboriginal museum and government officials present.

Indeed, Cranmer Webster credits Martin's potlatch with encouraging similar public demonstrations of pride back at home in Alert Bay. "In all probability," Cranmer Webster writes, "the success of Mungo Martin's potlatch encouraged people in Alert Bay to think about building their own big house. Various tribes contributed to the design and construction. The big house was completed in 1963 and was opened with a potlatch hosted by Chief James Knox of Fort Rupert. He was one of twenty people who had been imprisoned for two months in 1922, for potlatching."[65] While not the founder of the oft-cited "renaissance," Martin, following the revision of the Indian Act, was integral to enabling the Kwakwaka'wakw community to step beyond the limitations of the potlatch ban. The efforts of Scow, Martin, and others contributed to an important sense of identity and pride in the face of overwhelming economic and social marginalization.

In this sense, Martin's rigorous use of conventional early twentieth-century Kwakwaka'wakw two- and three-dimensional form, although a product of his training with Charlie James, played an important role in suggesting an unswerving sense of continuity between past and present. The bold and imposing painting on the front of the Wa'waditla house, with its elegantly angled shapes and immaculately balanced positive and negative spaces, is surely one of the most memorable of Victoria's downtown landmarks. Here, in vitally graphic terms, Kwakwaka'wakw culture springs up outside the containing walls of the museum.

The Wa'waditla potlatch served as a powerful reaffirmation of Kwakwaka'wakw culture both to the Kwakwaka'wakw themselves and to the government officials and general public who attended it. During one of the rehearsals, Omhid addressed the Kwakwaka'wakw crowd: "I wish to remind our young people to keep away from mischief during these ceremonies ... Any wrong move we might make, and these people here might make fun of us."[66]

Named "Wa'waditla," the house, as Tony Omhid described it, was not an imaginary reconstruction. Omhid owned the right to the name and then "sold," or transferred, that right to Martin during the potlatch. Referring to Martin, Omhid said:

> You all recognize this house, chiefs. This house is not just a made up house. Take a look at this, and that and that [the carved houseposts]. It is a copy of the first house that all you tribes used to gather in; the house that belonged to my chief; the house that belonged *naqa'penk'em*. That is the reason he can't take just anything up. After all, this house was planned long time ago. This house has a story.[67]

Through the potlatch speeches, the pride related to who the Kwakwaka'wakw were and the desire to conform to Kwakwaka'wakw ways emerge as consistent themes. Omhid addressed the rehearsal audience – "we should be proud of the people that we represent" – while warning Mungo Martin to "be careful for the few days that are coming. So, you will respect our gathering here, as it is well respected by our forefathers ... This I say because you are all trying out tonight. You are all trying out tonight, my children, so that I will see how you do; to see if there should be any faults in your actions."[68]

With regard to this, George Scow asked: "Why should we try to put a different dance from what we are supposed to do? We have to follow the rules of our dances, just as we talk our language, so that we will all understand one another. Because it has been told by our old people that we must never forget."[69] Through the speeches and dances, prerogatives were demonstrated and the house was named. Linking the past with the future, many of Martin's relatives were given names, notably his grandchildren, Ellen Neel, Neel's children, and Wilson Duff's daughter.[70] A ceremony of healing and reaffirmation upon the lifting of the potlatch ban, the Wa'waditla potlatch became a ceremony of hospitality and sharing when, on the third night, the doors were opened to the blocks-long line of curious Victorians.

An impression of Kwakwa̲ka̲'wakw strength and solidarity shone through the proceedings. As Omhid said at one point, "We have been successful now, all you tribes ... We are the right tribes to perform this. All these dances we would never have seen if our children had been weak."[71] Neither reduced to a simple commodity nor set simplistically within some European historicist tableau, at least for three nights the dances and speeches activated Wa'waditla and Martin's renovated poles. Within a stone's throw from the provincial legislature, Martin appropriated the space of the museum and pushed forward his agenda of maintaining the Kwakwa̲ka̲'wakw way, despite some seventy years of enforced and systematic assimilation. "You have put strength into me, for I was very weak all by myself away from home," he said to his Kwakwa̲ka̲'wakw audience. "And you have come to help, you with your famous names, you chiefs. You have strengthened me. Your fame will spread because you are down here, and brought your big names along with you. So you will finish what I want to do. You have strength, for you know everything."[72] "Kinship solidarity and sociability pervade all of life and are the bedrock upon which everything else is built," writes Marjorie Halpin of potlatching on the Coast. "Meaning is coeval with memory, or history, and an object's meaning is, so to speak, the sediments of memory that accumulate everytime it is 'brought out' in a potlatch and money distributed to 'memorize' and mark the legitimacy of the event."[73] Ironically, given the location of both Wa'waditla and its dedicatory potlatch, this memory was accumulated beyond the grasp of the museum. Despite the intent of the Indian Act and the professionalization of academic expertise in public institutions, the knowledge of First Nations objects, their histories and functions, still thrived in their communities of origin.

As for Mungo Martin, he was the central figure in a government-funded program aimed at "resurrecting" the production of "traditional" totem poles. In 1958 he personally attended the London presentation ceremony of a pole commissioned by the provincial government as a gift to Queen Elizabeth the Second, and when he died in 1962, his body was piped aboard the HMCS *Ottawa* and transferred, with a military honour guard, to Alert Bay for burial. He was posthumously awarded the Canada Council Medal for his "contribution to Canada's artistic, cultural and intellectual life."[74]

9
The Totem Pole Preservation Committee and the Case of the Gitanyow

The political significance of Mungo Martin's assertion of the continuity of Kwakwa̲ka̲'wakw authority through the Wa'waditla potlatch was paralleled by the BCPM's realization that Martin, as a carver willing to share his deep knowledge of the potlatch system, could almost single-handedly legitimize the museum and its activities. With Martin, the BCPM had something to offer the general public other than weekend and evening lectures and an empty repository space filled with historical odds and ends. Martin's potlatch, the *active* presence of Martin and the other carvers, enlivened what was otherwise a tomb. This opportunity had always existed, for the production of objects associated with the potlatch system had never completely ceased. Martin, for one, had been involved with this production. On the other hand, museum involvement was limited by a lack of resources and curatorial interest (or, perhaps, even awareness), assimilationist ideology, and the ceremonial restrictions imposed by the Indian Act. Because the museum was a public institution, it would have been difficult for curators to celebrate objects associated with a practice outlawed under Canadian federal law.

The growth of museum- and university-based First Nations studies in British Columbia in the 1950s thus seemed to satisfy a diversity of government needs. It superficially acknowledged First Nations identities and addressed the issues of poverty and employment while advertising the activities of the industrial sector and reaffirming the basis of governmental authority through revitalizing knowledge-producing public institutions. Central to the government's actions in the 1950s, and the focus of this chapter, was the Totem Pole Preservation Committee project, in which older poles were removed from their villages of origin, copied by Martin and his assistants, and re-erected in strategic touristic locations throughout the province. Of course, Mungo Martin and his Kwakwa̲ka̲'wakw relations were not alone in their interest in using "Western expertise" as a means of enshrining the symbolism of the totem pole through the potlatch system. A more explicit re-appropriation of the spaces of Euro-Canadian authority occurred with the

Totem Pole Preservation Committee's activities at the end of the 1950s, this time instigated by another "totem pole group" – one that had been the focus of federal attention in the 1920s: the Gitxsan.

Industrial Development and the Totem Pole Restoration Program

After provincial First Nations enfranchisement and the poorly received Indian Act revisions, provincial public arts institutions concentrated their promotional efforts on Martin, stressing the conformity to "tradition" evident in his work and, therefore, the "authenticity" of both Martin and the institutions' programs. Ultimately, this led to the marginalization of more "modern" First Nations artistic expression. Continuing the process of encouraging First Nations art, Duff and Hawthorn veered away from the easel painting styles pioneered in the Southwest and tentatively cultivated by the British Columbia Indian Arts and Welfare Society. Judith Morgan went to Cottey College in Missouri,[1] never again to enjoy the public attention in British Columbia that she had received as a high school student. François Batiste also disappeared from the public realm, and, although George Clutesi shared a 1967 commission for the exterior mural at the Indian Pavilion in Montreal's world exposition, after the 1940s his work was bought neither by the British Columbia Provincial Museum nor by the University of British Columbia. A "renaissance" demanded "authentic" form, not the "Western-style" illusionistic narratives of these artists. Part of this preference was rooted in the economics of the art market, and it contributed to erasing the era of assimilation from social memory. While it may not have been Hawthorn's or Duff's intention, or that of any of the anthropologists and art historians who followed them, to contribute to this erasure, the marginalization of Clutesi, Morgan, and some of the other modernist painters within the discourses around First Nations objects supports Blundell's assertion that "anthropologists [and art historians] can *unintentionally* reproduce presumptions by employing rhetorical devices and modes of speaking and writing that they have inherited from an earlier generation of disciplinary practitioners" (emphasis in original).[2]

Echoing the management procedures in the restructured forest industry after the provincial Royal Commission Inquiry into Forest Resources in 1944, the BCPM became a centralized processing plant in a new program of sustained yield for totem poles. It was part of the new economic cycle of harvest and renewal. Its spin-off benefits included production regulation, a growing private market, growing employment opportunities, and an altruistic appearance that obscured the ongoing denial of treaty negotiation and the parcelling off of traditional First Nations lands through forest management licences and public working circles.[3]

In 1952, under W.A.C. Bennett, the Social Credit party began its twenty years of government in British Columbia. Under Bennett, the province set out to provide "the necessary physical and economic infrastructure for profitable enterprise."[4] It built "an infrastructure of railways, roads, and electricity through government spending."[5] It also provided "a fiscal policy, a tax structure, and a legal framework which encouraged multinational corporations to invest in the forest and mining sectors."[6] The relationship between industry and the provincial government was close: up to 95 percent of the forest was on Crown land, which the government, in turn, allocated to companies according to long-term tenure arrangements. Almost 13 percent went to MacMillan-Bloedel alone.[7] Forestry itself was responsible for 40 percent of the value of production in British Columbia during the 1950s.[8] Such industries then aided the totem pole programs through public donations of materials and transportation facilities as well as by providing funding through the private philanthropic endeavours of their chief executive officers.

Technological improvements following the war also changed the range and scope of resource exploitation in the province. Areas previously inaccessible were now open to fishers or to the forestry and mining companies. It also became easier for both museums to extend their reach to previously "unharvested" areas, and the curators began to salvage more systematically the older, mostly abandoned villages off the main transportation routes. Museum collections were no longer restricted to the major rail lines. Curators like Duff felt that the poles from these villages were in great danger from mining and, most particularly, from the forest companies, who were dispersing their harvesting operations farther and farther into the provincial hinterlands. In addition to the advancing age and, consequently, advanced deterioration of the poles, many historic objects were becoming more vulnerable to unsanctioned removals by private collectors.

Greater accessibility and localized state-industry cooperation also meant that public institutions in British Columbia could, for the first time, realistically assemble a collection of monumental First Nations sculpture that would dazzle in scale and, eventually, surpass in quantity the collections of the eastern American museums. In this way, they fulfilled the federal aspirations of the Massey Commission by first housing and then reproducing a category, perhaps at the time the only category, of Canadian heritage acclaimed internationally.

The provincial Totem Pole Preservation Committee was formed in 1954 around the partnership of UBC's Harry Hawthorn and the BCPM's Wilson Duff. It consisted of former Massey commissioner and the then president of UBC, Norman MacKenzie, as honourary chairman; officials from UBC and the BCPM; and representatives from the DIA and the "general public." Hawthorn chaired the committee and Duff was its field director and secretary. In the preamble to a May 1954 brief, Duff defined for the committee the promotional touristic importance of the totem pole to non-Aboriginal British

Columbians: "Totem poles are the most distinctive symbols of our coast, extensively used to convey the atmosphere of this region."[9] In addition, he noted that "the best totem poles are also outstanding works of primitive art."[10] The corporate community, especially the forest industry, provided extensive support for the committee "in the interests of public relations and for the general good of the province."[11]

Although the BCPM and UBC had been taking their own tentative first steps towards an expanded totem pole replacement program, the more widely based provincial restoration program seems to have got its start in January 1952 with inquiries to Hawthorn from H.R. MacMillan. MacMillan, who coincidentally cited Barbeau's 1950 book, *Totem Poles*, wrote that he "was really upset to see how many of them had been taken by Canadians to various other countries at a time when good ones could be obtained, and also to note that practically none had been saved for British Columbia."[12] As provincial chief forester prior to the First World War and president of the largest forest company in the province, MacMillan had travelled the Coast extensively. He recalled that "I used to see many of them in 1907 to 1918 from about Comox north to the Queen Charlottes ... I was at Skidegate last year for the first time since 1918 and noticed that none was in sight ... If it is not too late to rescue a few more, and a little money would help you do it," he continued, "I would make a contribution."[13]

In Hawthorn's response, he outlined the carver training program at the museum in Victoria, noting that it was the intention of the program to branch out "into the training of several younger carvers in the various tribal traditions, who can then replace poles in Alert Bay, Skidegate, and other places."[14] Hawthorn then coolly promised to take MacMillan's proposition into consideration. Over the next four years, MacMillan's inquiry resulted in combining the carver training program with four salvage expeditions to outlying settlements. MacMillan's contribution only partly funded the project, although he did provide the committee a profitable funding lead in suggesting that it contact a number of forestry companies and sawmills, including Flavelle Cedar, who provided the replication program with materials. BC Forest Products and the Powell River Company also donated materials. MacMillan-Bloedel continued to donate logs for replication and Union Steamships contributed boats for transportation. MacMillan himself remained more or less a silent partner, contributing major portions of the funding while remaining anonymous in the committee's promotional literature.

Since MacMillan first approached UBC, the poles were salvaged cooperatively by the university and the BCPM. Using the resources of both, the committee then divided the poles evenly between the institutions. This led to the expansion of collections for both Totem Pole Park at UBC in Vancouver and for Thunderbird Park in Victoria. It also led to the hiring of a third full-time artist, Henry Hunt, at the BCPM.

Tanu and Skedans

With the assistance of Dr. Peter Kelly, United Church minister, graduate of Raley's Coqualeetza school, and an important leader in both the Allied Tribes and the Native Brotherhood, the Totem Pole Preservation Committee first targeted the abandoned villages of Tanu (sometimes spelled "Tanoo") and Skedans on Haida Gwaii (see Figures 35 to 37), which had been the sources for Newcombe's collecting for the BCPM prior to the First World War and for the CPR park in Prince Rupert during the 1930s.[15] Duff and Hawthorn traced the pole owners through Solomon Wilson, and the committee paid a nominal fifty-dollar fee per pole section, which was dramatically less than the peak price of $1,000 per pole demanded by Gitxsan and Nisga'a chiefs from Barbeau and Smith in the 1920s. Six poles were collected and delivered south to their new urban destinations. The expedition also received national attention through the Canadian Broadcasting Corporation, which sent an announcer of Haida descent – Bill Reid.

The following year, the hiring of Hunt and the program's unsuccessful gamble on additional private funding taxed its budget. When no additional

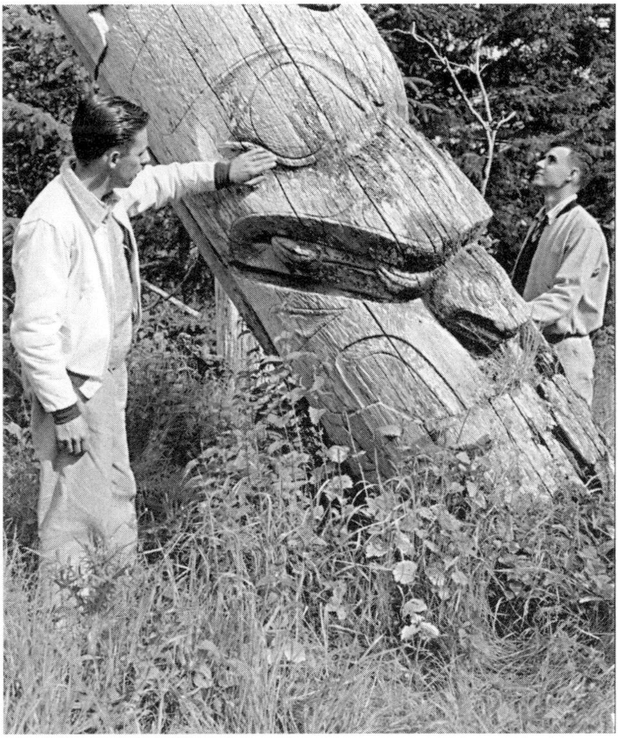

35 Totem Pole Preservation Committee members survey poles at Tanu, ca. 1955.

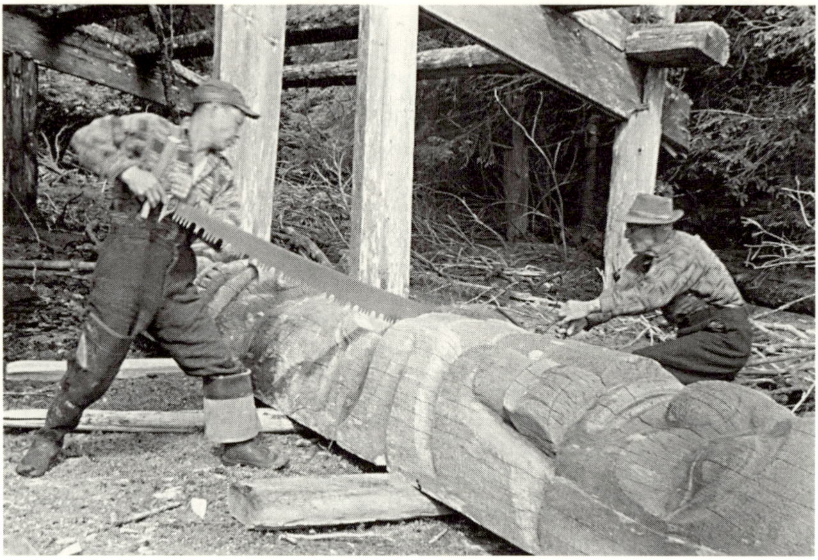

36 Tanu pole sawed in sections for removal, ca. 1955.

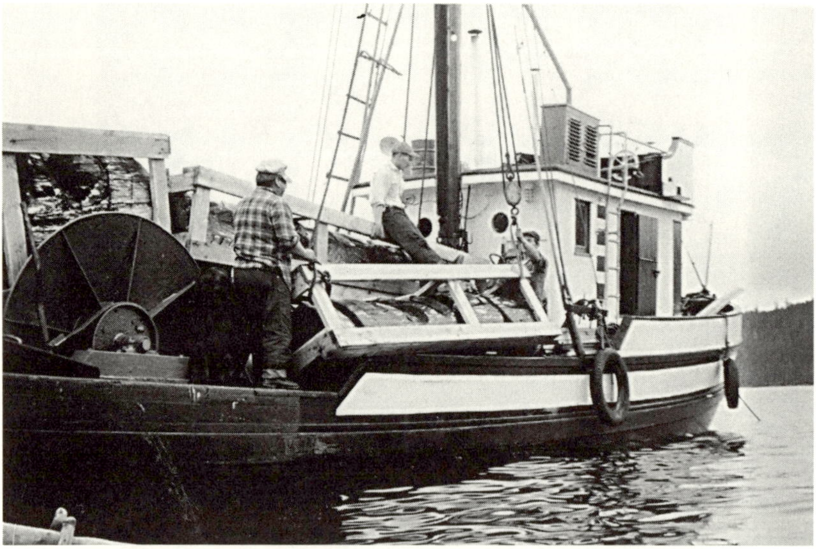

37 Tanu poles sectioned and crated for shipment on a seiner, ca. 1955.

funding was found, the museum laid off all three carvers from mid-December to the beginning of the next fiscal year in April 1956. However, the museum's active encouragement of corporate interest in totem poles allowed the carvers to remain working in Victoria for the rest of the winter. From January to April, all three carvers were commissioned to carve the world's tallest

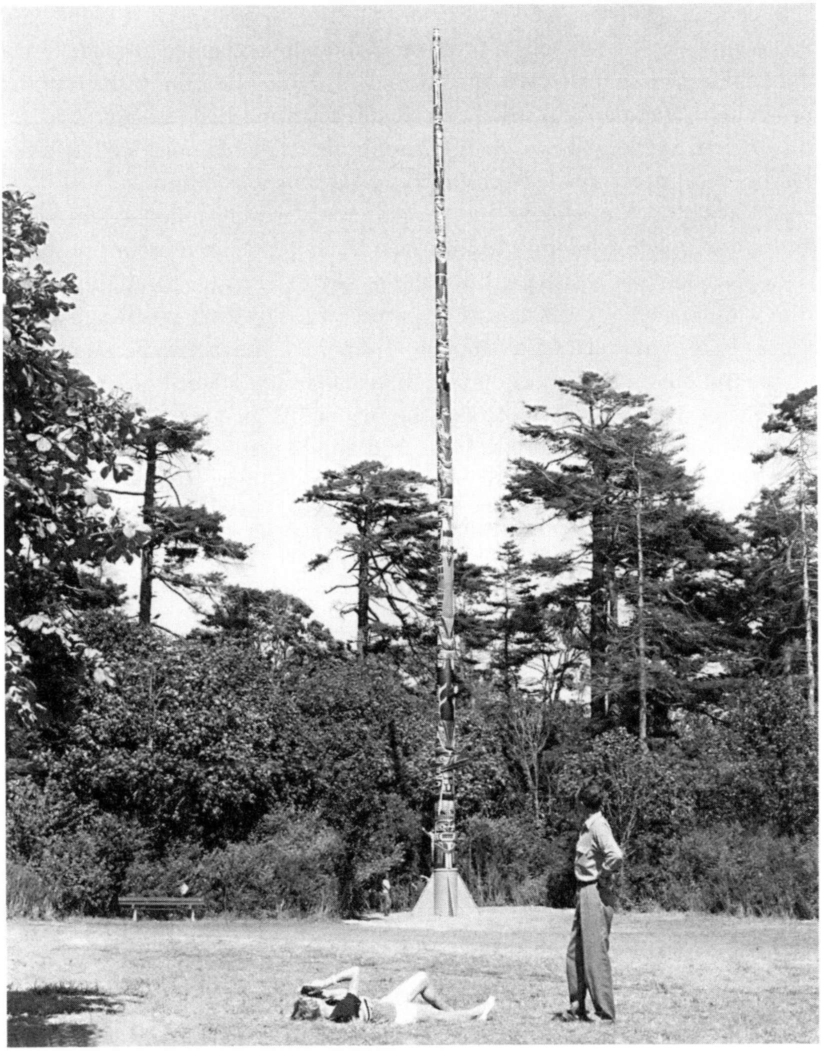

38 "World's tallest totem pole," Beacon Hill Park, Victoria.

totem pole for the city of Victoria. The touristic publicity stunt was sponsored by a local newspaper, *Victoria Daily Times*, which sold public shares and solicited corporate and individual donations. The museum donated space for the carving. Completed by mid-April, the pole was erected in July in another of Victoria's popular tourist spots, Beacon Hill Park,[16] only a few blocks southwest of Thunderbird Park and the museum. Like the Mathias Joe pole in Stanley Park, the "world's tallest totem pole" (see Figure 38) spun off a number of private copy commissions for the Martins and Hunt, including, for $150, a six-foot replica for the Victoria and Island Publicity Bureau in 1956.[17]

In general, 1956 was a busy year for both the carvers and BCPM officials. Radio announcer and soon-to-turn internationally acclaimed "Indian" artist Bill Reid was hired for six weeks to work with Mungo Martin in the training program at Thunderbird Park.[18] Already an accomplished jeweller, Reid got his first chance to work on the old monumental Haida poles with Mungo Martin, replicating a pole from the Tanu-Skedans expedition of 1954.[19]

Following on the heels of the very popular "world's tallest totem pole" and reiterating Totemland's tourist agenda, in 1956 the museum program set a precedent for redistributing poles at key tourist sites throughout British Columbia.[20] The replicated pole, partly carved by Reid, was set up at the tourist bureau at Peace Arch Park, which straddles the international boundary at the busy White Rock-Blaine, Canada-United States border crossing (see Figure 39). Since then, one of the first sights greeting tourists driving up from Washington State has been Reid and Martin's Haida pole. In general, the totem pole now loomed large as the primary symbol of British Columbia.

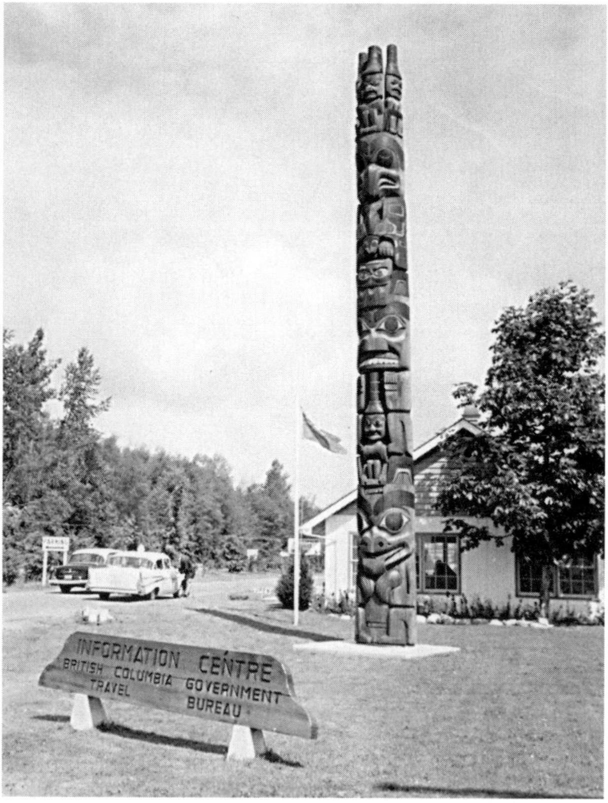

39 Replica Skedans pole carved by Mungo Martin and Bill Reid at the White Rock-Blaine border crossing.

A second pole replicated from the Tanu-Skedans salvage was erected at Exhibition Park (previously called Hastings Park) in Vancouver, and two poles were carved for Riley Park in Comox.[21] As replicated poles were erected in these various sites, the museum retained title to the works so as to guarantee their "proper display and maintenance."[22] As the museum's annual report for 1956 indicates, one of the objectives of this part of the program was to promote and to maintain quality control in the open market. Using a refrain common since the height of the late nineteenth-century museum collecting phase, they wrote: "We hope that this programme of putting excellent poles on display in various parts of the Province will increase the public appreciation of native art and counteract the effects of the atrocious totems so frequently seen."[23]

Hope and Gilford Islands, Rivers Inlet

The replication aspect of the totem pole restoration program was extended during bad weather to include a number of masks in the museum collection. As well, in 1956 Mungo Martin completed a series of eight two-dimensional paintings for the museum. His son David, in acknowledgment of the preservation committee's emphasis on promoting poles by erecting them in city public parks, attended the American Institute of Park Executives Conference in Seattle. David Martin also went (on loan) to UBC for a month in the spring in order to help restore some of the poles in its collection, and he was involved in the annual salvage expedition. He accompanied Michael Kew, whom the museum had recently hired and who would be a future professor in the UBC Department of Anthropology and Sociology, to Hope Island for a week.[24]

In addition to Hope Island, the BCPM used a $3,000 donation from H.R. MacMillan to send Kew to other Kwakwa̱ka̱'wakw sites on Gilford Island and at Rivers Inlet. During the salvage expedition, Kew supervised the purchase and removal of fourteen poles. Of the fourteen poles, eight houseposts from two houses came from Gilford Island and five more houseposts came from two houses on Hope Island. The final pole was a house frontal pole from Rivers Inlet.[25]

Early on in the planning for the expedition, Duff had been approached by Charlie Clair of Quatsino about purchasing some houseposts and four small figures. Duff was interested, even though, initially, they hadn't been targeted for purchase by the committee. In January 1956 he wrote Hawthorn about the possibility of drumming up additional funding. By the time Kew had been sent to the central coast, Clair had not contacted either the BCPM or UBC. The matter had been forgotten until March 1957, when the houseposts arrived in Vancouver, sent by Clair via Union Steamships, which he understood would not charge shipping costs due to the "educational purposes" of the project.[26] The budget was already stretched due to a $600 overdraft on the Kwakwaka'wakw salvage expedition (paid by MacMillan),[27] and Duff and Hawthorn were left scrambling to cover the additional cost of $1,600 for Clair's poles and figures as well as a transportation bill from Union Steamships. The private and anonymous financier for the committee's unexpected and unsolicited purchase was Czech immigrant lumber baron, art collector, and philanthropist, Walter Koerner.[28] Koerner's anonymous contributions would also ensure the next two seasons of salvage. (His patronage of Bill Reid and various donations to UBC eventually stimulated the construction of the new Arthur Erickson-designed Museum of Anthropology, which was opened in 1976.)[29]

Over the next two seasons, business continued as usual for the Totem Pole Preservation Committee. In 1957 the Martins and Hunt went on loan to the municipality of Courtenay in Kwakwaka'wakw territory on northern Vancouver Island, where they carved a pair of poles for the entrance to the city's Lewis Park.[30] While the city paid $1,000 to the British Columbia Totem Preservation Committee for the poles and their erection, the opening ceremony itself was turned over to local Kwakwaka'wakw First Nations. Under the direction of Chief Andrew Frank, the pole-raising shared similarities with Martin's Wa'waditla opening. Both followed a basic potlatch pattern, with the performance of traditional dances and songs, and with a chief giving and receiving ceremonial names.[31] Once again, First Nations control over the ceremonial proceedings led to an opening that was exotic and colourful to non-Aboriginal eyes and that demonstrated the vital, historically continuous presence of First Nations peoples. With the Courtenay ceremony being favourably covered by both the local mainstream press and the *Native Voice*, the preservation committee seemed one step closer to its earlier goal of spreading the restoration program out through the "old" centres of First Nations society.

Ninstints

Also in 1957 the salvage expedition returned to Haida Gwaii, again it seems on the suggestion of MacMillan,[32] although this time funded by a semi-anonymous $2,750 donation from Koerner.[33] Eleven poles were removed from Ninstints, which is located on Anthony Island. In gratitude for Koerner's financial assistance, the committee presented him with a "small token" of its appreciation at the end of the salvage in July 1957; namely, the six-foot long central watchman from the top of the Beaver House (House Number I) frontal pole at Ninstints.[34] Although this was never made public, UBC paid the internal bill for the figure. In presenting Koerner with this ostentatious gift, university officials had other projects in mind. A memorandum from Norman MacKenzie's deputy, G.C. Andrew, to Harry Hawthorn outlined Koerner's demonstrated interest in UBC and hinted at a kind of subsurface competition between the two primary institutions involved in the preservation committee. Andrew asked Hawthorn to cover the costs of the figure and to "indicate to Wilson [Duff] that the President and yourself have been in touch with Walter [Koerner] regarding this and other University developments."[35] After delineating Koerner as university territory, Andrew then counselled Hawthorn to show Koerner the university museum. "Walter told me incidentally that he has a collection of primitive artifacts which he was thinking of giving to the Provincial Museum," wrote Andrew. "He did not seem to be aware of our range of interests and this is one reason why I want him to visit the museum and see for himself our range of interests."[36]

The committee also displayed great urgency in its negotiations with the pole owners, especially when it came to the "legal" ownership of the poles. The committee's assertiveness was the direct result of Haida uneasiness at the museum's survey expedition to Ninstints in the summer of 1956. In December of the same year, the Skidegate council issued a resolution to W.S. Arneil, the DIA's Indian commissioner for British Columbia:

> Having read of the discovery by an expedition from the Provincial Museum of an ancient Indian village known as Ninstints, on Anthony Island, and of the finding of totem-poles and grave-poles here, we view with alarm the proposal to remove these grave-poles and other objects of our past culture from their present sites, and do request the Indian Department to have any further action in removing such objects immediately stopped. Descendants of the original inhabitants of this village are still living, and we ask that no further action be taken by the Provincial Museum or others until permission is granted by these people.[37]

The preservation committee's access to the poles was no longer a foregone conclusion. Previous salvage expeditions had called for careful negotiation, although this never seemed to entail great urgency. Some pole owners saw payment for these unused objects as an unexpected bonus. As before the war, for some First Nations the ownership of the crests and names themselves was much more important than was the ownership of their material manifestation in the form of frontal poles and houseposts. Others, like Charlie Clair, who dismantled the old house himself and delivered the four small figures to Vancouver on his own seiner, seemed almost anxious to get the objects off their land so they could rebuild. In short, there had not been any organized opposition to the committee's salvage efforts.

Nonetheless, for Duff and Hawthorn, the Skidegate resolution may not have been unexpected. In November 1956 they had received, via Arneil, a letter from Molly Stewart in Ketchikan, Alaska, who claimed a connection to the site and some of the poles through her great-great-grandfather, Elijah Ninstints. While she professed a willingness to reach "some mutual satisfactory agreement"[38] with the museum, she also derided it for having "no authority, according to our custom, and what I understand of the law, to go and take things that do not belong to the Museum. There was a lot of hard work involved in making the poles, and they were and are very sacred to myself."[39] In wording that echoed Harlan Smith's problems on the Skeena thirty years earlier, Stewart continued: "This matter is of great concern to myself, and my children, and I would appreciate it very much if you would contact the Museum and advise me if it is going to recognize my right and title to these poles, because if not, I will have to place the matter with legal counsel."[40]

Although Duff continued to follow the committee's policy of acknowledging individual ownership of the poles and the payment of a token price per pole unit as symbolic recognition of ownership, Arneil questioned the legal right of the Skidegate band council to administer payments for the poles. Because Anthony Island was not on official reserve land, technically, as an organ of the provincial government, the museum held legal title to the poles. On Arneil's suggestion, Duff contacted the Attorney General's Office, which presented him with some leverage in the negotiations. "We could rephrase the Anthony Island situation as follows," Duff wrote Arneil in May 1957:

> Anything fixed or attached to the land becomes part of the land and the property of the owners of the land. Therefore legally the totem poles are now the property of the Provincial Government. We are under no *legal* obligation to either the Skidegate band or the individuals who claim ownership of the poles. However we do wish to recognize the Indian ownership. Several individuals have some claim, but not all the claims are equally valid. The best body to judge the validity of the claims is the Skidegate band, acting through its council, and they have consented to do this.[41]

Because Duff and the committee symbolically acknowledged individual title to the poles, they managed to appease the Skidegate council. They also slipped out of assuming responsibility for deciding validity of title claims and avoided any legal dispute with individual claimants, including Molly Stewart. The final purchase price was $800 for all eleven poles, at fifty dollars per section.[42] The money went into trust while the Skidegate band council sorted out the individual claims. For the first time, the committee was pressed to solve the jurisdictional problem of ownership while satisfying both individuals and the band as a whole. The Skidegate resolution and the uncertainty it momentarily created served to prepare Duff and Hawthorn for their next salvage expedition.

Bill Reid and Totem Pole Park

The year 1958 was a climax of sorts for the promotion of First Nations art. Being the centennial of British Columbia's colonization, it coincided with the federal government's decision to fund universities without infringing on provincial jurisdiction over education. In 1956 the federal government had received $100 million dollars from the estates of Izaak Walton Killam and Sir James Dunn, which it used the following year to finally realize the Massey Commission's most important recommendation – the arm's-length federal granting agency, the Canada Council. Under Canada Council structure, significant monies were freed up for funding university building programs. As J.L. Granatstein reports, regionalism has been a fact of Canada Council life (and Canadian political life in general) since its inception. Coincidentally, as early as 1957 Norman MacKenzie complained that "the fact that Toronto has been given the bulk of our grants to date – while not a cent goes west of Winnipeg is well designed to develop instant bitterness and criticism."[43] To this end, MacKenzie's University of British Columbia received approval for a Canada Council grant for $700,000 in December 1957.[44] A small part of this was used to supplement MacMillan's funding of the 1958 hiring of Bill Reid and Doug Cranmer for the construction of a replica Haida village (see Figure 40), which consisted of seven poles and two houses, in the campus's Totem Pole Park (see Figure 41).[45] With the Canada Council

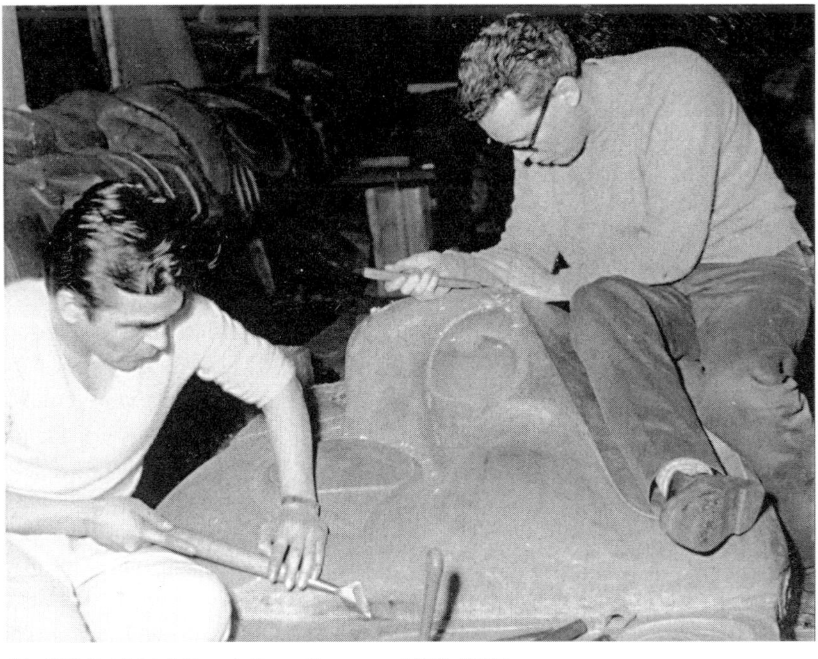

40 Bill Reid (right) and Doug Cranmer, UBC, 1957.

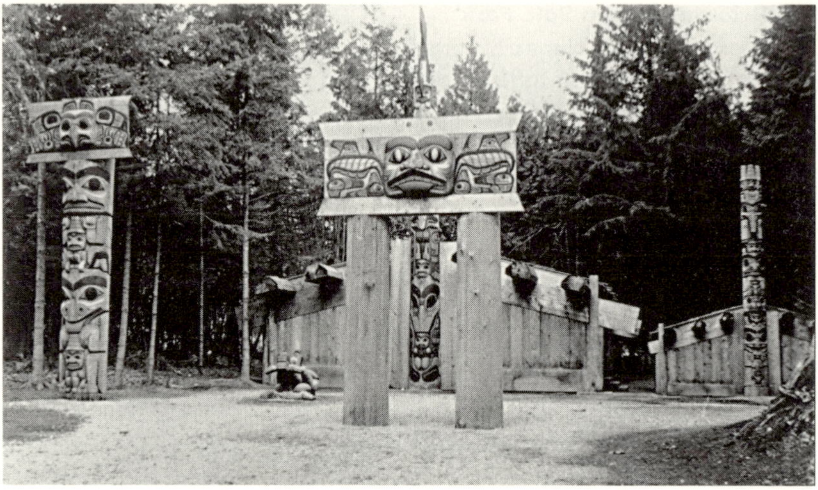

41 Replica Haida village by Bill Reid and Doug Cranmer, UBC.

funding the bulk of UBC's physical expansion, private donations could then be used to pursue secondary projects such as the reconstructed Haida village, which, in turn, reaffirmed the position of First Nations objects as the primary symbols of British Columbia and, thus, as an important symbol of Canada in general.

The historicist references that placed First Nations arts within the metaphorical social memory of modern industrialism that displaced a "primitive" past continued in the Reid-Cranmer village, especially as 1958 was British Columbia's centennial year. The village was also important with regard to establishing Reid's reputation as a *contemporary* artist. Reid, who was non-status, grew up only vaguely aware of his Haida heritage, and had neither the facility to nor the interest in potlatching the monuments he carved. He was nonetheless well versed in the language of modern art and spoke of Haida art in almost purely aesthetic terms.[46] The modernist concept of the universality of human genius reflected in the aesthetic beauty of the object appealed to a generation of scholars who were interested in First Nations art and who, with the public and private backing that social reformers like Raley and Ravenhill had earlier lacked, sought to use this notion as a major access point to Northwest Coast objects for the museum-going and art-buying public. Doris Shadbolt, who worked with Reid, Duff, and University of Washington art historian Bill Holm on the 1967 *Arts of the Raven* exhibition at the Vancouver Art Gallery, wrote: "Reid was becoming known in scholarly and journalistic circles as an unusual person, someone who had a root by blood in the Haida culture, but also a critical distance from it; someone knowledgeable, thoughtful, responsible, who could write and speak precise, poetic and eloquent English."[47]

In other words, Reid had the pedigree to legitimize his art and an attitude that endeared him to museum and gallery curators and, through them, to the non-Aboriginal art-buying public. Reid's most lasting contribution, then, may have been to personify the realization of three generations of institutional activity; that is, he was a "modern artist" whose technical mastery of Northwest Coast form enabled him to create "authentic"-looking objects that functioned not as indicators of social status within Northwest Coast societies but, rather, as luxury commodities primarily for circulation within non-Aboriginal Canada and as legitimators of Canada's various levels of government. Furthermore, apart from the village that he and Cranmer produced for UBC, the bulk of Reid's early work was drawn from the touristic curio production of people like Charles Edenshaw.[48] In short, Reid, following a trail already partly blazed by Ellen Neel and Mungo Martin, was the first of a new generation of professional artists recognized and promoted by Duff, Hawthorn, and their institutions.

Crosby says that "Reid could be described as the perfect model for the successful integration of the Indian. The western values for which he was praised – his education, articulate speech, and successful career – signal the possibility of the successful assimilation of other Canadian Indians into the progressive space of modernity."[49]

First Nations objects have historically fulfilled a diverse range of functions. The transformation of these objects, through Reid and some of the subsequent generations of artists, into mid-twentieth century modern art is not so much a break with tradition as it is simply an additional facet of an already complex and diverse artistic continuum. The UBC village was the first monumental commission for the artist who would replace Mungo Martin as a public metonym for the Northwest Coast, taking the non-Aboriginal reception of Northwest Coast objects yet another step towards the mainstream artistic directions of the 1960s and 1970s. In her groundbreaking analysis, Crosby states:

> Despite the way in which Reid privileged western values, form and aesthetics in relation to Northwest Coast cultures, his presence as a contemporary Haida artist of masterworks did open up some discourse on contemporary socio-political concerns – albeit in a limited way. At the same time, the experiences of Reid's historical displacement and his position as an "urban" Haida artist and curator point out the multiplicity of aboriginal communities that were formed not only through acts of colonialism, but through the invisibility of Canadian ideology. Today, Reid's position of cultural authority is not only located in western institutions and knowledge, but supported by representatives of the Haida nation – especially since his involvement in the land question in Haida Gwaii. The public image of him as an aboriginal artist of Haida descent has taken on new meanings according to

> the circumstances and contexts of various historical moments, blurring the boundaries of what constitutes Haida culture and politics.[50]

Many have cited the *Arts of the Raven* show as the birth of Northwest Coast art.[51] The catalogue for the exhibition suggests that contemporary Northwest Coast objects "are arts in a different sense. Though truly enough of Indian descent, they are now Canadian art, modern art, fine art."[52] Essentially, it was restating what Raley, Ravenhill, and even Eric Brown had said thirty and forty years earlier. Shadbolt may have thought that the exhibition was a shift, that it was saying something new to make "an explicit and emphatic statement"[53] defining Northwest Coast objects as "high art, not ethnology";[54] however, to paraphrase George Manuel, the "renaissance" of Reid and Shadbolt's day was the fruit of the accumulated labour of earlier generations.

And while Bill Reid began his ascent to the heights of artistic recognition, Mungo Martin's reputation as *the* totem pole carver in British Columbia was further enhanced in 1957 when he was asked by the provincial Centennial Committee to carve a 100-foot pole as a gift to Queen Elizabeth from the people of British Columbia. Every step of the process was ritualized by the Centennial Committee. With 300 witnesses, Lieutenant-Governor Frank Ross cut the first chip from the log for the pole and was presented by Martin with the name "Gwiutalas" ("Man of Great Hospitality") and a ceremonial blanket.[55] Various promotional organizations also used the pole to promote the province in general. Centennial Committee chairman J.L. Wallace presented the City of San Francisco with a Mungo Martin pole at a Lions International Meeting in August 1957. The Vancouver branch of the Centennial Committee out-muscled competing municipalities in acquiring Martin's 100-foot duplicate of the royal pole and, in order to qualify for the federal funding necessary for its acquisition, erecting it alongside the historic Royal Canadian Mounted Police ice breaker, the *St. Roch*. The municipal competition building over the poles even resulted in newspaper reports questioning the authenticity of rival poles. "Indian experts" in one Vancouver story suggested that Mungo Martin's pole in Beacon Hill Park was not "the largest authentic pole in Canada" but, rather, "a 'gimmick' pole ... and not a genuine Indian pole."[56]

Gitanyow (Kitwancool)

While Martin's contemporary pole was enshrined as the official symbol of the province at the London presentation ceremony, and Martin himself was heralded as "the proud Indian who revived world-wide interest in the native crafts of the west coast,"[57] back in British Columbia the preservation committee continued its harvest of historic poles. The Skeena River had long been seen by Euro-Canadians as the most important pole area in

British Columbia. Some of this recognition was the result of the national museum's program in the 1920s. In addition, Barbeau had already carefully documented the poles and published the information in *Totem Poles of the Gitksan, Upper Skeena River, British Columbia* (1929) and, more recently, in *Totem Poles* (1950). Their tempting accessibility, in conjunction with the Gitxsan's defiance of Euro-Canadian authority, further teased the committee. Duff and Hawthorn had surveyed the Gitxsan villages of the upper Skeena on their earliest cooperative venture in 1949 and were particularly interested in the poles at Gitanyow (prior to 1990 usually referred to in anthropological and art historical texts as Kitwancool), a village just north of the Skeena River and, therefore, away from the main CNR line and out of the range of the 1920s federal preservation program. Subsequent visits by Duff in 1952 and 1958 convinced him of the necessity of purchasing and removing poles before they all fell and completely disappeared.

In 1952 Duff wrote that Gitanyow "contains the largest and by far the finest group of old totem poles to be found in their native setting anywhere,"[58] and, although he recommended purchasing any poles or pole parts available for indoor storage in Victoria and Vancouver, for the first time he suggested that "where the natives refuse to part with ... poles, they be encouraged and assisted to find or construct adequate storage warehouse for them in the villages."[59] Duff preferred to have the poles housed in the southern museums, ostensibly because of rot and weather erosion.

In 1952 Duff met with Albert and Walter Douse to discuss the possible purchase of their poles. Sometimes referred to as a tribe, the Gitanyow are, as Duff would later note, "an amalgamation of several groups of people of different origins ... essentially ... made up of two matrilineal exogamous phratries – the Wolves and the Frogs."[60] Lacking a unifying leadership due to the village's structure of phratries and houses, the Gitanyow created the office of president in 1938 to provide a unified front against outside encroachment, swearing "to protect all the lands and natural resources belonging to the people of Kitwancool."[61] While Peter Williams was the president of the Gitanyow in 1958, Walter Douse was the primary chief of the Gwass-lam house of the Wolf phratry, and he and his brother Albert were, at that point, representing to museum officials the general Gitanyow views on the poles.

According to Albert Douse, what was at issue with the release of the poles was the lands and natural resources of the Gitanyow people. They categorically refused to sell their poles to Duff and the preservation committee because of the poles' connections to house territories and hunting grounds. Duff countered with an explanation of "the importance of these things as *art* by telling of books, shows, etc. on NWC (Northwest Coast) art."[62] But, as Duff noted in his field notes, articulating the sharp split in the objects' understanding that characterizes the history of British Columbia, "they seemed unable to divorce the concept of art from its social context. The *only* meaning of poles to them seems to be as a symbol of social position" (emphasis Duff).[63] According to Duff's notes, Douse responded to his proposal as follows: "Since your plan was not to preserve the poles in the village but to take them away, we have decided that we are unable to sell any poles. If we let one pole go it would be like letting go of everything that is ours."[64]

Duff noted six main points with regard to the Gitanyow's refusal to sell the crest poles. First, the Gitanyow outlined a "history of resistance to white encroachment"[65] and then noted that this was continuing, citing specifically the "taking of timber licenses."[66] He suggested that the Kitwancool were "still [the] most conservative, isolated, proud group in the area"[67] and that "here, more than elsewhere, totem poles are symbols of [the] whole Indian way of life."[68] With no elaboration, he also cited the "personality and background"[69] of Albert Douse as a factor in the Gitanyow refusal to sell. Finally, reiterating his earlier point, he noted the Gitanyow's "inability to divorce totem poles as art objects from their social background enough to let us take away the object of art. That would be taking away their crests."[70] He then questioned "whether they have the concept of art as art."[71] Later, in the more formal field report, Duff wrote of Albert Douse: "He agreed that it would be a good thing to preserve the poles, but interprets this as a preservation of the crests, traditions, privileges, rather than as a preservation of an object of art."[72]

Douse also brought up the question of money in a manner that surprised Duff. Douse asked, "if a clan had gained prestige by giving out large amounts of money when the pole was erected, could it receive money back for the pole without negating some of that prestige?"[73] While Mungo Martin and the Kwakwa̲ka̲'wakw had had little problem with this, feeling that the prerogatives symbolized in the carvings mattered more than the carvings themselves, clearly the connection between meaning and material was more pronounced among the Gitanyow. The symbolic acknowledgment proffered to the Haida during the Ninstints expedition would not accomplish the preservation committee's objectives, nor would the legal argument that the totem poles located off reserve land were Crown property. Not only were the poles on reserve land, but the Gitanyow also insisted "that they have never been party to any agreement to relinquish any of their rights over their territories. They have never made a treaty, nor have they been conquered. They have never admitted that the Government has any right to set aside plots of land for them as Indian reserves. In their view, all of their former territories still rightfully belong to them."[74] In short, Duff found himself acting as government representative in discussions with people who did not acknowledge the authority of state officials over any of their affairs. This was an unfortunate position, and it recalls Halpin's characterization of museum ethnologists as adopting a "professional attitude of disloyalty to their employing institutions"[75] in order to balance research and administrative needs.

Duff persevered. During Duff and Kew's April 1958 visit to Gitanyow, they suggested that the copies that would be made from poles removed to Victoria would be returned to Gitanyow and re-erected. In the wording of a later museum press release, the Gitanyow could "trade copies for the originals."[76] After a general meeting, the Gitanyow accepted the offer with one additional condition: "that their histories, territories, and laws were to be written down, published, and made available to the University for teaching purposes."[77] In short, the Gitanyow had decided to use the Euro-Canadian educational system as an outlet for their resistance to non-Aboriginal control. As asserted in the same press release, "through the years the Kitwancool ... have fought to keep their territories intact, using all means short of force. In 1927 and even earlier, they even occasionally resorted to force to keep surveyors and other intruders away. Now they have turned their faith to education – to educate white men by having their history published. The museum is delighted to help out in this because it is exactly our job."[78]

Museum officials were also delighted that they might finally obtain important Gitxsan poles for their collection. A contract was quickly drawn up for the removal of three poles: "(a) Chief Wiha's pole now lying beside the house of Mr. Walter Douse. (b) Chief Wiha's pole now standing in the old village. (c) Chief Guno's pole showing three frogs and now fallen in the old village."[79] Confusingly, three poles were actually removed and replicated in 1958, a fourth was removed in 1961, and another was removed in 1962. A mistake in rank-related etiquette was made in removing pole C, Gwen-nue's (also spelled "Guno") Nee-gamks pole, and not the pole of Chief Gam-lak-yeltqu (Solomon Marsden) (variously spelled "Gamlakyetlque," "Gam-lak-yeltk," or "Sam-lak-yelth"), the senior chief of another house within the Frog phratry.[80] This fourth pole was the Ha-ne-lal-gag pole[81] (see Figures 42 and 43), one of a grouping of three poles and considered "one of the most important in the village and ... the pole that ties the other poles together. It holds the power for the other two poles ... in other words, it represents all three poles, and is the pole of the Raven."[82] Although stories concerning Ha-ne-lal-gag and Gam-lak-yeltqu had been included in the final text, this oversight delayed the erection of the pole replicas from 1959 to 1961. As Gitanyow president Peter Williams indicated, "the honour of the Great head Chief Gamlakyeltque"[83] was at stake. Not wanting to contribute to a split in the community, and happy to get the opportunity to gain access to more poles, the preservation committee made arrangements for Ha-ne-lal-gag's removal and replication. A fifth pole, another in the Ha-ne-lal-gag grouping, named Thga-belathgum-gak ("Raven Soaring") was also removed, with a copy going to the new University of Victoria in 1966.[84]

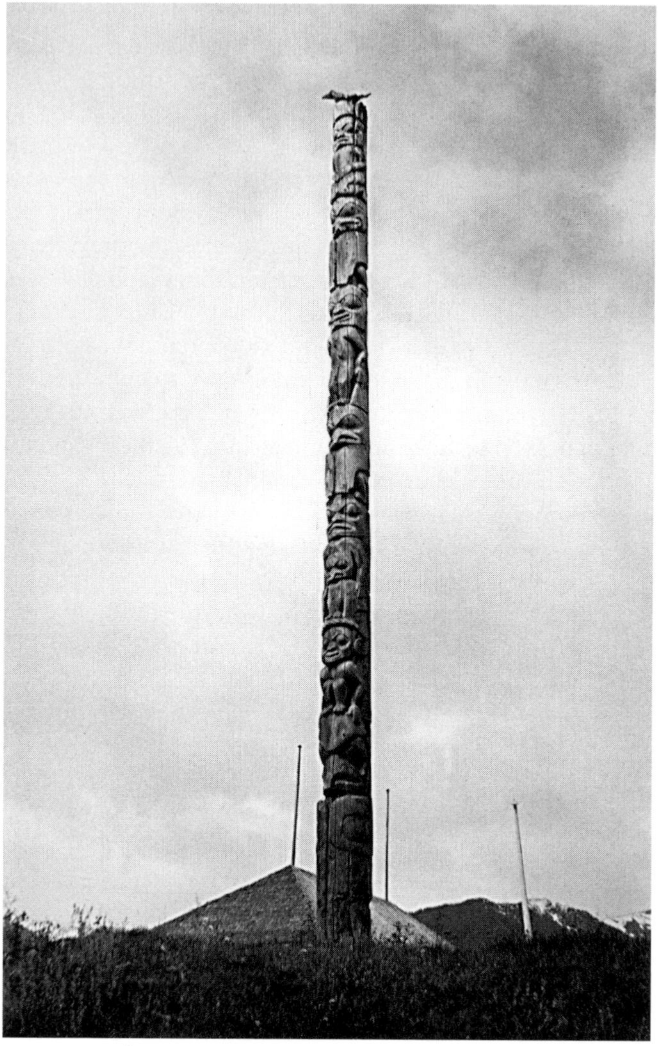

42 Ha-ne-lal-gag pole, Gitanyow.

In October 1958 Constance Cox, a former resident of Hazelton fluent in the Gitanyow language, was hired to record and translate the appropriate stories.[85] The manuscript for the subsequent publication, *Histories, Territories, and Laws of the Kitwancool* (1959), was prepared in typewritten form and resubmitted to the Gitanyow chiefs in November 1959. These chiefs asked that passages omitted from the recorded histories be incorporated into the final text, and they also asked that the provincial coat of arms be printed on the outside cover.[86]

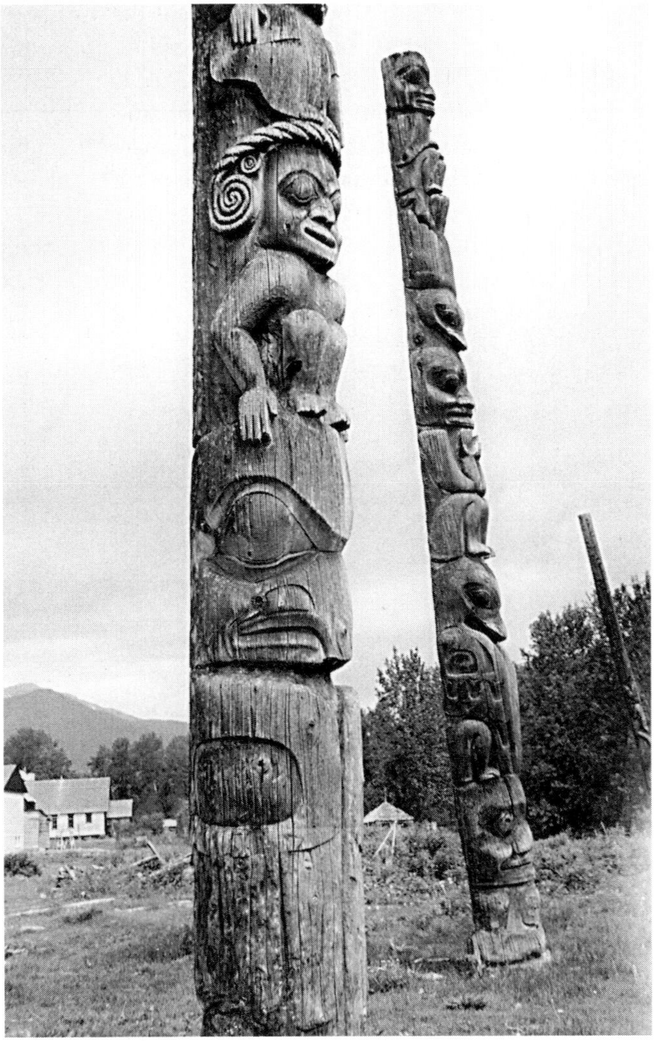

43 Detail of Ha-ne-lal-gag, Gitanyow.

The three poles covered in the agreement were removed in 1958. The museum paid the costs of replicating the poles, and Koerner funded their handling, transportation, and erection. The Canadian Navy was enlisted to transport them to Victoria. Koerner, as a condition of his donation, demanded that the poles go to UBC.

The stories of the two Wolf (Gilt-winth) poles, the Skim-sim and Will-a-daugh pole, and the Gaa-quk-dik-giat pole (see Figure 44), "which belong to the same crest and have the same stories,"[87] were told by the then holder of the Wee-kha title, Ernest Smith. These stories detail the Wee-kha house's "early home on the sea-coast at the site of the present Prince Rupert, of their travels up the Nass River, and their establishment in their present territory."[88] The poles relate closely to the political structure of the house, and the accompanying narrative note that "this house, unlike other houses, has two seats for the chiefs with the two heads on the pole."[89] The poles were also indicators of the history of the house's existence at Gitanyow and thus, presumably, of their rights to house territories and resources in the vicinity. Wee-kha emphasized that the first of the two poles was "the first erected in Kitwancool by the clan of the Wolves."[90] He further clarified the social structure to which these poles alluded:

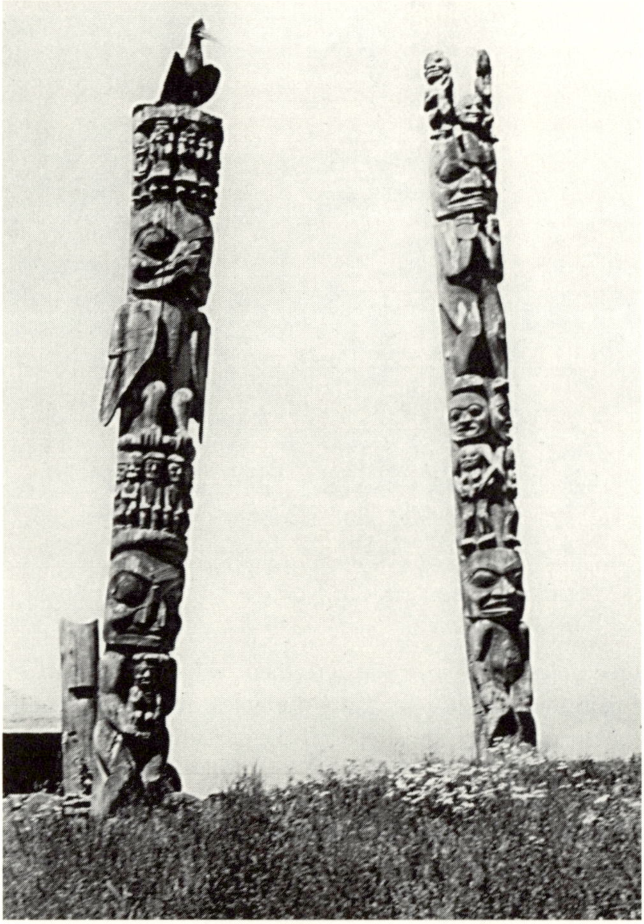

44 The two Wolf poles, Gitanyow.

When a pole decays (a pole lasts about 200 years), or at the death of a chief, a new pole is always erected in the same place. When these people migrated, they took along duplicates of their totem-poles and erected them in their new permanent villages. When a pole is erected or changed, it is erected at the same place. A feast is always given and the territories are discussed. They tell the people the size of their village, the mountains they own, their hunting and fishing grounds. They tell this so that each generation will know what they own. The new chief and his council divide the land. They tell each clan which mountains they can have, and what areas they can hunt and fish in.[91]

The story of the Nee-gamks pole of the Frog clan (see Figure 45), of which another copy was made and erected in front of a tourist bureau office in

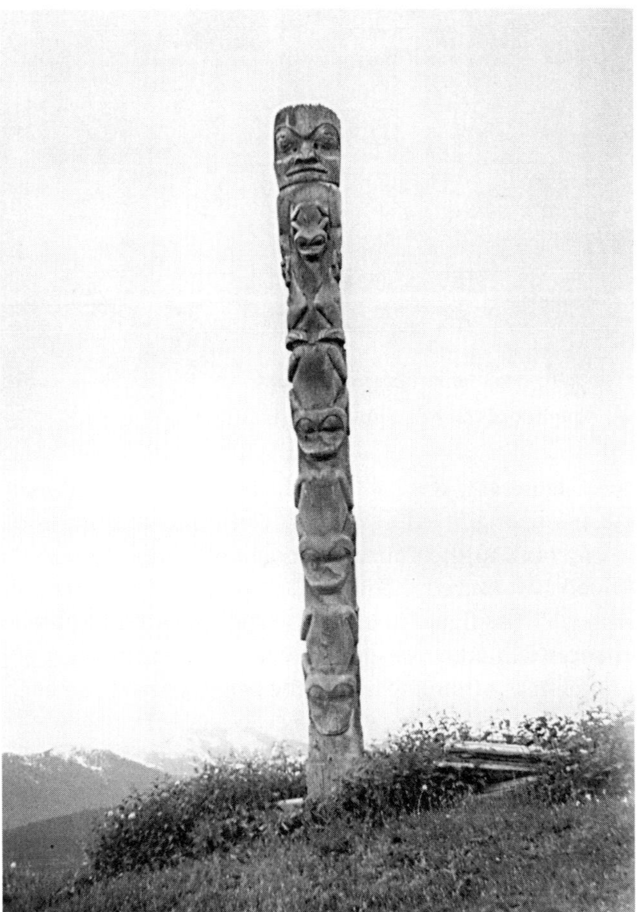

45 The Nee-gamks pole, Gitanyow.

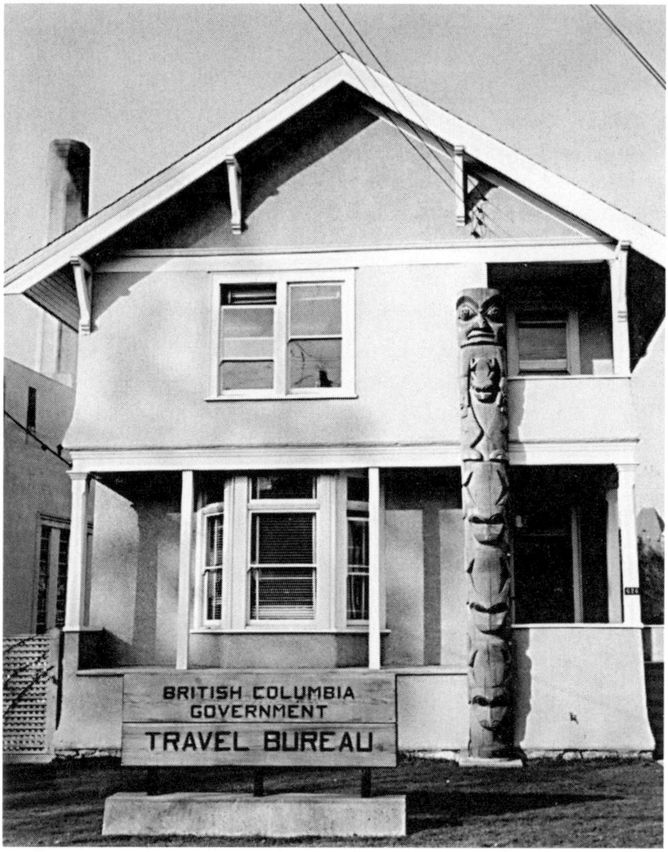

46 A replica of the Nee-gamks pole, in Victoria.

Victoria (see Figure 46), was told by Chief Gwen-nue (Godfrey Good). It also traces a house origin, telling of how "Gwen-nue and his people tried to find their way back to their ancestral home of Dam-la-am on the Skeena after the flood had carried them west to Alaska, and of their adventures along the way."[92] The figure holding a frog on her chest at the top of the pole is an ancestral figure, Nee-gamks, who married the chief of the frogs and who, when rising from the lake at the behest of her brother Gwen-nue, sung a funerary song. This song was sung each time the pole was re-erected. Below this figure are three smaller frogs representing Nee-gamks's children. According to Gwen-nue's narrative, the house valued "the pole very highly, as it represents the lost sister and the nieces and nephews of the clan."[93]

Ha-ne-lal-gag ("On Sleeps the Raven," or "Where the Raven Sleeps with Its Young"), which was illustrated in the text but not initially removed, was erected by the Frog phratry in 1910. Part of the lineage history of the house of Shen-dil, the right to discuss the history of the pole belonged, in 1958, to

Chief Less-say-gu (Mrs. Fred Good).[94] Ha-ne-lal-gag has on its top the nest of the Raven referred to in its name. The pole's story tells of an ancestral chief, Shen-dil, and traces his and his family's travels from their original village to Kitwancool. The story makes very specific reference to where they came from and where they went, and it includes the names of such specific places as Lak-wee-yep, the top of a mountain with a timber stand.[95]

> The reason they were traveling so much was that they were making their map, and on each piece of land when they stopped they had left their mark and their power, making it theirs ... The poles gave them their power ... and gave them the right of ownership of all the lands, mountains, lakes, and streams they had passed through or over and camped or built villages in. The power of these poles goes unto the lands they had discovered and taken as their own ... The power of the pole still goes on and belongs to Shen-dil.[96]

The location of the pole is also important. In 1958 it stood in front of the house of Albert Douse, the primary chief of the Gwass-lam house of the Gitanyow Wolf phratry, along with the two other poles originally not included in the original collection agreement by the Totem Pole Preservation Committee. At the foot of the pole is the mountain eagle, a crest loaned from Chiefs Wee-kha and Gwass-lam of the Wolf clan and carved on this particular Frog clan pole to honour to them. If the house were to be rebuilt or the pole recarved, then these crests would not be allowed to be represented on the new pole.[97]

Also included in the museum booklet was the story of the house of Mahley, which traces when and how the house had arrived and been accepted at Gitanyow. The story made specific references to a grizzly bear pole not included the museum's removal plans and not illustrated in the text. As with the other stories, this one too referred specifically to hunting grounds and other house lands.

The final text was published in 1959. It is divided into three main parts: (1) *Histories of the Kitwancool*, consisting of transcriptions from Cox's recordings of the histories of the poles, the main houses, the founding of the village of Gitanyow, related wars with the Tse-taut, and the subsequent peace that transformed Gitanyow into Kitwancool; (2) *Territories of the Kitwancool*, which outlines the territories and hunting grounds of the Gitanyow houses; and (3) *Laws and Customs of the Kitwancool*, which chronicles Gitanyow social structure and its relevant customs and life passages.[98]

Disputes between the BCPM, renamed the Royal British Columbia Museum in the 1980s, and UBC over the ownership of the poles continued until the late 1960s. At one point, Walter Koerner, on the basis of having paid the shipping costs, asked carver Gaylord Morrison to replicate the Gitanyow poles for presentation to UBC. Although museum officials in

Victoria sidestepped this issue, in an April 1960 letter to Cyril Belshaw (an anthropologist at UBC), Wilson Duff acknowledged the debt owed Koerner for the project funding and addressed Koerner's desire that the poles be displayed in Vancouver:

> The idea of preserving the old poles at the University was not part of the original agreement with the Kitwancool and is therefore not mentioned in the memoir. It was stated by Mr. Koerner, and in view of his contribution and our shortage of storage space, I agreed. I have carried on correspondence with Neil Harlow about a suitable place to put them (since I insist that they have proper indoor display space) ... I shall hold on to the poles until it becomes clear whether or not our carving programme is to be continued.[99]

In 1970 Duff, for his part, did use the Gitanyow histories as the basis for a course (Anthropology 301) after he obtained a teaching position at UBC in the mid-1960s. His lecture notes tied the preservation committee's Gitanyow project into the continuing Gitanyow struggle to maintain their territories in the face of land expropriation, tracing the history back to the 1880s and placing their protest within a contemporary context.[100] Duff understood the Gitanyow strategy of using Euro-Canadian institutions and, indeed, himself, in his capacities as museum curator and university professor, to publish their case through the museum and to disseminate it through the university. "Are you learning?" he asked his students.[101]

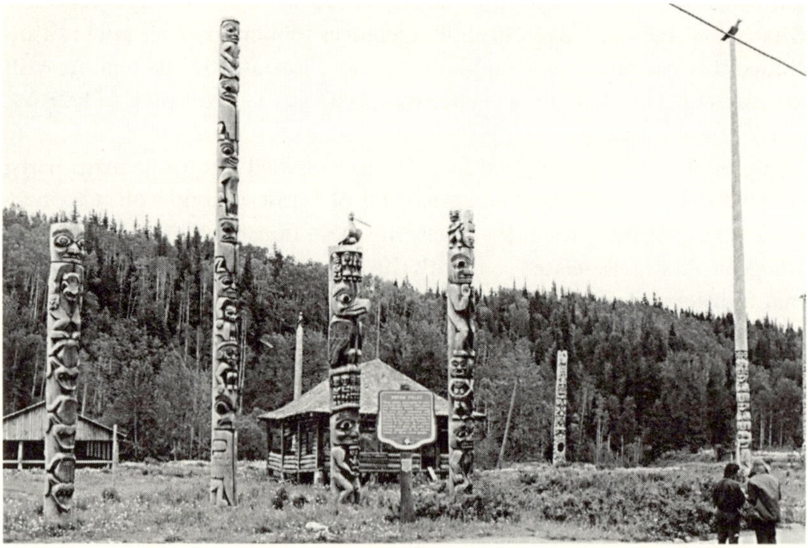

47 The four poles replicated for Gitanyow, ca. 1961.

The three replicated poles included in the contract, and the fourth collected and replicated later, were re-erected and grouped together (see Figure 47). In 1961 the completion of this phase of the project coincided with the federal enfranchisement of First Nations. Breaking the virtual lock that King and St. Laurent's Liberal party had maintained over the federal government since the mid-1930s, Prime Minister John Diefenbaker and his Conservative party had come to power in 1957 at the height of "totem" fever in British Columbia. With rhetorical references to Macdonald's national policy of almost a century earlier, Diefenbaker offered a program of northern development and "unhyphenated Canadianism." In addition to energy commissions and a federal interest in Arctic oil and gas, Diefenbaker took steps towards establishing a more pluralistic Canada by introducing the 1960 Bill for the Recognition and Protection of Human Rights and Fundamental Freedoms – a bill that officially rejected discrimination by reason of race, colour, national origin, religion, or sex. This led to another revision of the Indian Act, passed in 1961, which provided federal voting rights to First Nations individuals. In early 1962 the Charter of Rights also contributed to the elimination of racial discrimination and was a major feature of Canada's immigration policy. The era of assimilation, at least in theory, was officially over.[102] The postwar growth of the BCPM and UBC, and their role in promoting First Nations culture, was part of the policy shift from assimilation to integration. In reality, it was a continuation of the depoliticization of First Nations objects and the hinderance of First Nations claims. On an optimistic note, in the face of persistent attempts to erase or rework the histories of subjugated classes in Canada, the people of Gitanyow, like Mungo Martin at his Wa'waditla house opening, demonstrated an ability to use the system of government institutions in a way that enabled them to construct an oppositional discourse.

10
Tales of Ghosts That Hover in the World Like Fading Smoke

In 1977 Joan Vastokas, summarizing the thrust of most of the texts on Northwest Coast object production prior to 1990, argued that "decline in general quality as well as quantity may be attributed in large part to the loss of cultural meaning attached to the art works, since, for the most part, they came to serve no internal social purpose."[1] If this discursive trend is to be believed, then Northwest Coast peoples and their arts suffered from the "fatal impact" of European colonialism.

"A 'fatal impact' has ... been detected in European historiography far more frequently than it actually occurred," counters anthropologist Nicholas Thomas, noting that extinctions of "primitive" peoples have been reported worldwide. Thomas pinpoints one of the dangers of this construction: "Though generally sympathetic to the plight of the colonized, such perceptions frequently exaggerate colonial power, diminishing the extent to which colonial histories were shaped by indigenous resistance and accommodation."[2] Such a construction undermines the recognition of resistance while also contributing to depicting the achievements of colonized subjects as something that occurred in the past rather than as something that is occurring in the present.

In the 1920s the notion that Aboriginal traditions could no longer continue was at the heart of assimilationist policies. The intersection of the concept of the "fatal impact," assimilationist policies, disciplinary control, and the expansion of public museum collections was most explicitly illustrated in the 1922 Cranmer persecutions. At that time the Lekwiltok of Quadra Island, the Mamalillikulla of Village Island, and the Nimpkish of Alert Bay surrendered over seventeen cases of masks, dance paraphernalia, and coppers to Indian Agent William Halliday in exchange for suspended sentences for violating the Indian Act's potlatch ban. The masks and dance accoutrements were assessed according to curio market prices, and the Kwakwa̱ka̱'wakw owners were awarded a total of $1,456. No compensation was paid for the coppers. As mentioned earlier, Halliday sold thirty-five pieces to American collector George Heye before displaying the rest in the Alert Bay church hall and then shipping them to the national museum in Ottawa. In Ottawa, the head of ethnology, Edward Sapir, selected a number of items for display in Deputy Superintendent Scott's Department of Indian Affairs office.

This sequence of events added urgency to the fight for control over the meaning of Northwest Coast objects, which were increasingly being housed in American, European, and Canadian museums. It was a pivotal point in the public negotiation of the position of First Nations peoples in Canadian society and Canada's national "culture." As Paul Connerton argues, "the control of a society's memory largely conditions the hierarchy of power."[3] The government, by constructing a narrative of displacement through locating First Nations objects within museum displays, threatened the traditional roles of the totem poles, masks, coppers, and dance gear in legitimizing lineage, individual uses of terrestrial and spiritual resources, and fixing relations of inheritance and hierarchy in material form. Displacement through display affirmed government authority over the distribution and economic development of land and natural resources and was part of a larger strategy of transforming First Nations peoples into colonial subjects.

Within this general Anglo-Canadian ideological understanding of displacement, of social evolution from "primitive" to "modern," there emerged conflicting display projects. The history of institutional displays of Northwest Coast objects affirms Nicholas Thomas's notion that "meanings engendered by hegemonic codes and narratives do not exist in hermetic domains but are placed at risk, re-valued and distorted through being enacted and experienced."[4] The interests of local institutions, for example, conflicted with the interests of federal institutions. In the Art, Historical, and Scientific Association of Vancouver's (AHSAV) 1921 plan to promote an image of the city's progress by reconstructing a Kwakwa̱ka̱'wakw village in Vancouver's Stanley Park, association members obtained poles without the consent of the DIA. Their "incongruous appearance" in "public or private parks" was cited in governmental correspondence as justification for later federal intervention in the preservation of totem poles.[5] AHSAV also conflated ethnic divisions on the Coast, utilizing Kwakwa̱ka̱'wakw poles as metonyms for all Coastal peoples. In 1924 it then raised four free-standing Kwakwa̱ka̱'wakw poles on a historic village site, XwayXway, which was claimed by the Squamish people. This provoked Squamish intervention and ensured that the project did not realize its final objectives. It also raised the issue of Squamish claims to the park in the local media. The value of this attention was demonstrated in 1929 when the court acknowledged that land at XwayXway belonged to a Squamish woman popularly known as "Aunt Sally." This land was then purchased for $15,500.

By the 1920s totem poles were popular tourist attractions on the Inside Passage steamship routes from Washington State to Alaska and were increasingly seen as symbols of Canada. Beginning in 1924 the federal government hoped to utilize the poles in order to promote railway tourism on the newly nationalized CNR line through the Skeena River Valley in northwestern British Columbia. To this end, a committee was formed, its members coming from the DIA, the CNR, Canadian National Parks, the Ministry of Mines, and the national museum, to supervise the in situ preservation of poles in Gitxsan villages adjacent to the CNR line. Dogged by Gitxsan resistance and market gamesmanship over the prices of poles (in part provoked by the collecting activities of national museum ethnologist Marius Barbeau), the project nonetheless sought to give the sensation of time travel by constructing Gitxsan and Tsimshian life as part of the past. The Gitxsan, for their part, frequently refused to allow project members to touch their poles. Project correspondence explicitly cites the unsettled land question as one major impediment to cooperation.[6] "A few years ago," wrote National Museum anthropologist Harlan Smith, summarizing Gitxsan uneasiness with the museum's activities, "[the white men] had prohibited the erection of totem-poles; why did they wish now to preserve them?"[7]

Frustrated by Gitxsan resistance and unable to control the sale of poles to American museums and collectors, private commercial companies, and municipal parks, DIA Deputy Superintendent Scott and Diamond Jenness (Sapir's replacement at the National Museum) drew up a 1926 amendment to the Indian Act in order to prevent tampering with any "Indian grave-house, carved grave-pole, totem pole, carved house-post or large rock embellished with paintings or carvings."[8] A measure of the value these "heritage" objects held for officials in Ottawa, this amendment complemented other Indian Act amendments of the period that sought to suppress the potlatch and to limit the ability of First Nations to file land claims.

In conjunction with the preservation project, Barbeau and the National Museum, along with curator Eric Brown and the national gallery, held the travelling 1927-8 exhibition, *Exhibition of Canadian West Coast Art, Native and Modern,* in Ottawa, Toronto, and Montreal. The exhibit showed the affinity between First Nations subjects painted by Emily Carr, A.Y. Jackson, Langdon Kihn, and a number of other non-Aboriginal modernist artists and the "ancient" traditional arts of the Northwest Coast. Although this further entrenched First Nations artistic expression as something of *Canada's* past and constructed an evolutionary narrative culminating in the accomplishments of the modern, Euro-Canadian artistic community, the inclusion of two named First Nations artists – Frederick Alexie, who was still living, and Charles Edenshaw, who had passed away only seven years earlier – signalled a discursive instability. The inclusion of Alexie, in particular, despite his limited acceptance by the Canadian artistic status quo, provided the opportunity for a new category of producer: the living "Indian" artist.

However, federal museum and gallery activities on the Northwest Coast collapsed, along with the global economy, in 1929. The severe impact of the Great Depression brought with it a transitional phase in the representation and promotion of Northwest Coast objects. Social reformers like the Reverend George Raley in Vancouver and Alice Ravenhill in Victoria advocated the systematic support of contemporary First Nations artists as a means of providing them with employment during the 1930s. The arts also became a focal point for organizations lobbying for changes to the Indian Act and the DIA. "If it is an untrodden path we have to travel – if there is the ghost of a chance of it leading somewhere – we British pride ourselves upon the spirit of adventure," wrote Raley in the early 1930s. "Surely with our knowledge now is a time we should make it manifest and break away from any past accepted notions and policies which have not led us to a satisfactory condition or as Tennyson says we should 'leap the rotten poles of prejudice' and do something new, adventuring in reviving primitive crafts for the welfare of our own primitive people."[9] Raley modelled his proposals upon similar developments in the United States, which had taken place under Roosevelt's "New Deal"; however, due to his isolation from provincial authorities and lack of funding during the first half of the 1930s, they had little direct impact.

Raley also represented a new attitude towards Northwest Coast objects – one that conformed to the narratives of the earlier displays but that had a distinctive agenda. He saw the objects as metonyms for the people who produced them, and he valued them partly because of how he believed they contributed to "our understanding of our own historical trajectory";[10] however, he saw their metonymic value as the basis for their exchange value within a contemporary context. Thus, for him, the art of the past was valuable as a contemporary production. He saw this connection between past and present as the basis for a commodity market in First Nations arts production, and he advocated the development of programs that would create a demand (through education and marketing) and regulate production quality (through training). These recommendations became important aspects of later, better known marketing programs that, in the 1950s, were sponsored by state institutions.

Ravenhill was more directly influential than was Raley. She helped develop curriculum materials and training pertaining to First Nations issues for the public school system, in the process forming a growing partnership with the British Columbia Provincial Museum. In 1939 Ravenhill founded the British Columbia Indian Arts and Welfare Society (BCIAWS), which worked closely with the BCPM, holding exhibitions of student art and promoting a number of individual artists, including teenaged Gitxsan painter Judith Morgan; Nuu-chah-nulth writer, actor, and painter George Clutesi; and Kwakwa̲ka̲'wakw carver Ellen Neel.

The strategies of the BCIAWS were paternalistic. After the Second World War, it advocated "authenticity" as the basis for quality control in the burgeoning postwar "Indian art" market, suggesting that the BCPM establish the criteria and that the BCIAWS issue a "stamp of authenticity" in order to regulate the fluctuating quality of objects available for sale. Control over knowledge, its distribution, and application would, in this view, rest with government officials and associated or government-recognized organizations; it would certainly not rest with First Nations leaders or artists.

However, the BCIAWS complemented the individual and organized lobbying efforts of political organizations like the Native Brotherhood of British Columbia, which, in the 1930s and 1940s, were also pressuring the provincial and federal governments to acknowledge and respond to First Nations issues. In the variety of efforts directed towards asserting Aboriginal histories and claims and affirming pride in First Nations accomplishments, art played a significant role. "One of the challenges of contemporary anthropology and art history," concludes Jonaitis, "is to seek understanding of the active and affirmative responses that cultures make to their historical conditions in the modern world, and to deconstruct consciously our past biases which blinded us to those Native initiatives."[11]

In 1936 Squamish band member Mathias Joe carved the first free-standing Coast Salish pole as a way of publicizing the historical presence of the Squamish in Vancouver generally and Prospect Point (or "Chay-thoos") specifically. Located on a high point on the Stanley Park side of the entrance to Burrard Narrows, the Thunderbird Dynasty pole overlooked the site of the new Lions Gate Bridge connecting the city to the British Properties, a Guinness-owned subdivision developed in the late 1930s on land close to the Capilano reserve. As the 1929 Aunt Sally case demonstrated, any affirmation of historical presence could potentially contribute to valuable compensation.

The Native Brotherhood carried on the practice of using art publicly as a symbol of historical Aboriginal presence, thereby implying the legitimacy of claims to land and Aboriginal rights. It followed the 1929 example of Captain Jack in Yuquot on Vancouver Island and presented the governor general of Canada with a pole and ceremonial name from Kwakwa̲ka̲'wakw carver Mungo Martin. William Scow and the Brotherhood used art in educational contexts, presenting a pole carved by Kwakwa̲ka̲'wakw carver (and Martin's niece) Ellen Neel to UBC's Alma Mater Society in 1947. And George Clutesi, who exhibited his illusionary paintings with the BCIAWS and wrote articles for the *Native Voice*, addressed First Nations youth, calling for pride in heritage and professional training to facilitate greater First Nations control over their education and health.

These efforts, both Aboriginal and non-Aboriginal, were important with regard to pressuring different levels of government through parliamentary committees and commissions. In 1974 George Manuel and Michael Postuns wrote: "Indians had always been complaining. Now there were sophisticated, organized urban voters, whose view of the matter may have been entirely different from ours, but who were, nonetheless, pointing at the same problems and the same administration."[12] The movement culminated in the Conference on Native Indian Affairs held at UBC in April 1948. At this conference teacher and former BCIAWS member Anthony Walsh summarized the powerful role of art in the movement: "This group wouldn't be meeting today if it weren't for the art of the Indian. It has been the one approach for interpreting the culture of the Indian people to the public."[13]

But here once again there was conflict. At the same conference Neel delivered a memorable speech in which she contradicted the notion that Northwest Coast art needed reviving: "For if our art is dead, then it is fit only to be mummified, packed into mortuary boxes and tucked away into museums."[14] She also disagreed with the call for a reliance upon the collections of the past. "If the art of my people is to take its rightful place alongside other Canadian art," she stated, "it must be a living medium of expression. We, the Indian artists, must be allowed to create!"[15]

In 1947 the government, upon its return to representing and promoting First Nations arts, acknowledged Clutesi and the social reform movement when it bought seven of Clutesi's paintings in commemoration of the opening of UBC's Museum of Anthropology. In 1949 the provincial government bought paintings by Judith Morgan in commemoration of provincial enfranchisement. By the end of the 1940s the research phase of state restructuring had been completed, and federal officials began to implement a new vision of Canada – one based, in part, on the Keynesian economics of Roosevelt's New Deal. Officials were anxious to present a Canadian identity independent from its colonial past. Education and professional training, the expansion of a supportive government infrastructure, and the promotion of regional contributions to national "culture" all led to provincial programs aimed at preserving "traditional" Aboriginal "culture" as a source of employment within the expanding Canadian economy. These programs, in turn, led directly to the hiring of contemporary First Nations artists at public institutions in the province; first Ellen Neel and then Mungo Martin at UBC, and then Mungo Martin, his son David, and Henry Hunt at the BCPM.

By the early 1950s there was an unprecedented excitement about totem poles in British Columbia. The totem pole, with its evocation of place and its function as "primitive" counterpoint to booming postwar British Columbia, was being increasingly promoted in Euro-Canada as a symbol of the province. The mythical notion of history as progress still informed the totem pole's symbolism for Euro-Canadians. With public officials openly expressing interest in a resurgence of First Nations "arts and crafts" as a source of employment, the false and rather wishful suggestion that First Nations societies had expired could no longer be prolonged. The "Vanishing American" myth clearly was not true demographically,[16] and the public acceptance of Neel and Martin suggested that it was not true artistically. The social reform movement and First Nations political associations made concerted efforts to ensure the public recognition of this through the media. Given the wealth of academic and popular literature attesting to the reality of the myth of "vanishing Indian" and its long-time acceptance by the Euro-Canadian public, the presence of Martin and the other carvers within the museums thus implied a rebirth of First Nations society within the arms of the postwar Canadian state. In short, since state officials had told the Canadian public repeatedly that First Nations peoples and their "culture" had disappeared, the only logical way of explaining the new institutional interest was to proclaim a renaissance.

Marcia Crosby argues that the decision to issue this proclamation was not so much a shift in the direction of government policy as it was a way of consolidating state authority and undermining the seemingly new political power of "pan-Indian" associations like the Native Brotherhood. "The position of anthropologists, art historians, curators, and the like was not simply one of supplying an academic analysis," writes Crosby, "but was linked to the authority of western expertise that continues to be used in the courts of Canada both to establish and extinguish aboriginal land title."[17] While this may have been a view at least partly embraced by the new generation of museum anthropologists in the 1950s, it seems the relationship between Duff and his colleagues on one side and the Haida and the Gitanyow on the other may have reshaped anthropology in British Columbia. Thomas Berger of the Supreme Court of Canada, for one, wrote: "Wilson Duff played an important role in the development of native claims in British Columbia and in Canada in the 1960s and 1970s [and] ... was a key witness in two very important cases that were brought before the courts in support of aboriginal rights."[18] This initiative has recently been replicated in a number of high-profile court cases related to land claims and Aboriginal rights. The cohesiveness and sanctity of the Western expertise Crosby describes was not, and is not, secure.

Martin's participation became the basis for a carver training program. Objects from the BCPM or totem poles salvaged cooperatively by UBC and the BCPM under the auspices of the Totem Pole Preservation Committee were models for replica poles that the committee redistributed to tourist sites throughout the province. In museum promotional materials Martin was constructed as the "last great totem pole carver," as the person responsible for passing on traditional carving skills through the museum to the next generation of carvers. This has resulted in the impression that the BCPM was directly responsible for the continuation of the fragile art of monumental carving in British Columbia – an impression that, on two important occasions during the committees' programs, was severely disrupted.

First, in 1953, only two years after the dropping of the potlatch ban from the newly revised Indian Act, Mungo Martin and his kin demonstrated the continuing vitality of Kwakwa̱ka̱'wakw potlatch practices. Commissioned to reconstruct a traditional house for the BCPM, Martin illustrated that, despite the assimilationist intent of the Indian Act prior to its revision, Kwakwa̱ka̱'wakw ways persisted. Despite the move towards professionalizing First Nations art and emphasizing the academic expertise of institutional authorities, the knowledge of First Nations objects, their histories and functions, still thrived in their communities of origin. The house was given a ceremonial name and was celebrated with three consecutive nights of potlatching, first for Martin's family and invited guests, then for museum and public officials, and finally for the general public. Dan Cranmer's daughter, Gloria Cranmer Webster, retired director of the U'mista Cultural Centre in Alert Bay, states that Martin's Wa'waditla potlatch was the inspiration for the first public potlatch held in Alert Bay since the Cranmer prosecutions in 1963.[19]

Second, the Totem Pole Preservation Committee approached the Gitxsan community of Gitanyow (Kitwancool) for permission to remove poles so that they could be included in the salvage and replication program. The negotiations between curator Duff and the community illustrated the ongoing conflict regarding the significance of the poles. Part of Duff's argument in favour of their removal was that they were outstanding examples of "primitive art." Gitanyow negotiator Albert Douse thought that the sale of poles was linked to the relinquishment of traditional territories and stated that selling them would negate the prestige associated with their original erection. The final compromise saw the poles go to the committee for "permanent preservation," replication, and re-erection in Gitanyow. In return, the committee paid for the recording, transcription, translation, and publication of Gitanyow histories, laws, and territories, which implied an official endorsement of the legitimacy of Gitanyow claims. Furthermore, these laws and histories were to be taught at university (Duff did this at UBC).

The removal of the first four Gitanyow poles coincided with the end of assimilation as Canada's official policy towards First Nations. The four decades that separated the most intrusive attempt at assimilation – namely, the 1922 Cranmer potlatch prosecutions and the 1961 federal enfranchisement – had seen a growth in political infrastructures and the implementation of a range of strategies for asserting both Aboriginal and non-Aboriginal political agendas. Art played a significant role in many of these strategies and articulated different historical perspectives according to the context of display and the individuals and groups involved. The conflict over control of this multiplicity of meaning, however, remained constant.

The project of encouraging contemporary expression further affected the discourse of Northwest Coast art in a number of ways. One of the most important was the emphasis on individual artists. The potlatch ban had prompted caution and distrust in many First Nations individuals. Since, initially, museum officials only professed interest in the past and lacked the financial and political backing of the government to support and promote the arts as a source of employment, individual First Nations arts practitioners had not been celebrated as individual artists with the same enthusiasm their Euro-Canadian counterparts received prior to the Second World War. Even Euro-Canadian artists felt isolated and unappreciated prior to the Canadian Arts Council brief to the Turgeon Committee, but it is unlikely that any of them would have been as quickly forgotten as, for example, was Haida carver Mark Spence. Spence was from New Masset and, in 1940, was commissioned to carve entrance posts for the new Thunderbird Park in Victoria. In 1956 the posts were replaced with carvings by Martin and Hunt. By the time the Spence posts were removed to the officers' mess at the Naden naval base in Esquimalt in 1963, Wilson Duff had no information on Spence save that he was "an old Haida Indian ... living in Victoria."[20] There is now a photograph of Spence in the visual records department of the Royal British Columbia Museum. However, the negative for this photograph has been transferred to either the British Columbia Archives or the Vancouver Tourism Board, neither of which has any record of Spence in its computerized files. This says something of the low status allotted First Nations carvers prior to the 1950s. Duff was not aware of Spence because the museum's mandate in 1940, the era of his predecessors, did not include the promotion of individual artists.

The emphasis on describing formal design systems and the achievements of individual artists in Euro-American terms contributed to a postwar tension between the discourses of anthropology and art history. An important question was, to quote Wilson Duff, "whether [First Nations] have the concept of art as art."[21] Some objects, as Halpin and many others note, "have as their referents the beaches, rivers, mountains, and other properties whose ownership or transfer is being witnessed." She points out that "what you and I have labeled art not only *is* property, it is about property."[22] While cognizant of the difficulties of applying Boas's and Holm's universalist, and wholly modernist, formal approaches to Northwest Coast objects, many artists have intentionally made objects that will fit within non-Aboriginal categorizations of art. The paintings of George Clutesi and Judith Morgan are good examples of this and should not be dismissed as "inauthentic." To do this would be to deny their resonance not only with the times in which they were produced, but also with the vast network of kin relations through which property is inherited, asserted, and defended. With the growth in state intervention and industrial development, "fighting with property," as Helen Codere termed it in 1950,[23] took on new meaning. The network and the properties it contains had to be spoken about in new languages. It is for this reason that Mathias Joe adapted the Kwakwa̱ka̱'wakw carving style to his 1936 multi-figure pole – an act that reinforced the connection between monuments accepted and celebrated by non-Aboriginal Canadians and Joe's claims to the Squamish ownership of park lands. This is also why Morgan and Clutesi may have appropriated European illusionistic painting techniques in order to depict First Nations stories: it was a way of updating the imagery and making it relevant to current issues. Since the legitimacy of the potlatch system had been called into question in the last quarter of the nineteenth century, First Nations peoples found it necessary to expand the audiences for their claims. The recognition and promotion of Northwest Coast visual production, its institutionalization as "art" in Canada's new public spaces, provided one avenue for doing this – an avenue that enabled individuals with such diverse interests and intentions as Clutesi, Morgan, Joe, James, the Martins, Hunt, Neel, and a host of others to become active participants in the production of Northwest Coast art.

Rather than dismissing objects that do not conform to the definitions of "classic" art, I argue that what we should be doing is assessing the political use of these objects. I favour an understanding of First Nations visual production that sees it as a method for examining the profound entanglement of Aboriginal and non-Aboriginal societies and the consequent range of meaning formulated around objects at specific historical moments and within specific historical contexts. Far from Duncan Campbell Scott's notion of "tales of ghosts that hover in the world like fading smoke," these objects and images, and the ideas they represent, continue to exert a strong influence on the world we share. Our motivation for discussing them should be neither strictly promotional nor for the purposes of enacting some sense of closure; rather, it should be in order to understand the processes that inform the conflicting, and constantly shifting, discourses that speak through and around them.

Appendix A
First Nations Groups in British Columbia

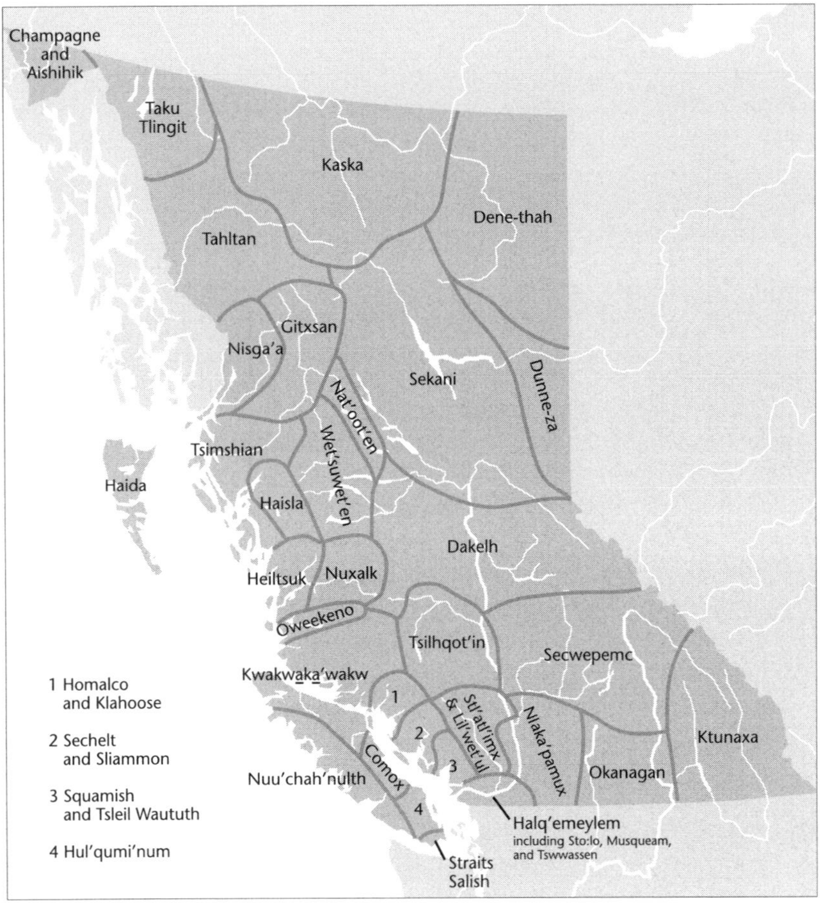

Appendix B
Chronology of First Nations Art in British Columbia, 1921-61

1921
Potlatch hosted by Dan Cranmer is held at Village Island.

1922
Indian Agent William Halliday from the Kwawkewlth agency charges participants in the Cranmer potlatch with violating the Indian Act.

The Lekwiltok of Quadra Island, the Mamalillikulla of Village Island, and the Nimpkish of Alert Bay agree to an informal plea bargain and surrender their coppers and dancing gear to Halliday in Alert Bay in return for suspended sentences. Halliday organizes a display of this material in the Alert Bay church hall.

Halliday subsequently sells thirty-five pieces to American collector George Heye for $291 and receives an official reprimand from his superiors for sending such valuable material to the United States.

Twenty-one potlatchers who had not agreed to the exchange offered by Halliday are imprisoned at Oakalla Prison in Burnaby. Twenty serve two-month sentences. Charlie Hunt, on his second conviction, serves six months. The Cranmer potlatch has now come to epitomize the draconian enforcement of the federal potlatch ban during the period of assimilation.

1923
The Cranmer material is catalogued by ethnologist Edward Sapir of the National Museum of Canada and sent to the National Museum and the Royal Ontario Museum. A selection of masks is also put aside for display in the office of Deputy Superintendent of Indian Affairs Duncan Campbell Scott.

The Art, Historical, and Scientific Association of Vancouver (AHSAV) acquires two freestanding crest poles from Alert Bay and two houseposts carved by Charlie James for Tsaweenok of Kingcombe Inlet. The association relocates them to Stanley Park in Vancouver as part of a plan to recreate an original First Nations village and a Hudson's Bay Trading Post.

The first recorded sale of a Gitxsan totem pole from the upper Skeena Valley is to New York's American Museum of Natural History.

1924
AHSAV expands its plan for the touristic village in Stanley Park to include the possibility of buying and relocating the entire village of Alert Bay.

A federal Totem Pole Preservation Committee is formed, composed of representatives of the Department of Indian Affairs, Ministry of Mines, Canadian National Parks, and the National Museum.

Funded by the Department of Indian Affairs and the Canadian National Railways, the committee's preservation work begins with National Museum ethnologist Marius Barbeau's survey of totem poles in Gitxsan villages adjacent to the Canadian National Railways line in the upper Skeena Valley.

1925
Protests by the Coast Salish Squamish people prevent AHSAV from continuing with its plans to reconstruct a First Nations village at Stanley Park's Lumberman's Arch site, previously a Squamish village site known as XwayXway.

1926
Wallis A. Olen of Clintonville, Wisconsin, contacts Harlan Smith and then Diamond Jenness, Sapir's replacement at the National Museum, about the possibility of purchasing a totem pole.

Chief Seamadaks of Kitwanga attempts to sell a pole and ten masks to the North West Biscuit Company of Edmonton.

These two incidents alert Jenness and Deputy Superintendent of Indian Affairs Scott to the need for protective government control over the sale of totem poles. Together Jenness and Scott draft legislation that makes it illegal to sell poles and other "heritage" objects without the permission of the Department of Indian Affairs.

1927
Canada's Silver Jubilee year.

A show of Canadian modernist paintings curated by National Gallery director Eric Brown opens at the Jeu de Paume museum in Paris and includes a selection of Northwest Coast carvings and fabrics.

A domestic version of the Paris exhibition, entitled *Exhibition of Canadian West Coast Art, Native and Modern,* opens at the National Gallery of Canada in Ottawa. It includes paintings by Langdon Kihn, Emily Carr, and A.Y. Jackson, traditional Northwest Coast carvings and textiles, and works by named First Nations artists Frederick Alexie and Charles Edenshaw. The inclusion of Alexie's paintings marks the first time that a named, living First Nations artist has been exhibited at the National Gallery.

Marius Barbeau begins collecting privately for other institutions, including the Royal Ontario Museum. His negotiations in the Nass River to purchase a pole for $1,000 forces an increase in prices in Kitsegukla, where the Totem Pole Preservation Committee is negotiating to preserve poles *in situ*. The bidding war that Barbeau sets off effectively ends the Totem Pole Preservation program's success in eliciting the cooperation of Gitxsan residents.

Franz Boas's *Primitive Art* is published.

1928
The *Exhibition of Canadian West Coast Art, Native and Modern* opens in Toronto and Montreal.

The National Museum publishes Marius Barbeau's *The Downfall of Temlaham.*

The Hoover Administration in the United States releases the Meriam Report, which calls for a reform of the Native American education system.

1929
The Great Depression begins.

Squamish resident "Aunt Sally" of the XwayXway or Lumberman's Arch site in Stanley Park, is the only resident able to establish a legal right to live in the park after parks authorities seek eviction notices to clean the park of "unwanted" residents. Her property is then purchased on behalf of the Parks Board by philanthropist W.C. Shelley for $15,500.

Chief Seamadaks of Kitwanga sells a pole to the Hudson's Bay Company for $300, without the consent of the Department of Indian Affairs. Seamadaks is assisted in the pole's removal by T.B. Campbell, an engineer with the Canadian National Railways assigned to the Totem Pole Preservation Committee.

Governor General Lord Willingdon travels to the Nuu-chah-nulth community of Yuquot on the west coast of Vancouver Island. Chief Captain Jack presents him with a rare free-standing monumental Nuu-chah-nulth crest pole. T.B. Campbell goes to Yuquot to supervise the pole's removal. After the costs for removing the pole to the governor general's residence at Rideau Hall in Ottawa proved prohibitive, Lord Willingdon ceremoniously returns the pole to the village of Yuquot for "safe-keeping."

1931
Native Brotherhood of British Columbia is founded.

1933
Democrat Franklin Delano Roosevelt is elected president of the United States on his influential New Deal policy platform.

Roosevelt appoints leading social reformer and campaigner for Native rights, John Collier, to the position of Commissioner of Indian Affairs.

1934
The Roosevelt administration announces the repeal of the assimilationist 1887 Dawes Act with the Wheeler-Howard Indian Rights bill, also known as the Indian Re-organization Act or the Indian New Deal. One objective of the bill is to promote Native American culture in the United States.

Vancouver resident and collector of Northwest Coast art, the Reverend George Raley, begins campaigning for a First Nations arts program to be supported by the federal government.

While initially negotiating to sell his collection to George Heye, Raley sells his collection to the city of Vancouver through local businessman Victor Spencer. This collection later serves as the basis for Vancouver's two important museums, the Vancouver Museum and the University of British Columbia's Museum of Anthropology.

The Provincial Museum obtains a Carnegie Fund grant to finance public lectures organized by Alice Ravenhill.

1935
The Bureau of Indian Affairs in the United States creates the Indian Arts and Crafts Board to promote Native American art.

1936
The Vancouver Golden Jubilee Committee commissions a free-standing monumental crest pole by Squamish carver Mathias Joe and erects it at Prospect Point in Stanley Park. They also erect three older, anonymous poles at the Lumberman's Arch site.

1938
The Provincial Museum publishes Alice Ravenhill's *The Native Tribes of British Columbia,* primarily for use in the province's grade schools.

1939
The Indian Arts and Crafts Board sponsors the exhibition of Native American objects as fine art at the Golden Gate Exposition in San Francisco. The exhibition is curated by Indian Arts and Crafts Board General Manager René d'Harnoncourt and Denver Art Museum Curator Frederic Douglas.

The Second World War begins.

Victoria resident and educational reformer, Alice Ravenhill, founds the British Columbia Indian Arts and Welfare Society (BCIAWS). This organization simultaneously campaigns for the reform of the Indian Act and First Nations education and government-supported social programs, while also advocating the promotion of First Nations arts as a source of employment.

1940
The Provincial Museum opens Thunderbird Park, an open air totem pole park in the heart of downtown Victoria.

1941
René d'Harnoncourt and Frederic Douglas organize the influential *Indian Art of the United States* exhibition at the Museum of Modern Art in New York.

The British Columbia Indian Arts and Welfare Society publishes *The Tale of the Nativity* and *Meet Mr. Coyote.*

1942
The BCIAWS submits a brief to the Department of Indian Affairs, entitled *Suggestions on the Encouragement of Arts and Crafts in the Indian Schools of British Columbia.*

The Native Brotherhood of British Columbia amalgamates with the Pacific Coast Fishermen's Association.

1943
An annual exhibition of First Nations student art at the Provincial Museum in Victoria begins. It sometimes includes the work of mature artists like George Clutesi and Ellen Neel as well.

The Okanagan Society for the Revival of Indian Arts and Crafts submits a brief to the federal Committee on Reconstruction and Re-establishment, entitled *Native Canadians: A Plan for the Rehabilitation of Indians.*

1944
The Provincial Museum publishes Alice Ravenhill's *A Cornerstone of Canadian Culture: An Outline of the Arts and Crafts of the Indian Tribes of British Columbia* "to provide teachers and students with a record of former tribal decorative arts and crafts which have possibilities of further development and utilization in modern life."

1945
The Second World War ends.

The Native Brotherhood of British Columbia incorporates itself under the British Columbia Societies Act.

1946
The Native Brotherhood of British Columbia commissions a pole from carver Mungo Martin for presentation to Governor General Viscount Alexander at the Kitsilano Indian Village as part of the city's Diamond Jubilee celebrations.

The Native Brotherhood of British Columbia launches its own newspaper, *Native Voice*.

The federal government passes the Canadian Citizenship Act, which, for the first time, creates a Canadian citizenship that is distinct from British subject status.

1946-9
The federal government appoints the Special Joint Committee on Revision of Indian Act.

The federal government selects the Native Brotherhood of British Columbia as the sole representative of British Columbian First Nations.

1947
Harry Hawthorn becomes the first anthropologist hired at the University of British Columbia (UBC).

UBC president and Massey Commissioner Norman MacKenzie appoints a committee to purchase totem poles for UBC. The committee contracts Marius Barbeau and Arthur Price to purchase eight free-standing poles and a housepost.

The Native Brotherhood of British Columbia proclaims the provincial government illegal for not allowing First Nations people to vote.

Federal laws prohibiting Asian immigration and banning Asian-Canadian voting rights are overturned.

At a collegiate football game, William Scow, president of the Native Brotherhood of British Columbia, presents the Alma Mater Society of UBC with a monumental pole carved by Ellen Neel. This presentation is part of a ceremony legitimizing the university sports teams' use of the moniker "Thunderbirds."

1948
The United Nations issues the Declaration of Human Rights.

UBC/BCIAWS co-sponsors a conference on Native Indian Affairs. Ellen Neel delivers the keynote address in the section on the arts.

Josephine Godman prepares a formal marketing strategy for the BCIAWS for the sale of First Nations arts.

Hunter Lewis, UBC English professor and national president of the Federation of Canadian Artists, undertakes a six-week research trip along the BC coast under a grant from the University Research Committee. He calls for government cooperation in pole restoration and copying.

The university hires Mungo Martin to restore the Barbeau poles for re-erection in UBC's Totem Pole Park.

In commemoration of the opening of the university's Museum of Anthropology, UBC buys seven paintings by George Clutesi.

1949
The federal government establishes the Royal Commission on National Development in the Arts, Letters and Sciences (Massey Commission) to chart the government's role in the postwar period in the promotion and support of postsecondary education, research, and the arts in Canada. Its final report is released in 1951.

First Nations peoples win provincial enfranchisement and participate in a provincial election for the first time. From this point on, the provincial government, primarily through the Provincial Museum, but with the cooperation of UBC, dominates the promotion of First Nations arts in the 1950s.

Nisga'a chief Frank Calder, formerly secretary of the Greenville branch of the Native Brotherhood of British Columbia and president of the Nishga Tribal Council, is elected the Cooperative Commonwealth Federation (CCF) member of the Legislative Assembly for the Atlin riding.

In celebration of provincial enfranchisement, the provincial government purchases five paintings by the young Gitxsan artist Judith Morgan.

BC Packers makes inquiries into purchasing Haida crest poles for removal to BC Packers plants.

Forester H.R. MacMillan is similarly interested in acquiring old crest poles. The UBC President's committee contacts MacMillan for financial/logistical help in recovering and restoring crest poles.

The provincial government announces that "both the Provincial and Federal Governments were interested in the advancement of Indian crafts, not only to preserve their culture, but also to help the natives make a livelihood."

Wilson Duff of the Provincial Museum and Harry Hawthorn of UBC make an ethnographic survey of the Nass and Skeena valleys.

The Provincial Museum begins its "Anthropology in BC" publication series.

1950
The National Museum publishes Marius Barbeau's *Totem Poles.*

The Massey Commission calls on Harry Hawthorn to prepare a report on the status of First Nations arts in Canada.

The Totemland Society is launched, adopting the thunderbird totem pole as its insignia and the slogan "totem land" to advertise the province. Totemland Society officers include Premier Byron Johnson, the attorney general, the mayor of Vancouver, the Minister of Trade and Industry, William Scow, and the Commissioner of the Victoria and Island Publicity Bureau.

Mayor Thompson of Vancouver gives an Ellen Neel pole to the mayor of Sydney on a promotional visit to Australia.

UBC's Totem Pole Park opens in October.

1951
A revised Indian Act that drops the prohibitions of the potlatch and land claim activities is passed in Parliament.

The Massey Commission releases its recommendations, including a need for "arm's length" government funding of both First Nations and mainstream Canadian artistic production.

A totem pole insignia is added to BC's automobile licence plates.

1952
W.A.C. Bennett and the Social Credit party begin twenty years of government in British Columbia. This administration will seek to expand the province's physical infrastructure through large-scale construction projects and to encourage multinational investment in forestry and mining.

Minister of Education and Provincial Secretary W.T. Straith announces a totem pole preservation program in the provincial legislature. The plan includes totem pole carving to be taught by Mungo Martin through the Ministry of Education in a workshop in Thunderbird Park. Cedar is provided by H.R. MacMillan.

Martin begins working on the restoration of poles in Thunderbird Park. His wife gives daily weaving demonstrations during the summer.

Wilson Duff and University of Washington graduate student George A. Cheney travel to the Gitxsan totem pole villages in the upper Skeena to study poles and examine potential problems in preserving them.

1953
Wa'waditla is completed and opens in Thunderbird Park with the first open, public potlatch since the Cranmer prosecutions. The event is hosted by Martin.

1954
The joint provincial Totem Pole Preservation Committee is formed. The committee immediately purchases and removes six poles from the Haida villages of Skedans and Tanu; three each go to the Provincial Museum and UBC.

The poles are reproduced by Martin and his apprentices for erection in Thunderbird Park.

Henry Hunt is hired as apprentice carver.

1955
Funded by H.R. MacMillan, the Preservation Committee surveys Kwakwa̱ka̱'wakw villages on the central coast.

Carvers are laid off from mid-December until the beginning of the following fiscal year (April) due to financial difficulties.

1956
Financed by MacMillan, the Preservation Committee removes fourteen poles from the Kwakwa̱ka̱'wakw villages surveyed in the previous year.

The Preservation Committee also surveys the Haida village of Ninstints on Anthony Island in Haida Gwaii.

Through the support of a local newspaper, Wilson Duff arranges for the carving of the "world's largest totem pole" to keep Martin and his helpers at work in Victoria during the winter.

Bill Reid spends ten days with Martin replicating poles salvaged from Ninstints in Victoria.

Under "a special financial arrangement," the carvers carve a pair of poles for the entrance to Riley Park in Courtenay. This is the beginning of the project expanding the pole copying program to areas outside the museum. They also complete poles at the Pacific National Exhibition in Vancouver and at the Tourist Bureau office at Peace Arch Park at the Canada-United States border crossing.

1957
The Preservation Committee removes eleven poles from Ninstints.

Mungo Martin and his helpers begin work on the centennial pole for presentation to Queen Elizabeth.

Godfrey Hunt is brought on as another apprentice carver.

John Diefenbaker is elected prime minister of Canada.

The Canada Council is established.

Bill Reid and Doug Cranmer are hired by UBC to reconstruct a Haida village on the university campus.

1958
British Columbia's centennial year. The federal government issues a commemorative silver dollar bearing the likeness of a Haida pole taken from a photograph in the Provincial Museum.

Martin and his helpers complete the 100-foot pole presented to the Queen. A copy is erected in Vancouver alongside the historic RCMP ice breaker, the *St. Roch*.

The Preservation Committee removes three poles from Gitanyow in an agreement that results in the publication of *Histories, Territories, and Laws of the Kitwancool* the following year.

Martin and Hunt carve an eight-foot pole for the Canadian Tourist Association Convention in Quebec City.

1960
The Diefenbaker administration passes the Bill for the Recognition and Protection of Human Rights and Fundamental Freedoms in Parliament, which officially rejects discrimination by reason of race, colour, national origin, religion, or sex.

1961
A revised Indian Act, which gives First Nations peoples federal voting rights, is passed in Parliament.

The fourth pole from Gitanyow is removed for replication in Victoria.

Notes

Chapter 1: Introduction

1 While prior to 1980 the misnomer "Indian" is frequently used in texts, in recognition of their political status the Aboriginal peoples of Canada are now usually referred to as First Nations or First Peoples. In the United States, the appellation Native American is more accepted.

2 See, for example, Barry Lord, *The History of Painting in Canada: Toward a People's Art* (Toronto: NC Press, 1974).

3 Following the definition put forward by Wayne Suttles, the Northwest Coast "culture area ... includes the north Pacific Coast of North America from the Copper River delta on the Gulf of Alaska to the Winchuk River near the Oregon-California border, extending inland to the Chugach and Saint Elias ranges of Alaska, the Coast Mountains of British Columbia, and the Cascade Region of Washington and Oregon." See Wayne Suttles, "Introduction," in *Handbook of North American Indians*, vol. 7, *Northwest Coast*, ed. Wayne Suttles (Washington, DC: Smithsonian Institution, 1990), 1. The First Nations language groups of British Columbia referred to under this rubric include, from north to south: Haida, Tsimshian, Nisga'a, Gitxsan (Gitksan), Haisla, Heiltsuk, Nuxalk, Oweekeno, Kwakwaka'wakw, Nuu-chah-nulth, Ditidaht, and the Salishan-speaking (Salish) Halkomelem, Squamish, and Straits Salish (Homalco, Klahoose, Sliammon, Comox, Qualicum, Se'shalt, Sne-Nay-Muxw, Squamish, Quwutsun', Sto:lo, Semiahmoo, Tsleil-Waututh, Musqueam, Tsswassen, T'Souke, Esquimalt, Songhees, Saanich, and Coquitlam). See "First Nations of British Columbia" (Vancouver: University of British Columbia Museum of Anthropology Map Project, 5 March 1996), n.p.

4 Bill Holm and George Irving Quimby, *Edward S. Curtis in the Land of the War Canoes: A Pioneer Cinematographer in the Pacific Northwest* (Vancouver: Douglas and McIntyre, 1980).

5 Phil Nuytten, *The Totem Carvers: Charlie James, Ellen Neel and Mungo Martin* (Vancouver: Panorama Publications, 1982), 29.

6 Marjorie M. Halpin, *Totem Poles: An Illustrated Guide*, Museum of Anthropology Museum Note No. 3 (Vancouver: UBC Press, 1981), 8.

7 Anthropologist Wilson Duff, for one, identified the artistic climax of the northern Northwest Coast as occurring between 1850 and 1880, and among the Kwakwaka'wakw between 1890 and 1920. See Wilson Duff, "Contexts of Northwest Coast Art," in *Arts of the Raven: Masterworks of the Northwest Coast Indian*, ed. Vancouver Art Gallery (Vancouver: Vancouver Art Gallery, 1965).

8 Tina Loo, "Dan Cranmer's Potlatch: Law as Coercion, Symbol and Rhetoric in British Columbia, 1884-1951," *Canadian Historical Review* 68, 2 (1992): 150-1.

9 One-quarter of the three million immigrants to Canada between 1896 and 1914 were from the non-Anglo-Celtic world. See Angus McLaren, *Our Own Master Race: Eugenics in Canada, 1885-1945* (Toronto: McClelland and Stewart, 1990); Reg Whitaker, *Canadian Immigration Policy since Confederation* (Ottawa: Canadian Historical Association Canada's Ethnic Groups

Booklet 15 1991); Howard H. Palmer, *Cultural Diversity and Canadian Education* (Ottawa: Carleton University Press, 1984), 21-40.

10 As British Columbia premier Simon Fraser Tolmie announced in 1928: "We are anxious to keep this a British country. We want British Columbia British and nothing else." Quoted in Patricia E. Roy, "British Columbia's Fear of Asians, 1900-1950," *Histoire Sociale/Social History* 13, 25: 162.

11 Paul Connerton, *How Societies Remember* (Cambridge: Cambridge University Press 1989), 1.

12 Marius Barbeau, quoting Indian Agent Todd, writing from Metlakatla in 1899 on "the principal objection amongst the Christianized Indians to the potlatch," in C.M. Barbeau, "The Potlatch among the B.C. Indians and Section 149 of the Indian Act," unpublished (Canadian Museum of Civilization 11007.13, B12, F2, VII-X-46M, 1934), 49.

13 Margaret B. Blackman, "Haida: Traditional Culture," in *Handbook of North American Indians,* vol. 7, *Northwest Coast,* ed. Wayne Suttles (Washington, DC: Smithsonian Institution, 1990), 248. Although Blackman reports that, in the 1970s, the Masset Haida stated that halibut banks were named but not owned (249), I think it is important that, in the era of the potlatch ban, published accounts report that this resource was owned by lineages.

14 The crests were "the most important incorporeal lineage properties" and "were the identifying symbols of the lineages and, in cases where an individual claimed exclusive right to a crest, it was indicative of individual rank within the lineage" (Blackman, "Haida," 249). These crests were carved on totem poles, household utensils, boxes, and feast dishes, all of which, beginning in the 1870s, were the focus of museum collecting. See Douglas Cole, *Captured Heritage: The Scramble for Northwest Coast Artifacts* (Vancouver and Toronto: Douglas and McIntyre, 1985; rpt. UBC Press, 1995). See also Blackman, "Haida," 249, on tattoos and body painting.

15 Blackman, "Haida," 248-9. This general summary is based on Haida society as described by Blackman. For other groups in British Columbia see: Marjorie M. Halpin and Margaret Seguin, "Tsimshian Peoples: Southern Tsimshian, Coast Tsimshian, Nishga, and Gitksan," 267-84; Charles Hamori-Torok, "Haisla," 306-11; Suzanne F. Hilton, "Haihais, Bella-Bella, and Oowekeeno," 312-22; Dorothy I.D. Kennedy and Randall T. Bouchard, "Bella Coola," 323-39; Helen Codere, "Kwakiutl: Traditional Culture," 359-77; Eugene Arima and John Dewhirst, "Nootkans of Vancouver Island," 391-411; Dorothy I.D. Kennedy and Randall T. Bouchard, "Northern Coast Salish," 441-52; and Wayne Suttles, "Central Coast Salish," 453-75. All of the preceding appear in Suttles, *Handbook.*

16 Gisday Wa and Delgam Uukw, *The Spirit in the Land: The Opening Statement of the Gitksan and Wet'suwet'en Hereditary Chiefs in the Supreme Court of British Columbia* (Gabriola, BC: Reflections, 1989), 7-8.

17 Codere, "Kwakiutl: Traditional Culture," 359 and 364.

18 Ibid., 366-72.

19 Bill Holm, "Art," in Suttles, *Handbook,* 618.

20 Paul Tennant, *Aboriginal Peoples and Politics: The Indian Land Question, 1849-1989* (Vancouver: UBC Press, 1992), 84-113.

21 Cole, *Captured Heritage,* 278.

22 Because First Nations peoples had been allocated status as wards of the state through the Indian Act, they did not have the rights of citizenship. See, for example, John Leslie and Ron Maguire, eds., *The Historical Development of the Indian Act* (Ottawa: Indian and Northern Affairs Canada, 1978); and Tennant, *Aboriginal Peoples and Politics.*

23 Edwin S. Hall, Margaret B. Blackman, and Vincent Rickard, *Northwest Coast Indian Graphics: An Introduction to Silk Screen Prints* (Vancouver: Douglas and MacIntyre, 1981), 45.

24 Peter Macnair, "Trends in Northwest Coast Indian Art, 1880-1959: Decline and Expansion," in Canadian Museum of Civilization, *In the Shadow of the Sun: Perspectives on Contemporary Native Art* (Ottawa: Canadian Ethnology Service, Mercury Series Paper 124, 1993), 51.

25 Ibid., 57.

26 Martine Reid, "In Search of Things Past, Remembered, Retraced, and Reinvented," in Canadian Museum of Civilization, *In the Shadow of the Sun,* 76. Here, Reid uses a semiotic framework based on an underlying paradigm of precontact height and contact contamination –

a paradigm that is effectively refuted in Bennetta Jules-Rosette, *The Messages of Tourist Art: An African Semiotic System in Comparative Perspective* (New York: Plenum Press, 1984), 219.

27 Halpin, *Totem Poles*, 2.

28 Tom Hill, "Indian Art in Canada: An Historical Perspective," in *Norval Morrisseau and the Emergence of the Image Makers* (Toronto: Art Gallery of Ontario, 1985), 20-1.

29 Bill Holm, "Will the Real Charles Edenshaw Please Stand Up? The Problem of Attribution in Northwest Coast Indian Art," in *The World Is as Sharp as a Knife: An Anthology in Honour of Wilson Duff*, ed. Donald Abbott (Victoria: British Columbia Provincial Museum, 1981), 177.

30 The term "formline" and the system of representation to which it alludes was most systematically defined by Bill Holm in *Northwest Coast Art: An Analysis of Form* (Seattle: University of Washington Press 1965). Holm had considerable influence on the direction of the *Arts of the Raven* show. He referred to *Northwest Coast Art: An Analysis of Form* as "a turning point ... which became a primer for the artists struggling for an understanding of their ancestors' art." See Holm, "Art," 630.

31 This show significantly influenced the perception of Northwest Coast objects over the next decade. Writing in 1975, for example, Marjorie Halpin linked the consideration of Northwest Coast objects as art specifically to the *Arts of the Raven* exhibit. See Marjorie Halpin, "The Uses of Collections," in *Northwest Coast Indian Artifacts from the H.R. MacMillan Collections in the Museum of Anthropology, University of British Columbia,* ed. University of British Columbia Museum of Anthropology (Vancouver: UBC Press, 1975), 43.

32 'Ksan Association, *'Ksan, Hazelton, B.C.* (Hazelton, BC: 'Ksan Association, 1970), 12-24.

33 Schafer and Fortier report that several million federal dollars were allocated to national and international artistic events, including Expo '67, all of which were seen as adjuncts to the centennial celebrations. See Paul D. Schafer and André Fortier, *Review of Federal Policies for the Arts in Canada, 1944-1988* (Ottawa: Canadian Conference of the Arts, 1989). Both government and corporate sponsors were acknowledged on the inside covers of the *Arts of the Raven* catalogue. These included the Canada Council, the Centennial Commission, the Vancouver Foundation, BC Tel, Canadian Forest Products, the Japan External Trade Organization, and MacMillan-Bloedel.

34 Wayne Suttles and Aldona Jonaitis, "History of Research in Ethnology," in Suttles, *Handbook*, 82.

35 George Woodcock writes of 'Ksan as one of the "programs of dissemination that were artistically and ethnographically educative without having any identifiable political intent" begun by the Trudeau administration in the late 1960s. See George Woodcock, *Strange Bedfellows: The State and the Arts in Canada* (Vancouver and Toronto: Douglas and McIntyre, 1985), 105.

36 This "democratization and decentralization" was announced by Secretary of State Gérard Pelletier at a seminar organized by the Canadian Conference of the Arts and the United States Associated Council of Arts in 1969. The objectives of the program as a state cultural policy were to spread cultural institutions and the management of cultural industries outside of Ottawa and central Canada and, at the same time, to foster cultural pluralism in Canada and both federal-provincial and international cooperation in the promotion of Canadian arts. See Schafer and Fortier, *Review of Federal Policies for the Arts in Canada.*

37 In announcing multiculturalism as state policy on 8 October 1971, then prime minister Pierre Trudeau stated: "The policy I am announcing today accepts the contention of the other cultural communities that they, too, are essential elements in Canada and deserve government assistance in order to contribute to regional and national life in ways that derive from their heritage and yet are distinctly Canadian." Quoted in Valerie Knowles, *Strangers at Our Gates: Canadian Immigration and Immigration Policy, 1540-1990* (Toronto: Dundurn Press, 1992), 168.

38 Hill, "Indian Art in Canada," 20-1.

39 Federal Cultural Policy Review Committee, *Summary of Briefs and Hearings* (Ottawa: Ministry of Supply and Services, n.d.), 5.

40 Ibid.

41 Bill Holm ("Art," 630) singles out the Kwakwaka'wakw (Kwakiutl) as continuing the production of ceremonial objects, and this contention is supported by other texts examining the Kwakwaka'wakw's open flaunting of the potlatch ban. See, for example, Douglas Cole and Ira Chaikin, *An Iron Hand upon the People: The Law against the Potlatch on the Northwest Coast* (Vancouver/Seattle: Douglas and McIntyre/University of Washington Press, 1990). According to Barbeau, the Gitxsan continued to erect and potlatch poles into the 1940s. Spirit dancing among the Coast Salish peoples of southern Vancouver Island was documented by Duff in the 1940s, and Nuu-chah-nulth individuals, like Ron Hamilton and Joe David, have challenged the suggestion that ceremonialism died out among their peoples. The supposition that First Nations ceremonies had to be revived needs closer, more critical examination.

42 Ellen Neel, in *Report of Conference on Native Indian Affairs,* ed. H.B. Hawthorn (Victoria: British Columbia Indian Arts and Welfare Society, 1948), 12.

43 Tony Hunt and Jo-Anne Birnie Danzker, "Personal Perspectives," in *Vancouver: Art and Artists 1931-1983,* ed. Vancouver Art Gallery (Vancouver: Vancouver Art Gallery, 1983), 266.

44 George Manuel and Michael Postuns, *The Fourth World: An Indian Reality* (Don Mills, ON: Collier-Macmillan, 1974), 69-70.

45 Aldona Jonaitis, "Traders of Tradition: The History of Haida Art," in *Robert Davidson: Eagle of the Dawn,* ed. Ian M. Thom (Seattle: University of Washington Press, 1993), 3.

46 Ibid., 3-4.

47 Ibid., 4.

48 Nelson Graburn, "The Fourth World and Fourth World Art," in Canadian Museum of Civilization, *In the Shadow of the Sun,* 2.

49 Valda Blundell, "Speaking the Art of Canada's Native Peoples: Anthropological Discourse and the Media," *Australian Canadian Studies* 7, 1 (1989): 25.

50 Nicholas Thomas, *Colonialism's Culture: Anthropology, Travel and Government* (Princeton: Princeton University Press, 1994), 32.

51 Virginia Dominguez, "Invoking Culture: The Messy Side of 'Cultural Politics,'" *South Atlantic Quarterly* 91, 1 (Winter 1992): 20. According to Northrop Frye: "Perhaps only intellectuals worry about cultural distinctiveness, and perhaps only because they have invented most of it themselves." See Northrop Frye, "National Conciousness in Canadian Culture," in *Divisions on a Ground: Essays on Canadian Culture,* ed. James Polk (Toronto: Anansi, 1982), 42. In the case of First Nations peoples in Canada, however, cultural distinctiveness is crucial to asserting a historical presence and, thus, the legitimacy of claims to an authority over land and resources that precede the European presence and its institutions.

52 Dominguez, "Invoking Culture," 21.

53 Ibid.

54 Ibid.

55 While the anti-industrial nostalgic tone of the "Vanishing American" paradigm implies a critical stance towards industrial modernity, Jackson Lears argues that such ideology "unknowingly provided part of the psychological foundation for a streamlined liberal culture appropriate to twentieth century consumer capitalism ... by creating an 'evasive banality' of 'official culture' ... The common pattern of culture involved a denial of the conflicts in modern capitalist society, an affirmation of continuing harmony and progress." See Jackson Lears, *No Place of Grace: Antimodernism and the Transformation of American Culture, 1880-1920* (New York: Pantheon Books, 1981), 4-17.

56 Walter Benn Michaels, "The Vanishing American," *American Literary History* 2, 2 (1990): 220-41.

57 Marvin Cohodas, *Basketweavers for the California Curio Trade: Elizabeth and Louise Hickox* (Tucson: University of Arizona Press, 1997), 48.

58 For example, in 1975 Marjorie Halpin outlined two fundamental categories under which Northwest Coast objects can be considered: (1) art, which she dated to the aesthetic appreciation of ceremonial objects at the 1967 *Arts of the Raven* show, and (2) anthropology, which she described as "the attempt of Western people, using the tools of science and scholarship, to understand other cultures in their own terms. Thus, the imposition of our category of 'art' ... can ... be seen as antithetical to the purposes of anthropology." See

Halpin, "The Uses of Collections," 45. Earlier examples of discursive disagreement might include the differing application of the terms "handicraft" and "industry" in relation to First Nations objects.

59 Nicholas Thomas, *Entangled Objects: Exchange, Material Culture and Colonialism in the Pacific* (Cambridge, MA: Harvard University Press, 1991), 4.

60 Ibid.

61 "Biographies of things," writes Igor Kopytoff, "can make salient what might otherwise remain obscure. For example, in situations of culture contact, they can show what anthropologists have so often stressed: that what is significant about the adoption of alien objects – as of alien ideas – is not the fact that they are adopted, but the way they are culturally redefined and put to use." See Igor Kopytoff, "The Cultural Biography of Things: Commoditization as Process," in *The Social Life of Things: Commodities in Cultural Perspective,* ed. Arjun Appadurai (Cambridge: Cambridge University Press, 1986), 67.

62 Paul Litt traces this to the effect of the Royal Commission on National Development in the Arts, Letters and Sciences (the Massey Commission), which sat from 1949 to 1951. The findings of the Massey Commission "showed that Canadian cultural development would have to come to terms not just with biculturalism, but multiculturalism as well." See Paul Litt, *The Muses, the Masses, and the Massey Commission* (Toronto: University of Toronto Press, 1992), 113.

63 Ibid., 17.

64 Halpin, *Totem Poles,* 2.

65 Thomas, *Colonialism's Culture,* 4-5.

66 Ibid.

67 The Duff Papers at the University of British Columbia Museum of Anthropology contain anthropologist Wilson Duff's documentation of Salish spirit dancing in the late 1940s.

68 See, for example, Ronald W. Hawker, "In the Way of the White Man's Totem Poles: Tsimshian Gravestones, 1879-1920" (MA thesis, University of Victoria, 1988); and Margaret B. Blackman, "Totems to Tombstones: Culture Change as Viewed through the Haida Mortuary Complex," *Ethnology* 12 (1973): 47-56.

69 David reports the use of apple boxes and other temporary, cheap, and easily accessible materials to construct wolf masks during the potlatch ban. According to him, the idea was to make masks that could be quickly discarded in case of a government raid. See Joe David, Fine Arts 369 lecture, Department of Fine Arts, University of British Columbia, January 1994.

70 For First Nations perspectives, see: Crosby, "The Imaginary Indian"; Doreen Jensen, *Topographies* (Vancouver: Vancouver Art Gallery, 1997); and essays by First Nations artists, writers, and curators in Diana Nemiroff, Robert Houle, and Charlotte Townsend-Gault, *Land Spirit Power: First Nations at the National Gallery of Canada* (Ottawa: National Gallery of Canada, 1992); Gerald McMaster and Lee-Ann Martin, eds., *Indigena: Contemporary Native Perspectives* (Ottawa: Canadian Museum of Civilization, 1992); Doreen Jensen and Cheryl Brooks, eds., *In Celebration of Our Survival* (Vancouver: UBC Press, 1991); and Canadian Museum of Civilization, *In the Shadow of the Sun.*

71 Marjorie Halpin, "The Structure of Tsimshian Totemism," in *The Tsimshian and Their Neighbors of the North Pacific Coast,* ed. Jay Miller and Carol M. Eastman (Seattle: University of Washington Press, 1984), 35.

Chapter 2: The Cranmer Potlatch and Indian Agent Halliday's Display

1 Duncan Campbell Scott, "Indian Place Names," in *Duncan Campbell Scott: Selected Poetry,* ed. Glenn Clever (Ottawa: Tecumseh Press, 1974), 36. (Originally published in *New World Lyrics and Ballads,* 1905.)

2 George H. Raley, "Canadian Indian Art and Industries: An Economic Problem of Today," *Journal of the Royal Society of Arts* 83 (September 1935): 993.

3 Clever, *Duncan Campbell Scott,* 36.

4 Boas made twelve field trips to the Northwest Coast. He worked exclusively with the Kwakwa̱ka̱'wakw on five of these, non-exclusively with them on three further trips. He also worked with the Kwakwa̱ka̱'wakw at the World Columbian Exposition in Chicago in 1893, in New York in 1903 (when George Hunt assisted him with exhibits at the American

Museum of Natural History), and in 1931 (when he and Dan Cranmer worked on a Kwakwala language project). See Helen Codere, "Introduction," in Franz Boas, *Kwakiutl Ethnography*, ed. Helen Codere (Chicago and London: University of Chicago Press, 1966), xxxi.

5 The earliest form of the legislated ban was not clear enough in its definition of the potlatch. The first successful prosecution did not occur until 1896. See Douglas Cole and Ira Chaikin, *An Iron Hand upon the People: The Law against the Potlatch on the Northwest Coast* (Vancouver/Seattle: Douglas and McIntyre/University of Washington Press, 1990), 36-44.

6 Ibid., 63.

7 Ibid., 92.

8 The most important of these, tabled in the House of Commons by Minister of the Interior Arthur Meighen in 1918, made potlatching a summary offence and thus allowed the Indian Agent to act as both prosecutor and judge. See Cole and Chaikin, *An Iron Hand,* 102.

9 A number of successful prosecutions preceded the Cranmer case. What distinguishes the Cranmer case, then, is partly the number of people charged and partly the plea bargain discussed in detail below.

10 According to Marjorie Halpin, *Totem Poles: An Illustrated Guide,* Museum of Anthropology Museum Note No. 3 (Vancouver: UBC Press, 1981), 10: "There have been many explanations for the ritual occasion that involved potlatch giftgiving – that it converted wealth into prestige through the principles of conspicuous demonstration (the giver deriving social prestige through the size of his gifts); that it served as an economic investment through the redistribution of resources between groups owning territories of different and variable productivity; that it maintained society by reinforcing social bonds between family groups; and that, through the rivalry of aggressive giftgiving, 'fighting with property' was substituted for 'fighting with weapons.' The scholarly debate [like the popular debate] has gone on for decades and likely will continue."

11 Quoted in Cole and Chaikin, *An Iron Hand,* 15.

12 Helen Codere, *Fighting with Property: A Study of Kwakiutl Potlatching and Warfare, 1792-1930* (New York: J.J. Augustin, 1951), 127. Codere quotes "Kwakiutl statements on fighting with property" in the potlatch system: "When I was young I have seen streams of blood shed in war. But since that time the white man came and stopped up that stream of blood with wealth" (129).

13 Ibid., 10.

14 William Halliday, quoted in Cole and Chaikin, *An Iron Hand,* 95.

15 C.M. Barbeau, "The Potlatch among the B.C. Indians and Section 149 of the Indian Act," unpublished (Canadian Museum of Civilization 11007.13, B12, F2, VII-X-46M, 1934), 49.

16 Ibid., 59.

17 Codere, "Kwakiutl," in *Handbook of North American Indians,* vol. 7, *Northwest Coast,* ed. Wayne Suttles (Washington, DC: Smithsonian Institution, 1990), 359.

18 Ibid., 366.

19 Irving Goldman, *The Mouth of Heaven: An Introduction to Kwakiutl Religious Thought* (New York: John Wiley and Sons, 1975), 25.

20 Ibid., 26.

21 Halpin, *Totem Poles,* 8.

22 According to Goldman, *Mouth of Heaven,* 51: "Basic rank defines a position held in the name of a lineage, and is linked with the particular name known as the 'house name.' All other names held by a person convey special ritual privileges, and represent various ancestral and supernatural beings. Only the house name, which carries the special privileges of distributing property and the office of chief, reifies directly a lineage ancestor. Since all lineage ancestors were men, all ancestral house names are masculine. Thus though women inherit basic rank names through primogeniture, they act as temporary conveyors of a purely male line ... The system of descent is dual. Basic rank through male names is but part of the cargo of supernatural treasures carried down the generations by chiefs. Another part is acquired only through marriage and is a matrilineal contribution to a man's children. Each line transmits its own type of powers, and makes its own contribution to the totality of status."

23 William Halliday, quoted in Cole and Chaikin, *An Iron Hand,* 81.

24 Charles Nowell, in Clellan Ford, *Smoke from Their Fires: The Life of a Kwakiutl Chief* (Hamden, CT: Archon Books, 1968), 156.
25 Barbeau, "The Potlatch," 65.
26 Goldman, *Mouth of Heaven*, 48.
27 In 1849 the Hudson's Bay Company established a coal mine and trading post at Fort Rupert on Beaver Harbour. Four tribes settled at the site, making Fort Rupert the largest Kwakwa̱ka̱'wakw settlement. It was a centre of ceremonial activity until its eclipse by the establishment of the salmon cannery at Alert Bay on Queen Charlotte Strait in 1870, and the beginning a long tradition of resettlement and tribal amalgamation. Alert Bay, with its Anglican mission, sawmill, residential and industrial schools, and Kwawkewlth Indian Agency office was also at the centre of many of the social and economic changes introduced in the late nineteenth and early twentieth centuries. See Goldman, *Mouth of Heaven*, 363.
28 Philip Drucker and Robert F. Heizer, *To Make My Name Good: A Reexamination of the Southern Kwakiutl Potlatch* (Berkeley and Los Angeles: University of California Press, 1967), 31.
29 Ibid., 3-34.
30 Cole and Chaikin, *An Iron Hand*, 119.
31 Goldman, *Mouth of Heaven*, 80.
32 After the initial marriage had been sealed by the distribution of gifts, which "functioned as a payment to the members of the [groom's] village who had accompanied him to witness the marriage ... The parents of the bride ... sought to amass as much wealth as possible. The young couple also accumulated property with the assistance of the groom's father and turned it over to the girl's parents. Three or four years after the wedding, when the bride's family had acquired enough wealth, they brought it in canoes to the groom's family. An important part of this property was a copper, referred to as the 'mast of the canoe,' which was given to the groom. The groom later distributed the property in a potlatch to those tribes who had come to witness the transaction. The amount thus paid by the bride's father was many times the amount originally received by him at the wedding; he attempted to return as much as he could for by his liberality he gained prestige and honour." See Ford, *Smoke from Their Fires*, 37-8.
33 Cole and Chaikin, *An Iron Hand*, 119.
34 Copper shields were important symbols of wealth and were displayed, transferred, and sometimes broken in Kwakwa̱ka̱'wakw potlatches. See Cole and Chaikin, *An Iron Hand*, 150-1.
35 Ibid., 119.
36 Ibid., 119-20. Although unidentified in the main text of Cole and Chaikin's book, the likely source for this is the 1975 film *Potlatch: A Strict Law Bids Us Dance*, 16 mm, 53 min. (Alert Bay, BC: U'mista Cultural Society, 1975), cited in Cole and Chaikin's bibliography (222).
37 Daisy Sewid-Smith, *Persecution or Prosecution* (Cape Mudge, BC: Nu-Yum-Balees, 1979), 55-7.
38 Tina Loo, "Dan Cranmer's Potlatch: Law as Coercion, Symbol and Rhetoric in British Columbia, 1884-1951," *Canadian Historical Review* 68, 2 (1992): 159-60.
39 Ibid.
40 Ibid.
41 Ibid.
42 For example, in 1914 Johnny Bagwany and Ned Harris had been given suspended sentences. Cessahollis of Kingcome Inlet was given a suspended sentence the following year. Likiosa (Johnnie Seaweed) and Kwosteetsas (Japanese Charlie) received the minimum penalty in 1919 but were released after their employers, BC Packers, provided bail bonds for $1,000 each. The posting of two RCMP officers in Alert Bay late in 1919 resulted in eight people being sent to Burnaby's Oakalla Prison over the next two years. One of these people was Charles Nowell, who was released on probation after six weeks. See Cole and Chaikin, *An Iron Hand*, 108-18.
43 Loo, "Dan Cranmer's Potlatch," 120.
44 Quoted in Sewid-Smith, *Persecution or Prosecution*, 47.
45 Cole and Chaikin, *An Iron Hand*, 108-18.

46 Sewid-Smith, *Persecution or Prosecution*, 4.
47 Ibid., 4-6.
48 Cole and Chaikin, *An Iron Hand*, 122.
49 Douglas Cole, *Captured Heritage: The Scramble for Northwest Coast Artifacts* (Vancouver: Douglas and McIntyre, 1985; rpt. UBC Press, 1995), 71.
50 Nicholas Thomas, *Colonialism's Culture: Anthropology, Travel and Government* (Princeton: Princeton University Press, 1994), 4.
51 Goldman, *Mouth of Heaven*, 107.
52 Bill Holm, *Smoky-Top: The Art and Times of Willie Seaweed* (Vancouver: Douglas and McIntyre, 1983), 94-117.
53 Ki-ke-in (Ron Hamilton), "Box of Darkness," in *In Celebration of Our Survival: The First Nations of British Columbia*, ed. Doreen Jensen and Cheryl Brooks (Vancouver: UBC Press, 1991), 63. Hamilton makes a point similar to that made by Martine Reid when she talks about "a sign without a signifier," although the former is writing of the masks being relocated to museums and attributes the loss of meaning to the workings of non-Aboriginal anthropologists and curators. See "In Search of Things Past, Remembered, Retraced, and Reinvented," in Canadian Museum of Civilization, *In the Shadow of the Sun: Perspectives on Contemporary Native Art* (Ottawa: Canadian Ethnology Service, Mercury Series Paper 124, 1993), 76.
54 Annie E. Coombes, *Reinventing Africa: Museums, Material Culture and Popular Imagination in Late Victorian and Edwardian England* (New Haven and London: Yale University Press, 1994), 214.
55 Ibid., 109.
56 Cole, *Captured Heritage*, 251.
57 Quoted in Sewid-Smith, *Persecution or Prosecution*, 75.
58 See Barbeau, "The Potlatch."
59 Coombes, *Reinventing Africa*, 111-12.
60 Cole and Chaikin, *An Iron Hand*, 122-3.
61 Edward Sapir to Duncan Campbell Scott, 29 January 1923, from Canadian Museum of Civilization, Sapir Correspondence, box 429, file 58.
62 W.M. Halliday, *Potlatch and Totem and the Recollections of an Indian Agent* (London and Toronto: J.M. Dent, 1935), 192-3.
63 Through the 1920s a number of government actions attacked any deviation from the concept of a core British Canadian identity. The federal government enacted the Chinese Immigration Act, 1923, which virtually halted Chinese immigration until after the Second World War. The imposition of mandatory schooling saw the burning of nine schools in British Columbia between 1923 and 1925, and the provincial government's invocation of the Infants Act, 1929, enabled it to seize Doukhobor children as wards of the state. See John P.S. McLaren, "'New Canadians' or 'Slaves of Satan'? The Law and the Education of Doukhobor Children, 1911-1935," unpublished document, November 1994. In an order in council, the federal government also prohibited the entry of Doukhobors, Mennonites, and Hutterites because of the "peculiar customs, habits, modes of life and method of holding property, and because of their probable inability to become readily assimilated or to assume the duties and responsibilities of Canadian citizenship within a reasonable time after their entry." Quoted in Valerie Knowles, *Strangers at Our Gates: Canadian Immigration and Immigration Policy, 1540-1990* (Toronto: Dundurn Press, 1992), 100.
64 Duncan Campbell Scott to Edward Sapir, 9 October 1922, from Canadian Museum of Civilization, Sapir Correspondence, box 429, file 58.
65 Edward Sapir to Duncan Campbell Scott, 29 January 1923, from Canadian Museum of Civilization, Sapir Correspondence, box 429, file 58.
66 Cole, *Captured Heritage*, 254.
67 Duncan Campbell Scott to Edward Sapir, 17 March 1923, from Canadian Museum of Civilization, Sapir Correspondence, box 429, file 58.
68 Given this description, it is more likely that this was an echo or *Sopali* mask. Referred to as "dialogue masks" by Hawthorn, these "carried on a light banter and humorous conversation with each other and with the spectators ... Some of these *Sopali* masks, and all

of the echo masks, were fitted with sets of wooden mouthpieces representing different characters." See Audrey Hawthorn, *Art of the Kwakiutl Indians and Other Northwest Coast Tribes* (Seattle: University of Washington Press, 1967), 283.

69 Cole, *Captured Heritage*, 253.

70 "List of potlatch paraphernalia surrendered at Alert Bay and shipped to Ottawa," from Canadian Museum of Civilization, Sapir Correspondence, box 429, file 58.

71 Edward Sapir to Duncan Campbell Scott, 14 May 1923, from Canadian Museum of Civilization, Sapir Correspondence, box 429, file 58.

72 Secretary to the Deputy to Edward Sapir, 16 May 1923, from Canadian Museum of Civilization, Sapir Correspondence, box 429, file 58.

73 Stan Dragland, *Floating Voice: Duncan Campbell Scott and the Literature of Treaty 9* (Concord, ON: Anansi, 1994), 5.

74 Thomas, *Colonialism's Culture*, 2-3.

75 Cole and Chaikin, *An Iron Hand*, 125.

76 Margaret Ormsby, *British Columbia: A History* (Toronto: Macmillan, 1958), 439-69.

77 Boas reports that "grease feasts are given in order to destroy the prestige of the rival." See Boas, *Kwakiutl Ethnography*, 96.

78 Sewid-Smith, *Persecution or Prosecution*, 63.

79 Cole and Chaikin, *An Iron Hand*, 122.

80 Drucker and Heizer, *To Make My Name Good*, 33.

81 Ibid., 147.

82 See Phil Nuytten, *The Totem Carvers: Charlie James, Ellen Neel and Mungo Martin* (Vancouver: Panorama Publications, 1982); and Bill Holm, *Smoky-Top*.

83 Aldona Jonaitis, *From the Land of the Totem Poles: The Northwest Coast Indian Art Collection at the American Museum of Natural History* (New York/Vancouver and Toronto: American Museum of Natural History/Douglas and McIntyre, 1991), 71-3.

84 Art, Historical, and Scientific Association of Vancouver Directors Meeting, 4 May 1926, CAV Add. MSS. 336.

85 Brian Titley, *A Narrow Vision: Duncan Campbell Scott and the Administration of Indian Affairs* (Vancouver: UBC Press, 1986), 204.

Chapter 3: Totem Poles in Stanley Park

1 Douglas Cole, *Captured Heritage: The Scramble for Northwest Coast Artifacts* (Vancouver and Toronto: Douglas and McIntyre, 1985; rpt. UBC Press, 1995).

2 John Oliver, the province's Liberal premier, had built his administration on the expansion of British Columbia's road network, which emanated outward from Vancouver. Through the early 1920s the provincial revenues rose through the sale of motor and liquor licences. The recently completed South Okanagan irrigation project spurred on increases in fruit revenues, while the fisheries and lumber industries were booming due to geographic and technological expansion and diversification. See Dianne Newell, *Tangled Webs of History: Indians and the Law in Canada's Pacific Coast Fisheries* (Toronto: University of Toronto Press, 1993), 98; and Walter Hardwick, *Geography of the Forest Industry of Coastal British Columbia* (Vancouver: Canadian Association of Geographers, Occasional Papers in Geography, 1963), 1-15.

3 Originally government reserve land, the 1,000 acres of parkland was, with the 1886 announcement that Port Moody was to be the terminus for the transcontinental Canadian Pacific Railway (CPR), considered too far removed from the original town of Granville (centred to the east along Burrard Inlet in what is now the city's Gastown neighbourhood) to be of any value. Steele believes that the city council's petition to create the park when the area lacked adequate docks, roads, schools, and health facilities was part of a ploy to ensure low land prices until the CPR moved its terminus to Vancouver and adjacent to the park land, thus guaranteeing high profits for the landowners between Granville and the park. Stanley Park was officially opened in September 1888. See Mike Steele, *Stanley Park* (Surrey: Heritage House, 1993), 12-15.

4 While the area north of Point Grey is generally identified as Squamish territory, Wayne Suttles suggests that, prior to 1850, Capilano, Mission, Seymour Creek, False Creek, and Lumberman's Arch may have been Musqueam (who are downriver Halkomelem). See Wayne

Suttles, "Central Coast Salish," in *Handbook of North American Indians,* vol. 7, *Northwest Coast,* ed. Wayne Suttles (Washington, DC: Smithsonian Institution, 1990), 455. This confusion is exacerbated by the forceable removal of XwayXway residents from Lumberman's Arch in the late 1880s and the consequent probable movement of people both north and south.

5 Steele, *Stanley Park,* 47-50.

6 Ibid.

7 XwayXway – variously spelled whoi-whoi, sxwaysway, sxwayxwey, xwexwe, and qwee-qwee – is an important cleansing ceremony among the Salish peoples. Normally, it is the ritual property of a kin group and is performed by two or more young men wearing distinctive costumes and masks. See Suttles, "Central Coast Salish," 468.

8 This is likely an anglicized variant of XwayXway.

9 Steele, *Stanley Park,* 47-50.

10 Robert A.J. McDonald, *Making Vancouver: Class, Status, and Social Boundaries* (Vancouver: UBC Press, 1996), 166.

11 Ibid., 169.

12 "Mawson offered three plans: one to retain a tree-fringed waterline on the north side of a lagoon at the park entrance; another, far more utilitarian than the first, to create playgrounds for children and playing fields for adults by filling the upper end of Coal Harbour; and a third, designed in the 'Grand Manner,' to feature three majestic neoclassical buildings surrounding a circular pond. At the centre was to be a statue atop a 'great shaft.'" See McDonald, *Making Vancouver,* 170.

13 Ibid., 168.

14 Art, Historical, and Scientific Association of Vancouver Constitution, 1894, CAV Add. MSS. 336.

15 Minutes from AHSAV Annual Meeting, 25 January 1921, CAV Add. MSS. 336.

16 Ibid.

17 AHSAV Annual Meeting Minutes, January 1923, CAV Add. MSS. 336.

18 Charlie James was born Charles Jameson in Port Townsend, Washington, around 1867. His father, Thomas Jameson, was an Anglo-American sawmill operator. His mother, 'Kugwisi'la'ogwa, was Kwakwa̲ka̲'wakw from Fort Rupert. She died when James was ten years old, and he was raised by his maternal grandmother in Victoria and Fort Rupert. When he was young, an accidental shotgun discharge left him with only the thumb and the major part of his forefinger on his left hand. This physical impairment prevented his participation in the forestry and fishing industries, and he was thus one of the few full-time Kwakwa̲ka̲'wakw carvers, producing canoes and poles, masks and other work for both the potlatch system and the curio market. Around 1895 he married Sara Nina in a Kwakwaka'wakw ceremony in Fort Rupert. Sara Nina had four sons from a previous marriage to 'Yax'nukwalas, (known to Euro-Canadians simply as Martin), including Herbert and Spruce Martin, important participants in the Cranmer potlatch, and Mungo Martin, who James taught how to carve. See Phil Nuytten, *The Totem Carvers: Charlie James, Ellen Neel and Mungo Martin* (Vancouver: Panorama Publications, 1982), 13-15.

19 Ibid., 29.

20 Of the three poles used for Curtis's outside set on Deer Island, two are now at the University of British Columbia's Museum of Anthropology. The third may or may not be in Stanley Park. Holm and Quimby suggest that the pole in the Curtis film was a copy of the one now in the park: "Whether it exists today is not known, but it was a magnificent one, inspired by the great Raven pole of Wakyas, the first fully carved tall pole at Alert Bay, which now stands extensively restored in Vancouver's Stanley Park. The Raven frontal pole at Deer Island was probably made for the film (it doesn't appear in any photographs of Fort Rupert or other villages), and it seems to be newly carved and painted in Curtis' pictures." The two houseposts appear in a number of interior shots in the film as well. Citing the Hunt ledgers given to George Hunt, Holm and Quimby suggest that George Hunt purchased them for Curtis in Fort Rupert on 16 June 1913 for $90.50 and $75.00. See Bill Holm and George Irving Quimby, *Edward S. Curtis in the Land of the War Canoes: A Pioneer Cinematographer in the Pacific Northwest* (Vancouver: Douglas and McIntyre, 1980). Nuytten reports that Ellen

Neel, James's granddaughter and a well recognized carver in her own right, had said that the owner of the houseposts "lived in Alert Bay and refused to sell the poles, but offered to rent them out instead ... Ellen laughed as she related how 'Old –' had boasted for years of the fine bargain he had made. He not only got the agreed rental payment, but also a brand new paint job – by Charlie James – paid for by the film maker." See Nuytten, *Totem Carvers,* 29. Although Nuytten confesses that he cannot remember the name of the houseposts' owner, presumably it was Tsa-wee-nok.

21 Ibid.

22 The story of Se-wid is repeated in Nuytten, *Totem Carvers,* 30.

23 S.W.A. Gunn, *A Complete Guide to the Totem Poles in Stanley Park, Vancouver, B.C.* (Vancouver: W.E.G. MacDonald, 1965), 19. Transcribed as Qolos by Goldman, this figure is sometimes described as the brother of Thunderbird. See Irving Goldman, *The Mouth of Heaven: An Introduction to Kwakiutl Religious Thought* (New York: John Wiley and Sons, 1975), 76.

24 Gunn, *Totem Poles,* 19.

25 Nuytten, *Totem Carvers,* 30.

26 Gunn supports this by stating that Ellen Neel presented him with a small carved "sea egg" as a wedding gift. See Gunn, *Totem Poles,* 19.

27 Ibid., 30.

28 Ibid., 15.

29 "Great Ancestor of Chief Wakias. In 1893, at a great potlatch ... on Turnour Island, Wakias dedicated a miniature model of the mythical Speakers Staff of the Wise Man. Since then the pole has come to be known as Wakias' Talking Stick, telling the legend of Nan-wa-kawie and his sons outwitting the Great Cannibal." See Gunn, *Totem Poles,* 16.

30 One of the Kwakwa̱ka̱'wakw birds of heaven; more recently Bill Holm spells it *huxwhukw.* See Bill Holm, *Smoky-Top: The Art and Times of Willie Seaweed* (Vancouver and Toronto: Douglas and McIntyre, 1983), 94.

31 Gunn, *Totem Poles,* 15-7.

32 Ibid.

33 Franz Boas, *Kwakiutl Culture as Reflected in Mythology* (New York: American Folk-lore Society, 1935), 2

34 Ibid., 2.

35 Ibid., 3.

36 Codere writes: "Fort Rupert maintained its central position until about 1900, when it was superseded by Alert Bay as the centre for the people of Queen Charlotte Strait. Alert Bay had its start in 1870, when two White men established a salmon cannery there and sought Indian labour. In 1877 the Reverend A.J. Hall began to work at Fort Rupert but soon moved to Alert Bay. By 1881 he had a school there and a home large enough to accommodate several young girls taught 'domestic duties' by his wife, and by 1888 he had built a sawmill to provide employment and lumber for single-family houses. In 1881 the federal government established a Kwawkewlth Agency at Fort Rupert, but this too moved to Alert Bay. In 1894 the Department of Indian Affairs opened an industrial school for boys at Alert Bay ... Meanwhile, Mrs. Hall's program had grown into a residential school for girls ... The Kwakiutl were also becoming assimilated into the Canadian economy and dependent on money income. This development led to a period of great prosperity between 1900 and the mid-1920s. Wealth became widespread, primarily because the old organization of production, knowledge of local resources, and industrious habits fit the new opportunities offered." See Helen Codere, "Kwakiutl," in *Handbook of North American Indians,* vol. 7, *Northwest Coast,* ed. Wayne Suttles (Washington, DC: Smithsonian Institution, 1990), 365.

37 The most common form of Central Coast Salish monumental sculpture was the housepost depicting "mythical creatures associated with family history, notable ancestors, events which displayed ancestors' spirit powers, or magical privileges of the family. They faced into the large winter houses declaiming to occupants and guests alike the long history, wealth, and high status of the family." See J.E. Michael Kew, *Sculpture and Engraving of the Central Coast Salish Indians* (Vancouver: University of British Columbia Museum of Anthropology Museum Note No. 9, 1980), n.p.

38 Renato Rosaldo, "Imperialist Nostalgia," *Representations* 26 (Spring 1989): 116.

39 Ibid.

40 According to Helen Codere, *Fighting with Property: A Study of Kwakiutl Potlatching and Warfare, 1792-1930* (New York: J.J. Augustin, 1951), 88: "These 'private' potlatches were a relatively late development as a means of continuing potlatching in the face of the law. It is exceptionally interesting that a written record seems to have made 'private' potlatches possible, since one of the functions of publicity in this non-literate society had always been to make important transactions like potlatch distributions a matter of record before many witnesses."

41 Codere, "Kwakiutl," 364, reports that "Kwakiutl prosperity suffered a setback in the 1920s with the difficulty of financing power boats (introduced in 1911). Difficulties lasted through the Depression but prosperity was restored by the boom in the fishing industry during World War II."

42 Boas, *Kwakiutl Culture*, 2.

43 Codere, *Fighting with Property*, 88.

44 Holm, *Smoky-Top*, 29.

45 Jonaitis writes that Boas and Swanton, "despite their conscious intentions to celebrate Indian art and promote the equality of all races, nevertheless ended up contributing to the design of an invented culture and reinforcing a process in which the display of Indian art functions in a larger context of major ideological significance that had less to do with Native Americans than with communicating the power, authority, and dominance of the elite class – largely to immigrant workers." See Aldona Jonaitis, "Franz Boas, John Swanton, and the New Haida Sculpture at the American Museum of Natural History," in *The Early Years of Native American Art History: The Politics of Scholarship and Collecting*, ed. Janet Catherine Berlo (Seattle/Vancouver: University of Washington Press/UBC Press, 1992), 23.

46 Boas's field assistant, George Hunt, was willing to build the facsimile village for a salary of $150 per month. See AHSAV Directors' Meeting Minutes, 22 March 1923, CAV Add. MSS. 336.

47 AHSAV Annual Meeting Minutes, January 1924, CAV Add. MSS. 336.

48 John C. Goodfellow, *The Totem Poles in Stanley Park, Vancouver* (Vancouver: Art, Historical, and Scientific Association of Vancouver, n.d.), 15.

49 Paul Tennant, *Aboriginal Peoples and Politics: The Indian Land Question in British Columbia, 1849-1989* (Vancouver: UBC Press, 1992), 89, 94, and 120.

50 AHSAV Directors' Meeting Minutes, 9 October 1925, CAV Add. MSS. 336.

51 Ibid.

52 Ibid.

53 Ibid.

54 Steele, *Stanley Park*, 32 and 50-1.

55 Gunn, *Totem Poles*, 13.

56 AHSAV Annual Meeting Minutes, January 1924, CAV Add. MSS. 336.

57 Rosalind C. Morris, *New Worlds from Fragments: Film, Ethnography and the Representation of Northwest Coast Cultures* (Boulder, CO: Westview Press, 1994), 55.

Chapter 4: Northwest Coast Art as National Heritage

1 Edward L. Keithahn, *Monuments in Cedar* (Ketchikan, AL: Roy Anderson, 1945), 128.

2 Douglas Cole, *Captured Heritage: The Scramble for Northwest Coast Artifacts* (Vancouver and Toronto: Douglas and McIntyre, 1985; rpt. UBC Press, 1995), 228.

3 Ibid., 229.

4 Ibid.

5 Ibid., 228-31.

6 Ibid., 267.

7 See Charles Marius Barbeau, "The Indians of the Prairies and the Rockies: A Theme for Modern Painters," *University of Toronto Quarterly* 1, 2 (1932); and "Backgrounds in Canadian Art," *Proceedings and Transactions of the Royal Society of Canada*, 3rd ser., 35 (1941).

8 John Murray Gibbon, *Canadian Mosaic: The Making of a Northern Nation* (Toronto: McClelland and Stewart, 1938), vii.

9 Charles Marius Barbeau, "I was a Pioneer," *Oracle* 44 (1982): n.p.

10 Robert Bothwell, Ian Drummond, and John English, *Canada 1900-1945* (Toronto: University of Toronto Press, 1987), 229-39.
11 Angus McLaren, *Our Own Master Race: Eugenics in Canada, 1885-1945* (Toronto: McClelland and Stewart, 1990), 46.
12 Clifford Sifton, minister of the interior from 1896 to 1905, announced an "open door" immigration policy that led to an immigration wave that ended in 1913. While the federal government sought specifically British agricultural immigrants, their lack of success forced the relaxation of ethnically based immigration quotas. "Our desire," said Sifton in 1901, "is to promote the immigration of farmers and farm labourers. We have not been disposed to exclude foreigners of any nationality who seemed likely to become successful agriculturalists." See Valerie Knowles, *Strangers at Our Gates: Canadian Immigration and Immigration Policy, 1540-1990* (Toronto: Dundurn Press, 1992), 58-9.
13 Quoted in Patricia E. Roy, "British Columbia's Fear of Asians, 1900-1950," *Histoire Sociale/ Social History* 13, 25: 162.
14 William Halliday to J.D. McLean, 8 December 1921, from Indian Affairs, Black Series, reel C-10185, vol. 4086, file 507787.
15 Charles Stewart to Arthur Conan Doyle, 29 August 1924, from Indian Affairs, Black Series, reel C-10185, vol. 4086, file 507787.
16 Ann Morrison, "Canadian Art and Cultural Appropriation: Emily Carr and the Exhibition of West Coast Art, Native and Modern" (MA thesis, University of British Columbia, 1991), 94.
17 Ibid., 94.
18 Cole, *Captured Heritage*, 271-3.
19 *Daily Colonist*, 19 July 1929, 2.
20 When the Grand Trunk Pacific Railway first drew up plans for Prince Rupert and the Skeena rail line, it claimed Prince Rupert as the best natural harbour on the entire Pacific coast. It was two days closer to the Orient than either Vancouver or San Francisco and, thus, between its train and steamship lines, gave the railway claim to the shortest round-the-world route. Promotional material recounted glowing reports of the possibilities for fishing and logging industries along the coast and for farming in the interior. Landscape architects Brett and Hall of Boston were hired to make Prince Rupert the most beautiful city in North America. See Phylis Bowman, *Whistling through the Wind* (Prince Rupert: P. Bowman, 1980).
21 Cole, *Captured Heritage*, 272.
22 Harlan Smith, quoted in Cole, *Captured Heritage*, 271.
23 Bothwell et al., *Canada 1900-1945*, 179.
24 Cole, *Captured Heritage*, 272.
25 C. Marius Barbeau, *The Downfall of Temlaham* (Toronto: Macmillan, 1928). See also, Maureen Cassidy, "The Skeena River Uprising of 1888," *British Columbia Historical News* 16, 3 (Spring 1983).
26 Harlan I. Smith to Duncan Campbell Scott, 11 November 1925, from Indian Affairs, Black Series, RG10, vol. 4086, file 507787-2.
27 Collins to Scott, 19 March 1932.
28 Edward Sapir, quoting Harlan I. Smith, to Duncan Campbell Scott, 15 June 1925, from Indian Affairs, Black Series, RG10, vol. 4086, file 507787-2.
29 Harlan I. Smith, "Restoration of Totem Poles in British Columbia," in *National Museum of Canada Annual Report for 1926* (Ottawa: King's Printer, 1928).
30 Ibid.
31 Ibid.
32 Ibid.
33 Harlan I. Smith, field report, Kitwanga, 22 July 1925, 4, Canadian Museum of Civilization, Sapir Correspondence, box 429, file 83.
34 Harlan I. Smith, field reports, Hazelton, 15 June 1925, 1-3; and Kitwanga, 22 July 1925, 1-5, Canadian Museum of Civilization, Sapir Correspondence, box 429, file 83.
35 Diamond Jenness to Duncan Campbell Scott, 8 and 10 April 1926; Duncan Campbell Scott to Diamond Jenness, 9 April 1926, from Canadian Museum of Civilization, Sapir Correspondence, box 432, file 34.

36 Duncan Campbell Scott to Diamond Jenness, 9 April 1926, from Canadian Museum of Civilization, Sapir Correspondence, box 432, file 34.
37 Chief Seamadaks to Harlan I. Smith, 7 October 1926; Harlan I. Smith to Duncan Campbell Scott, 10 November 1926 and 21 July 1926; Duncan Campbell Scott to Chief Seamadaks, 15 November 1926; and Duncan Campbell Scott to North West Biscuit Company, 22 July 1926, from Indian Affairs, Black Series, reel C-10186, vol. 4086, file 507787-2.
38 Diamond Jenness to Duncan Campbell Scott, 28 April 1926; Duncan Campbell Scott to Diamond Jenness, 26 April 1926 and 5 May 1926, from Canadian Museum of Civilization, Sapir Correspondence, box 432, file 34.
39 Ibid.
40 Cole, *Captured Heritage*, 278.
41 Report of Royal Canadian Mounted Police Constable T.E.E. Greenfield, Kitwanga, 10 October 1928, and 29 November 1928 (statement of Ada Fowler), from Indian Affairs, Black Series, reel C-10186, vol. 4086, file 507787-2.
42 Edgar Hyde to Duncan Campbell Scott, 31 January 1929, from Indian Affairs, Black Series, reel C-10186, vol. 4086, file 507787-2.
43 Duncan Campbell Scott to Edgar Hyde, 9 January 1929, from Indian Affairs, Black Series, reel C-10186, vol. 4086, file 507787-2.
44 Paul Tennant, *Aboriginal Peoples and Politics: The Indian Land Question, 1849-1989* (Vancouver: UBC Press, 1992), 157.
45 W. Langdon Kihn, an American, had twelve canvases, mostly portraits, included in the National Gallery's 1927 *Exhibition of Canadian West Coast Art, Native and Modern*. Kihn had gone to the Skeena in 1924 with Barbeau and stayed in Kitwancool for nine months. Morrison suggests that the original impetus for the exhibition was Barbeau's idea of exhibiting Kihn's paintings alongside Northwest Coast objects, an idea that was then expanded by Eric Brown and the gallery's board of trustees to include Canadian painters. See Morrison, "Canadian Art and Cultural Appropriation," 12-28.
46 Cole, *Captured Heritage*, 275.
47 Edgar Hyde to Duncan Campbell Scott, 25 June 1927, from Indian Affairs, Black Series, reel C-10186, vol. 4086, file 507787-2.
48 Cole, *Captured Heritage*, 275.
49 Edgar Hyde to Duncan Campbell Scott, 31 January 1929, from Indian Affairs, Black Series, reel C-10186, vol. 4086, file 507787-2.
50 Cole, *Captured Heritage*, 268-9.
51 Ibid., 269.
52 Marius Barbeau to Duncan Campbell Scott, 1 May 1930, from Indian Affairs, Black Series, reel C-10186, vol. 4086, file 507787-2.
53 G.C. Mortimer to Duncan Campbell Scott, 3 December 1930, from Indian Affairs, Black Series, reel C-10186, vol. 4086, file 507787-2.
54 Cole, *Captured Heritage*, 276.
55 Ibid., 269.
56 Rosalind C. Morris, *New Worlds from Fragments: Film, Ethnography and the Representation of Northwest Coast Cultures* (Boulder, CO: Westview Press, 1994), 66-77.
57 Ibid.
58 Ibid., 69.
59 Ibid.
60 Ibid., 55.
61 Cole, *Captured Heritage*, 276-7.
62 The National Museum's annual report of 1926-27 states that "nine of the best examples of British Columbia native carvings were lent to the National Gallery for exhibition at Paris, France, with the Wembley collection of Canadian paintings."
63 Diamond Jenness to Duncan Campbell Scott, 25 March 1927, from Canadian Museum of Civilization, Jenness Correspondence, box 432, file 34.
64 Translated and quoted in *Annual Report of the Board of Trustees for the Fiscal Year 1927-28* (Ottawa: National Gallery of Canada, 1928), 14.
65 Daniel Miller, "Primitive Art and the Necessity of Primitivism to Art," in *The Myth of Primitivism: Perspectives on Art*, ed. Susan Hiller (London and New York: Routledge, 1991), 58.

66 Bothwell et al., *Canada 1900-1945*, 229-44.

67 This exhibition is also discussed in Diana Nemiroff, "Modernism, Nationalism and Beyond: A Critical History of Exhibitions of First Nations Art," in *Land, Spirit, Power: First Nations Art at the National Gallery of Canada*, ed. Diana Nemiroff, Robert Houle, and Charlotte Townsend-Gault (Ottawa: National Gallery of Canada, 1992), 15-41.

68 National Museum of Canada, *Annual Report* 1927-28.

69 Emily Carr, *Hundreds and Thousands: The Journals of Emily Carr* (Toronto and Vancouver: Clarke, Irwin and Company, 1966), 11-12.

70 Ibid., 12.

71 Ibid., 9-12.

72 Ibid.

73 Eric Brown, in National Gallery of Canada, *Exhibition of Canadian West Coast Art, Native and Modern* (Ottawa: National Gallery of Canada, 1927), 3.

74 Franz Boas, *Primitive Art* (Cambridge, MA: Harvard University Press, 1927; rpt. New York: Dover Publications, 1955).

75 Barbeau, in National Gallery of Canada, *Exhibition of Canadian West Coast Art,* 80.

76 Marianna Torgovnick, *Gone Primitive: Savage Intellects, Modern Lives* (Chicago and London: University of Chicago Press, 1990), 83.

77 National Gallery of Canada, *Exhibition of Canadian West Coast Art*, 7.

78 Ibid., 4.

79 Ibid.

80 Ibid., 9.

81 Ibid., 11.

82 Ibid. The description of a competition between Edenshaw and his "faithful Tlingit slave" does not appear anywhere else in the literature, including, most significantly, Margaret B. Blackman, *During My Time: Florence Edenshaw Davidson, a Haida Woman* (Seattle: University of Washington Press, 1982).

83 Bill Holm, "Will the Real Charles Edenshaw Please Stand Up? The Problem of Attribution in Northwest Coast Indian Art," in *The World Is as Sharp as a Knife: An Anthology in Honour of Wilson Duff*, ed. Donald Abbott (Victoria: British Columbia Provincial Museum, 1981), 177.

84 Aldona Jonaitis, "Franz Boas, John Swanton, and the New Haida Sculpture at the American Museum of Natural History," in *The Early Years of Native American Art History: The Politics of Scholarship and Collecting*, ed. Janet Catherine Berlo (Seattle/Vancouver: University of Washington Press/UBC Press, 1992), 22-61.

85 Boas, *Primitive Art*, 158, 193, 201, 212, and 275.

86 National Gallery of Canada, *Exhibition of Canadian West Coast Art*, 13.

87 Ibid., 13.

88 See Marius Barbeau, "Frederick Alexie: A Primitive," *Canadian Review of Music and Art* 3, 11 and 12 (1945): 19-22. Barbeau received his information in a letter from William Benyon dated 17 November 1944 and now found in the Barbeau Northwest Coast Files at the Centre for the Study of Canadian Folklore, Canadian Museum of Civilization (Reference: B-F-159.4). Alexie is also discussed in Ronald W. Hawker, "Frederick Alexie: Euro-Canadian Discussions of a First Nations Artist," *Canadian Journal of Native Studies* 11, 2 (1991): 229-52; and Deidre (Tedds) Simmons, "History of Contemporary Canadian Indian Art," *European Review of Native American Studies* 5, 1 (1991).

89 Ibid.

90 Viola Garfield, "Wood Carving and Painting," unpublished manuscript, August-September 1934, 102. This manuscript was forwarded to me by George MacDonald, director of the Canadian Museum of Civilization, who identified the source for the paper as the University of Washington Archives.

91 Alexie is variously spelled "Alexcee," "Alexei," "Alexee," and "Alexie" in both published texts and museum files.

92 National Gallery of Canada, *Exhibition of Canadian West Coast Art*, 13.

93 Barbeau, "Frederick Alexie," 21.

94 National Gallery, *Exhibition of Canadian West Coast Art*, 13.

95 Ibid., 13.

96 Morrison, "Canadian Art and Cultural Appropriation," 65.

Chapter 5: The New Deals

1 Brian Titley, *A Narrow Vision: Duncan Campbell Scott and the Administration of Indian Affairs* (Vancouver: UBC Press, 1986), 78-83.

2 Helen Codere, *Fighting with Property: A Study of Kwakiutl Potlatching and Warfare, 1792-1930* (New York: J.J. Augustin, 1951), 20-1.

3 Duncan Campbell Scott, "Indian Place-Names," in *Powassan's Drum: Poems of Duncan Campbell Scott*, eds. Raymond Souster and Douglas Lochhead (Ottawa: Tecumseh Press, 1985), 17.

4 Marius Barbeau, *Totem Poles of the Gitksan, Upper Skeena River, British Columbia* (Ottawa: National Museum of Canada Bulletin 61, Anthropological Series, no. 12, 1929), 1.

5 Diamond Jenness, quoted in Ann Morrison, "Canadian Art and Cultural Appropriation: Emily Carr and the Exhibition of West Coast Art, Native and Modern" (MA thesis, University of British Columbia, 1991), 23.

6 Ibid.

7 Edward L. Keithahn, *Monuments in Cedar* (Ketchikan, AL: Roy Anderson, 1945), 119.

8 Ibid.

9 Ibid.

10 Marius Barbeau, *Totem Poles*, vol. 1 (Ottawa: Canadian Museum of Civilization, 1990), 403-4.

11 Keithahn, *Monuments in Cedar*, 120.

12 Ibid., 120.

13 Ibid., 120-2.

14 Molly Mullin argues that the Southwest became the focal point of American cultural nationalists because it was where they "were most apt to encounter Indians, [and because it] held promising possibilities for remapping the geography and aesthetics of American identity – away from Europe and from colonial New England – by virtue of monuments of comparable antiquity and landscapes, commodities, and people appearing startlingly unique." See Molly M. Mullin, "The Patronage of Difference: Making Indian Art 'Art, Not Ethnology,'" in *The Traffic in Culture: Refiguring Art and Anthropology*, ed. George E. Marcus and Fred R. Myers (Berkeley and Los Angeles: University of California Press, 1995), 169.

15 Robert Fay Schrader, *The Indian Arts and Crafts Board: An Aspect of New Deal Indian Policy* (Albuquerque, NM: University of New Mexico Press, 1983).

16 Ibid., 3.

17 J.J. Brody, *Indian Painters and White Patrons* (Albuquerque, NM: University of New Mexico Press, 1971); and "Pueblo Fine Arts," *Handbook*, vol. 9, *Southwest*, ed. Alfonso Ortiz (Washington, DC: Smithsonian Institution, 1979).

18 Ruth Roessel, "Navajo Arts and Crafts," in *Handbook of North American Indians*, vol. 10, *Southwest*, ed. Alfonso Ortiz (Washington, DC: Smithsonian Institution, 1983).

19 William Jackson Rushing, "Native American Art and Culture and the New York Avant-garde, 1910-1950" (PhD diss., University of Texas at Austin, 1989).

20 Brian W. Dippie, *The Vanishing American: White Attitudes and United States Indian Policy* (Middletown, CT: Wesleyan University Press, 1982), 285.

21 As Ellis W. Hawley explains, one of the legacies of the New Deal "was the rapid rise of an organizational economy, which brought with it large areas of 'private government,' new bureaucratic-scientific-professional values, and a persistent search for order and stability, primarily through the creation of ever larger associative and hierarchic structures, the infusing of these with a new set of managerial attitudes and group loyalties, and the use of the state, where necessary and expedient, to further the process ... The other major aspect of the ... New Deal was the expansion and nationalization of social services, exemplified particularly in the Social Security Act, the work relief program, the housing and conservation activities, and the protective labour and rural rehabilitation measures. In one sense now, 'welfare capitalism,' community-centred welfare, and the patronage-oriented welfare were all giving way to a larger and broader 'welfare statism.' Yet again, significant as this change was, the patterns adopted worked in some respects to strengthen rather than displace existing institutions." See Ellis W. Hawley, "The New Deal and Business," in *The New Deal: The National Level*, ed. John Braeman, Robert H. Bremner, and David Brody (Columbus, OH: Ohio State University Press, 1975), 52 and 87.

22 John Braeman, Robert H. Bremner, and David Brody, "Introduction," in *New Deal,* x.
23 Dippie, *The Vanishing American,* 327-34.
24 Quoted in ibid., 325.
25 Polly Miller, *Lost Heritage of Alaska: The Adventure and Art of the Alaskan Coastal Indians* (Cleveland and New York: World Publishing Company, 1967), 253.
26 Ibid., 262.
27 Ibid.
28 Ibid., 253.
29 The exhibition is discussed in detail in W. Jackson Rushing's "Marketing the Affinity of the Primitive and the Modern: René d'Harnoncourt and 'Indian Art of the United States,'" in *The Early Years of Native American Art History: The Politics of Scholarship and Collecting,* ed. Janet Catherine Berlo (Seattle/Vancouver: University of Washington Press/UBC Press, 1992), 191-238.
30 Frederic H. Douglas and René d'Harnoncourt, *Indian Art of the United States* (New York: Museum of Modern Art, 1941), 15.
31 Very quickly the term "New Deal" became something of a political cliché in both the United States and Canada. T.W.L. MacDermot, writing in 1933, stated that the "principles of political organization and evolution ... constitute a real significance of the experiment for a studious Canada," including, specifically, the principle of unification. According to MacDermot: "The New Deal is based on a centralized, organic view of the national life, in which all its principal parts are to be organized and integrated for the common task of building a shattered society ... Canada is far from being a genuine national unity as yet, either in constitutional, economic, or political respects, and the utilization of this principle in all these respects could be of profound moment to the Dominion." See T.W.L. MacDermot, "The Significance for Canada of the American 'New Deal,'" in *The Dirty Thirties: Canadians in the Great Depression,* ed. Michiel Horn (Toronto: Copp Clark, 1972), 486. In 1935, in an unsuccessful bid for re-election, Canadian prime minister R.B. Bennett announced the failure of laissez-faire capitalism and introduced a reform package, which was instantly labelled a New Deal. See Michael Bliss, *Right Honourable Men: The Descent of Canadian Politics from MacDonald to Mulroney* (Toronto: Harper-Collins, 1994), 115. British Columbia premier T. Dufferin Pattullo also sought re-election in 1933 under a reform package he termed the "Little New Deal." See Margaret Ormsby, "T. Dufferin Pattullo and the Little New Deal," in Horn, *The Dirty Thirties,* 620-34.
32 Michiel Horn, *The Great Depression of the 1930s in Canada* (Ottawa: Canadian Historical Association Historical Booklet no. 39, 1984), 4-7.
33 Margaret Ormsby, *British Columbia: A History* (Toronto: Macmillan, 1958), 439-69.
34 Ibid., 469.
35 UBC MOA Parallel Accession Files.
36 Paul Tennant calls George Manuel "the pre-eminent leader of the peoples of the interior." See Paul Tennant, *Aboriginal Peoples and Politics: The Indian Land Question, 1849-1989* (Vancouver: UBC Press, 1992), 125. Manuel helped found the Aboriginal Native Rights Committee of the Interior Tribes of British Columbia in 1959 as well as the North American Indian Brotherhood in 1960, and he was an important member of the Native Brotherhood of British Columbia. See Tennant, *Aboriginal Peoples and Politics,* 127-32.
37 An ordained Methodist and later United Church minister, Peter Kelly was a leader in the Allied Tribes of British Columbia and the Native Brotherhood of British Columbia. See Tennant, *Aboriginal Peoples and Politics,* 77, 94, 117-29.
38 See G.H. Raley, "Important Considerations Involved in the Treatise on 'Canadian Indian Art and Industries,'" unpublished, n.d., PABC Raley Papers, HD R13 R13.3 (II).
39 See Gerald McMaster, "Tenuous Lines of Descent: Indian Art and Craft of the Reservation Period," in *In the Shadow of the Sun: Perspectives on Contemporary Native Art,* ed. Canadian Museum of Civilization (Ottawa: Canadian Ethnology Service, Mercury Series Paper 124, 1993), 93-120.
40 Ibid., 2.
41 Ibid., 36.
42 As Schrader, *The Indian Arts and Crafts Board,* 245, demonstrates, Raley had to be careful if he wanted to get the general public to accept his programs. Similarly, liberal reformers in

the United States were dismissed by New Deal opponents as enforcing "nothing more or less than communism as practiced in Soviet Russia."

43 George H. Raley to A.O.N. Daunt, Indian Agent, New Westminster, 4 May 1934, PABC Raley Papers.
44 Douglas and d'Harnoncourt, *Indian Art.*
45 Raley, "Important Considerations," 9.
46 Ibid., 6.
47 Ibid.
48 Ibid., 13.
49 Ibid., 10-11.
50 Ibid., 40.
51 Ibid., 23.
52 G.H. Raley to G.S. Matthews, correspondence dated 6 October 1934, PABC Raley Papers.
53 J.S. Matthews, "A Shameful Repudiation," 24 June 1945, VCA.
54 Ibid., 554.
55 Raley, "Canadian Indian Art and Industries," 992.
56 Ibid.
57 Ibid.
58 Ibid.
59 Ibid.
60 Ibid., 996.
61 Ibid., 997.
62 Ibid., 997-1001.
63 Raley, "Important Considerations," 50.
64 Between the wars, the call against the Japanese and their "devious" economic subversion of Canadian industries was an oft-cited racist cliché in British Columbia.
65 Raley, "Important Considerations," 50.

Chapter 6: Alice Ravenhill and the BCIAWS

1 Paul Tennant, *Aboriginal Peoples and Politics: The Indian Land Question, 1849-1989* (Vancouver: UBC Press, 1992), 39-52.
2 The Putnam-Weir Report released in 1925, for example, proposed a far-ranging series of reforms for education in British Columbia, some of which were implemented immediately and some of which took a decade to implement. See F. Henry Johnson, *A History of Public Education in British Columbia* (Vancouver: UBC Press, 1964), 101-15.
3 Titley writes: "Some of the more critical reinterpretations of Canadian educational history suggest that universal schooling made its appearance, not so much as an adjunct on onward marching democracy, but rather as an instrument of social control. Dominant groups perceived the school as an effective mechanism for fostering loyalty to the prevailing political, economic, and social order among less advantaged groups." See Brian Titley, *A Narrow Vision: Duncan Campbell Scott and the Administration of Indian Affairs* (Vancouver: UBC Press, 1986), 92.
4 Alice Ravenhill, *Alice Ravenhill: The Memoirs of an Educational Pioneer* (Toronto and Vancouver: J.M. Dent and Sons, 1951), 73.
5 Ibid.
6 Ibid.
7 The tension created by a racial hierarchy that privileged European accomplishments is illustrated here in the assignment of First Nations material to the realm of natural, as opposed to human, history.
8 Francis Kermode, *Report of the Provincial Museum of Natural History for the Year 1934* (Victoria: Provincial Museum of Natural History, 1934), H6.
9 Malcolm S. Knowles, *A History of the Adult Education Movement in the United States* (Malabar, FL: Robert E. Krieger Publishing, 1977), 130.
10 Ibid.
11 Ibid.
12 Ravenhill, *Memoirs*, 211.

13 Alice Ravenhill, *Native Tribes of British Columbia* (Victoria: C.R. Banfield, 1938), 10.
14 Ibid.
15 Ibid.
16 Jenness stayed with Ravenhill at her home at Shawnigan Lake on an early visit to Vancouver Island. See Ravenhill, *Memoirs*, 181.
17 Ravenhill, *Native Tribes*, 10.
18 Ibid.
19 Ibid.
20 Ibid.
21 Provincial Museum of Natural History, *Report of the Provincial Museum of Natural History for the Year 1945* (Victoria: Provincial Museum of Natural History, 1945), 7.
22 The temporal ranking of non-European societies in social evolutionist thinking and the prevalent view that non-industrial societies were doomed to extinction in the course of the "natural" progression from "primitive" to "modern" informed a Western scientific concern with "salvaging" the remnants of "primitive" peoples within the spaces of anthropology and anthropological museums. This concern is discussed in detail in James Clifford, *The Predicament of Culture: Twentieth Century Ethnography, Literature and Art* (Cambridge, MA: Harvard University Press, 1988).
23 The Society for the Furtherance of British Columbia Indian Arts and Welfare, *Objects of the Society* (Victoria: N.p., 1939). PABC BCIAWS Papers, Add. MSS. 2720.
24 Ravenhill, *Memoirs*, 216.
25 Ibid., 216-19.
26 Ibid.
27 Gordon Selman, "The Adult Educator: Change Agent or Program Technician?" *Canadian Journal of University Continuing Education* 9, 2 (1985).
28 In June 1948 a suggestion was put forward by the society for the sale of Aboriginal objects in national parks through the National Parks Service. See "Recommendations of the B.C. Indian Arts and Welfare Society," *Native Voice*, June 1948, 13.
29 Anthony Walsh, "Introduction," *The Tale of the Nativity as Told by the Indian Children of Inkameep* (Victoria: Society for the Furtherance of British Columbia Indian Arts and Welfare, 1942), 5.
30 Ravenhill, *Memoirs*, 216-17. Batiste and classmate Johnny Stalkia were singled out by Anthony Walsh as star students. Batiste had attended school in Santa Fe and, in the early 1940s, had exhibitions arranged through Walsh and the Okanagan chapter of the BCIAWS at the Windemere Hotel, the Vancouver Art Gallery, and an unspecified location in Victoria. See PABC, BCIAWS Papers, Add. MSS. 2720, Anthony Walsh to Elizabeth Newton, 18 February 940; *Brief Statement of the Efforts and Attainments since Formation December 1939* (Victoria: BCIAWS, unpublished, n.d., n.p.); Arthur Lismer to Alice Ravenhill, 28 May 1940; and Alice Ravenhill to Mildred Thornton, August 1941.
31 Ernie Crey, "The Children of Tomorrow's Great Potlatch," in *In Celebration of Our Survival: The First Nations of British Columbia*, ed. Doreen Jensen and Cheryl Brooks (Vancouver: UBC Press, 1991), 154.
32 Ibid.
33 Crey quotes a Salish elder, Henry Castle, whose "classmates were caught speaking their language one day at Colqualeeza [where Raley was principal] ... they had their mouths pried open and sewing needles driven through their tongues into the bottom of their mouths by their caretakers." See Crey, *In Celebration*, 153.
34 From Alice Ravenhill, *A Cornerstone of Canadian Culture: An Outline of the Arts and Crafts of the Indian Tribes of British Columbia* (Victoria: British Columbia Provincial Museum, Occasional Paper No. 5, 1944), n.p.
35 Ibid.
36 Doris Shadbolt, *Bill Reid* (Vancouver and Toronto: Douglas and McIntyre, 1986), 96.
37 *Report of the Provincial Museum of Natural History for the Year 1943* (Victoria: Provincial Museum of Natural History, 1943).
38 See J.J. Brody, *Indian Painters and White Patrons* (Albuquerque, NM: University of New Mexico Press, 1971).

39 "Indian Girl's Paintings Have Been Purchased by the British Columbia Government," *Native Voice*, August 1949, 1-2; and "Portland Art Museum Displays Young Native Art," *Native Voice*, October 1947, 11.
40 Walsh, "Introduction," 6.
41 The Okanagan Society for the Revival of Indian Arts and Crafts, *Native Canadians: A Plan for the Rehabilitation of Indians* (Oliver, BC: unpublished, n.d.), in University of British Columbia, Special Collections.
42 Ibid., 5.
43 Shirley Joseph, "Assimilation Tools: Then and Now," in Jensen and Brooks, *In Celebration*, 65.
44 Alice Ravenhill, "Address to the Royal Commission of Senators and Members of the House of Commons Appointed to Inquire into All Phases of the Affairs of Canadian Indians in May and October 1946," in University of British Columbia, Special Collections, SPAM 571A.
45 Discussed in Brody, *Indian Painters*.
46 "The Conference on Native Indian Affairs Successful," *Native Voice*, April 1948, 2.
47 "Nootka Basket Makers," *Native Voice*, October 1947, 11.
48 Ibid.
49 Report of J. Godman on marketing activities, submitted in November 1948 and read at the Annual Meeting of the British Columbia Indian Arts and Welfare Society, January 1949. See PABC, BCIAWS Papers, Add. MSS. 2720.
50 Ibid.
51 H.B. Hawthorn, ed., *Report of Conference on Native Indian Affairs* (Victoria: BCIAWS, 1948), 16.
52 Ibid., 4.
53 Ibid., 5.
54 Ibid., 7.
55 Ibid., 9.
56 Ibid.
57 Ibid., 10.
58 Ibid., 11.
59 Phil Nuytten, *The Totem Carvers: Charlie James, Ellen Neel and Mungo Martin* (Vancouver: Panorama Publications, 1982), 43-73.
60 Hawthorn, *Report of Conference*, 12.
61 Ibid., 12.
62 Ibid., 14.
63 Ibid., 15. This idea had been implemented by the Indian Arts and Crafts Board in the United States. See Robert Fay Schrader, *The Indian Arts and Crafts Board: An Aspect of New Deal Indian Policy* (Albuquerque, NM: University of New Mexico Press, 1983), 133.
64 Ibid., 18. Ellen Neel took up carving full-time after her husband suffered from a stroke and could no longer work. Mungo Martin shot himself by accident as a boy and had an injured leg. Charlie James had a mutilated hand. Full-time art production was the work of those individuals unable to participate in more physically demanding and more financially rewarding employment (like forestry or fishing). Curiously, this corresponds to what Graburn reports among the Inuit during the same time period. He interviewed "most of the adult men about their carving activities and all but one of them ... said they loathed the activity as an occupation and that they only carved for the money it brought them, which was very little in terms of the long hours needed to make a carving. Most of the men would rather go hunting even with a smaller return whenever the weather was good. Carving has become the activity of the disabled and infirm and in times of bad weather." See Nelson H.H. Graburn, *Eskimos without Igloos: Social and Economic Development in Sugluk* (Boston: Little, Brown, 1969), 158-9. While the Inuit and Northwest Coast peoples are two vastly different societies, they seem to share certain similarities due to having to face a similar economic situation.
65 Hawthorn, *Report of Conference*, 19.

Chapter 7: Mathias Joe, Mungo Martin, and George Clutesi

1 Noel Dyck and James B. Waldram, "Anthropology in Public Policy and Native Peoples: An Introduction to the Issues," in *Anthropology, Public Policy and Native Peoples in Canada*, ed.

Noel Dyck and James B. Waldram (Montreal and Kingston: McGill-Queen's University Press, 1993), 3-38; and Robert Paine, "Ethnodrama and the 'Fourth World': The Saami Action Group in Norway," in *Indigenous Peoples and the Nation-State: Fourth World Politics in Canada, Australia, and Norway*, ed. Robert Paine (St. John's: Institute of Social and Economic Research, Memorial University of Newfoundland, 1985), 191-235.

2 Ron Hamilton, "Button Blankets on the West Coast?" in *Robes of Power: Totem Poles on Cloth*, ed. Doreen Jensen and Polly Sargent (Vancouver: University of British Columbia Museum of Anthropology Museum Note 17, 1986), 67.

3 *Daily Colonist*, 19 July 1929, 2.

4 From the *Revised Statutes of Canada*, 1927, vol. 2, chap. 98, no. 140, p. 2218, quoted in Daisy Sewid-Smith, *Persecution or Prosecution* (Cape Mudge, BC: Nu-Yum-Balees, 1979), 1.

5 "Totem Pole to Grace Rideau Hall Gardens: Ancient Relic to be Removed to Ottawa; gift to Governor-General from Indians," *Victoria Daily Times*, 24 June 1929, 8.

6 *Daily Colonist*, 19 July 1929.

7 Indian Affairs, RG 10, vol. 4086, file 507, 787-2, D.C. Scott to W.E. Ditchburn, 30 July 1929; Scott to Mieville, 23 August 1929.

8 The Royal Proclamation, as Brian Slattery has suggested, "has profound significance for modern Canada. Under its terms aboriginal peoples hold continuing rights to their lands except where those rights have been extinguished by voluntary cession ... In technical terms, the Indian interest constitutes a legal burden on the Crown's ultimate title until surrendered." Quoted in Paul Tennant, *Aboriginal Peoples and Politics: The Indian Land Question, 1849-1989* (Vancouver: UBC Press, 1992), 11.

9 Indian Affairs, RG 10, vol. 4086, file 507, 787-2, E. Frost, Indian Agent, Port Alberni, to W.E. Ditchburn, 10 July 1929; Mieville to Scott, 30 August 1929.

10 VCA, Vancouver Golden Jubilee Committee (VGJC), VCA, AM 177, vol. 1, file 6, G.G. McGeer, Mayor and Chairman, Vancouver Golden Jubilee Committee, to Charles E. Thompson, Deputy Chairman, VGJC.

11 "Detailed Outline of Programme for Vancouver Golden Jubilee Committee," VCA, AM 177, vol. 1, file 6.

12 VCA, AM 177, vol. 7.

13 G.H. Raley, *Our Totem Poles: A Souvenir of Vancouver* (Vancouver: Lumberman, 1937), 10-11, 16-17, and 20-1.

14 VCA, Vancouver Golden Jubilee Committee, VCA, AM 177, vol. 1, file 3.

15 Golden Jubilee Committee Clippings Book, VCA, Add. MSS. 177, vol. 6.

16 F.C. Ball, Indian Agent, to G.H. Raley, Indian Committee, Golden Jubilee Committee, Raley Papers PABC, HD R13 B77.

17 Stanley Park is subject to the overlapping claims of the Squamish and Musqueam peoples.

18 VCA, Vancouver Golden Jubilee Committee, VCA, AM 177, vol. 1, file 1, Managing Board Meeting, 16 January 1936.

19 Major J.S. Matthews, *Conversations with Khahtsahlano, 1932-1954* (Vancouver: Vancouver City Archives, 1955), 32.

20 Kitsilano is the name of a neighbourhood in Vancouver located on the south side of the mouth of False Creek.

21 Matthews, *Conversations*, 32.

22 Ibid., 32.

23 Ibid.

24 Raymond Hull, Gordon Soules, and Christine Soules, *Vancouver's Past* (Vancouver: Gordon Soules Economic and Marketing Research, 1974), 81.

25 Marius Barbeau, *Totem Poles of the Gitksan, Upper Skeena River, British Columbia* (Ottawa: National Museum of Canada Bulletin 61, Anthropological Series, no. 12, 1929), 163.

26 S.W.A. Gunn, *A Complete Guide to the Totem Poles in Stanley Park, Vancouver, B.C.* (Vancouver: W.E.G. MacDonald, 1965), 22.

27 Ibid.

28 Ibid.

29 Ibid., 23.

30 Ibid.

31 Ibid.
32 Ibid.
33 Ibid.
34 Ibid.
35 Raley, *Our Totem Poles*, 8.
36 Gunn, *Totem Poles in Stanley Park*, 23.
37 Ibid., 22.
38 Wayne Suttles, "Productivity and Its Constraints: A Coast Salish Case," in *Coast Salish Essays* (Vancouver/Seattle: Talonbooks/University of Washington Press, 1987), 104.
39 Bill Holm and Bill Reid, *Form and Freedom: A Dialogue on Northwest Coast Indian Art* (Houston: Rice University Press, 1975), 58-61.
40 Suttles, "Productivity and Its Constraints," 131.
41 Ibid., 132.
42 Ibid.
43 Ibid.
44 Golden Jubilee Committee Clippings Book, VCA, Add. MSS. 177, vol. 6.
45 Ibid.
46 Ibid.
47 Ibid.
48 Ibid.
49 Ibid.
50 An example of what now seems to be Joe's campy yet subversive sense of humour appears in a newspaper report dated 11 July 1936 and found in a Vancouver City Archives clippings book: "Those who conducted the ceremonies which inducted Mayor G.G. McGeer as a chief of the Squamish tribe may have committed a linguistic faux pas, it was revealed at the city hall this morning." The mayor was given the name Tlassala, translated at the time as "Sun Rising in the East." Typed in the margin next to the clipping by J.S. Matthews, City Archivist, and dated October 1936, is: "August Jack Haatsalano [sic] says the name given 'Tlassala' means in the Squamish tongue, 'a cloud,' and in the language of the Fort Rupert Indians a 'mink' (small, furred animal). In narrating the details of the incident of making his Worship a chief, he (August Jack Khatsahlano, a member of the Musqueam nation) was very much amused and said 'don't tell anybody, or it will spoil it all.'" See VCA, Add. MSS. 177, vol. 6.
51 Ibid.
52 Ibid.
53 Quoted in Jacqueline P. O'Donnell, "The Native Brotherhood of British Columbia, 1931-1950: A New Phase in Native Political Organization" (MA thesis, University of British Columbia, 1985), 114.
54 Rae Murphy, *The Essentials of Canadian History: Canada since 1867, the Post-Confederate Nation* (Piscataway, NJ: Research and Education Association, 1993), 70-1.
55 O'Donnell, "Native Brotherhood," 46.
56 Ibid.
57 Ibid.
58 According to Paul Tennant, "the Brotherhood came to play a major role in keeping officials and Indians informed about one another's concerns and in maintaining an atmosphere of some cordiality between the two groups." See Tennant, *Aboriginal Peoples and Politics*, 118.
59 Dianne Newell, *Tangled Webs of History: Indians and the Law in Canada's Pacific Coast Fisheries* (Toronto: University of Toronto Press, 1993), 115-20.
60 Tennant, *Aboriginal Peoples and Politics*, 121.
61 George Manuel and Michael Postuns, *The Fourth World: An Indian Reality* (Don Mills, ON: Collier-Macmillan, 1974), 129.
62 Nancy Fraser, *Unruly Practices: Power, Discourse, and Gender in Contemporary Social Theory* (Minneapolis: University of Minnesota Press, 1989), 164-5.
63 As early as 1899, Clifford Sifton, in his capacity as minister of the interior, advised that, "while the Department of Indian Affairs would consider Indian views as far as possible, the right of Indians to control the action of the Department would not be recognized 'under

any circumstances.'" Quoted in J. Rick Ponting and Roger Gibbons, *Out of Irrelevance: A Socio-Political Introduction to Indian Affairs in Canada* (Toronto: Butterworths, 1980), 17. This pattern was critical to the maintenance of government authority.

64 Mackenzie King was cautiously introducing state intervention similar to that outlined in Roosevelt's American New Deal. Commissions were the main vehicle for enlisting both individual support and input from the vast network of industry, voluntary organizations, and non-governmental interest groups. This led poet Frank Scott to write of King in 1954, "the height of his ambition / was to pile a Parliamentary Committee on a Royal Commission." Quoted in Michael Bliss, *Right Honourable Men: The Descent of Canadian Politics from Macdonald to Mulroney* (Toronto: Harper-Collins, 1994), 125. This was a jibe that, even in 1947, seemed aptly to describe state ambitions in general.

65 In 1950 Masset was the home of a large and largely Haida-owned seine boat fleet. See Mary Lee Stearns, "Haida since 1960," in *Handbook of North American Indians,* vol. 7, *Northwest Coast,* ed. Wayne Suttles (Washington, DC: Smithsonian Institution, 1990), 263. Important logging operations commenced in the Nass Valley in the late 1940s, long after the impact of the First World War had impeded non-Nisga'a settlement in the valley. See Gordon B. Inglis, Douglas R. Hudson, Barbara R. Rigsby, and Bruce Rigsby, "The Tsimshian of British Columbia since 1900," in *Handbook of North American Indians,* vol. 7, *Northwest Coast,* ed. Wayne Suttles (Washington, DC: Smithsonian Institution, 1990), 289.

66 Tennant, *Aboriginal Peoples and Politics*, 121.

67 Robert F. Harney, "'So Great a Heritage as Ours': Immigration and the Survival of the Canadian Polity," in *If One Were to Write a History: Selected Writings by Robert F. Harney*, ed. Pierre Anctil and Bruno Ramirez (Toronto: Multicultural History Society of Ontario, 1991), 228.

68 Even here, despite the pretense of an open-door policy, Canadian officials continued an informal hierarchical immigration policy. According to Harney: "Canadian Jews and Ukrainians lobbied the government to help their kinsmen who either survived the death camps or were in displaced-person camps. Such lobbies would prove that in a democracy, existing groups must be heard, but immigration officials were often more interested in developing systematic recruitment in Holland, Scandinavia and the United Kingdom." See Harney, "So Great a Heritage," 232.

69 Robert Bothwell, Ian Drummond, and John English, *Canada since 1945* (Toronto: University of Toronto Press, 1987), 117-31.

70 Canada tried to secure access to these markets through the attempted formation of the International Trading Organization. The Marshall Plan of 1947 eventually established the capital necessary for European reconstruction and contributed to a boom in the export of Canadian raw materials. See Bothwell, Drummond, and English, *Canada since 1945,* 65, 71-2.

71 Tennant, *Aboriginal Peoples and Politics*, 121.

72 Audrey Hawthorn, *A Labour of Love: The Making of the Museum of Anthropology, UBC – The First Three Decades, 1947-1976* (Vancouver: University of British Columbia Museum of Anthropology Museum Note 33, 1993), 4.

73 Ibid., 122.

74 "Indian Girl's Paintings Have Been Purchased by the British Columbia Government," *Native Voice*, August 1949, 1-2.

75 Ibid.; "Portland Art Museum Displays Young Native Art," *Native Voice*, October 1947, 11.

76 Quotes and other material on the Kitsilano Village and the Diamond Jubilee are located in CVA M6141.

77 Ibid.

78 Ibid.

79 Ibid.

80 Ibid.

81 Ibid.

82 Ibid.

83 Ibid.

84 Ibid.

85 The presentation is illustrated in the *Native Voice*, December 1946, 1.

86 CVA M6141.
87 Ibid.
88 Ibid.
89 *Native Voice*, December 1946, 1.
90 Ibid.
91 In a speech at the 1953 opening of Martin's reconstructed house at the British Columbia Provincial Museum (translated by Helen Hunt and transcribed by Wilson Duff), Tony Omhid identifies 'naqa'penk'em' as the owner of the original house that Martin copied for the museum. In 1967 Audrey Hawthorn also identified Martin as "Chief Nakapenkem of Fort Rupert of the Ma'mtagila clan." See Audrey Hawthorn, *Art of the Kwakiutl Indians and Other Northwest Coast Tribes* (Seattle: University of Washington Press, 1967), vii. Phil Nuytten, following the orthography developed by the U'mista Cultural Centre in Alert Bay, spells this "N*aka'*pank*a*m." See Phil Nuytten, *The Totem Carvers: Charlie James, Ellen Neel and Mungo Martin* (Vancouver: Panorama Publications, 1982), 11. Ironically, the previous holder of the prerogative was Mungo's brother, Spruce, who was imprisoned after the Cranmer potlatch of 1921. See "Potlatch Transcript: Mungo Martin's Thunderbird Park Potlatch, December 13-15, 1953," located in the Duff Files at the Royal British Columbia Museum. The story of the name was recorded by George Hunt and published in Franz Boas, *Contributions to the Ethnology of the Kwakiutl* (New York: Columbia University Contributions to Ethnology 3, 1925).
92 "As the eyes of hundreds of citizens at Kitsilano Indian Village Saturday night were fixed on the robed figure of Governor-General Alexander on the chief's dais or the garish masks of native dancers on the giant tom-tom stage," went one report, "a craftsman of a dying art was working within a few yards of them unnoticed ... Peering through an ancient pair of wire-rimmed glasses, he worked until gathering darkness called a halt, then he took a mild interest in the proceedings. As usual, he said little." CVA M6141.
93 Nuytten, *Totem Carvers*, 51.
94 *Native Voice*, December 1946, 1.
95 CVA M6141.
96 Peter Macnair, "Trends in Northwest Coast Indian Art, 1880-1959: Decline and Expansion," in *In the Shadow of the Sun: Perspectives on Contemporary Native Art*, ed. Canadian Museum of Civilization (Ottawa: Canadian Ethnology Service Mercury Series Paper 124, 1993), 51.
97 George Clutesi was born into the Wolf Clan of the Tse-shaht near Port Alberni in 1905. Active as a writer, radio broadcaster, artist, dancer, and actor, Clutesi was best known for his paintings, which were displayed in the Indian Pavilion at Expo '67 in Montreal. He published a series of children's books, including *Son of Raven, Son of Deer* (1967), *Potlatch* (1969), and *Stand Tall, My Son* (1990). He received an honourary doctorate from the University of Victoria in 1971, the Order of Canada in 1973, and an ACTRA award for Best Actor in 1975 for his role in the film *Dreamspeaker*. He died in 1988. This information is taken from George Clutesi, *Stand Tall, My Son* (Victoria: Newport Bay, 1990), 6.
98 George Clutesi, "The Force of Propaganda," *Native Voice*, November 1947.
99 G.E. Mortimore, "Indian Artist Makes Eloquent Plea," *Native Voice*, December 1949, 9.
100 George Clutesi, "The Urge to Create," *Native Voice*, June 1947, 14.
101 Hazel W. Hertzberg, *The Search for an American Indian Identity: Modern Pan-Indian Movements* (Syracuse: Syracuse University Press, 1971), 31.
102 Tennant, *Aboriginal Peoples and Politics*, 69.
103 Clutesi, "The Urge to Create."
104 George Clutesi, *Son of Raven, Son of Deer* (Sidney, BC: Gray's Publishing, 1967), 13.

Chapter 8: UBC, the BCPM, and the Totem Pole Carver Training Program

1 Paul D. Schafer and André Fortier, *Review of Federal Policies for the Arts in Canada, 1944-1988* (Ottawa: Canadian Conference of the Arts, 1989).
2 For a more detailed discussion, see Albert A. Shea, ed., *Culture in Canada: A Study of the Findings of the Royal Commission on National Development in the Arts, Letters, and Sciences, 1949-1951* (Toronto: Core, 1952); and Paul Litt, *The Muses, the Masses, and the Massey Commission* (Toronto: University of Toronto Press, 1992).

3 Audrey Hawthorn, *A Labour of Love: The Making of the Museum of Anthropology, UBC – The First Three Decades, 1947-1976* (Vancouver: University of British Columbia Museum of Anthropology Museum Note 33, 1993), 1.
4 Robert Bothwell, Ian Drummond, and John English, *Canada since 1945* (Toronto: University of Toronto Press, 1987), 46.
5 Schafer and Fortier, *Review of Federal Policies.*
6 Litt, *The Muses*, 17.
7 Shea, *Culture in Canada*, 13.
8 Ibid.
9 Ibid.
10 Ibid.
11 Quoted in Canada, *Special Joint Committee of the Indian Act, Minutes of Proceedings and Evidence* (Ottawa: King's Printer, 1950), 25.
12 Ibid., 55.
13 Ibid.
14 See, for example, Marjorie M. Halpin, *Jack Shadbolt and the Coastal Indian Image* (Vancouver: UBC Press, 1986).
15 Archibald A. Day, Secretary of the Commission, to Harry Hawthorn, 20 March 1950, UBC Archives, Norman MacKenzie Papers, box 194, file 3.
16 Ibid., 113.
17 Marcia Crosby, "Indian Art/Aboriginal Title" (Vancouver: MA thesis, UBC, 1994), 50.
18 Even in 1927, Brown and Barbeau's *Exhibition of West Coast Art, Native and Modern* was partly a response to the accusation that the National Gallery did not speak for all of Canada but, rather, for Ontario and Quebec.
19 Bothwell, Drummond, and English, *Canada since 1945*, 3-105.
20 Ibid.
21 Hawthorn, *Labour of Love*, 1.
22 BCPM, *Report of the Provincial Museum for the Year 1949* (Victoria: King's Printer, 1950), B16.
23 Audrey Hawthorn outlines her methodology for the preparation of this brief as follows: "With ethnographic atlases I was able to establish the locations of several linguistic groups in what had been the major ethnographic areas ... I mailed out lists of items of material culture and I appended questionnaires to find out what was still being made." See Hawthorn, *Labour of Love*, 7.
24 Ibid., 1.
25 Ibid.
26 The brief is contained in UBC Archives, Lewis Family Papers, box 7, file 9.
27 UBC Archives, Lewis Family Papers, box 1, files 7-8.
28 Douglas Cole, *Captured Heritage: The Scramble for Northwest Coast Artifacts* (Vancouver and Toronto: Douglas and McIntyre, 1985; rpt. UBC Press, 1995), 278.
29 Arthur Price to Marius Barbeau, 14 and 17 October 1947, CMC, Marius Barbeau's Correspondence, folder Price (Arthur), temp. box 45.
30 Ibid.
31 Ibid.
32 Ibid.
33 Ibid.
34 Ibid.
35 Ibid.
36 Ibid.
37 Phil Nuytten, *The Totem Carvers: Charlie James, Ellen Neel and Mungo Martin* (Vancouver: Panorama Publications, 1982), 51-4.
38 Ibid., 45-52.
39 Ibid.
40 Ibid., 75-116.
41 Peter Macnair, Alan L. Hoover, and Kevin Neary, *The Legacy: Continuing Traditions of Canadian Northwest Coast Indian Art* (Victoria: British Columbia Provincial Museum, 1980), 73.
42 Audrey Hawthorn, *Art of the Kwakiutl Indians and Other Northwest Coast Tribes* (Seattle: University of Washington Press, 1967), vii.

43 Ibid.; and Audrey Hawthorn, *Kwakiutl Art* (Seattle: University of Washington Press, 1979).
44 Ellen Neel, "Ancient Art Being Preserved," *Native Voice*, September 1949, 1.
45 Nuytten, *Totem Carvers*, 51-2.
46 The society also included the attorney-general, the mayor of Vancouver, the provincial minister of trade and industry, the commissioner of the Victoria and Island Publicity Bureau, various well-known local businessmen, and Native Brotherhood president William Scow. See Nuytten, *Totem Carvers,* 48.
47 Marius Barbeau, *Totem Poles of the Gitksan, Upper Skeena River, British Columbia* (Ottawa: National Museum of Canada Bulletin 61, Anthropological Series, no. 12, 1929).
48 H.R. MacMillan to K. Fraser, 23 August 1949, UBC MOA, Hawthorn Papers, box 12, ser. 5, file 1.
49 *BCPM, Report, 1949,* 7.
50 Ibid.
51 Wilson Duff to W.T. Straith, 16 August 1951, RBCM, Duff Papers.
52 Ibid.
53 Ibid.
54 Ibid.
55 BCPM, *Provincial Museum Annual Report for the year 1951* (Victoria: King's Printer, 1952), 7.
56 Ibid., 21.
57 Ibid.
58 Ibid.
59 Ibid.
60 *Vancouver News Herald,* 13 June 1950, UBC Archives, Lewis Family Papers, box 7, file 9.
61 Ibid.
62 Canada, Department of Mines and Resources, *Report of Indian Affairs Branch for the Fiscal Year Ended March 1950* (Ottawa: King's Printer, 1951), 73.
63 Gloria Cranmer Webster, "The Contemporary Potlatch," in *Chiefly Feasts: The Enduring Kwakiutl Potlatch,* ed. Aldona Jonaitis (New York: American Museum of Natural History, 1991), 227.
64 Diane MacEachern Barwick, "'A Grand Old Man at 35': Wilson Duff as Curator," in *The World Is as Sharp as a Knife: An Anthology in Honour of Wilson Duff,* ed. Donald Abbott (Victoria: British Columbia Provincial Museum, 1981), 25.
65 Cranmer Webster, "Contemporary Potlatch," 227.
66 "Potlatch Transcript: Mungo Martin's Thunderbird Park Potlatch, December 12-15, 1953," RBCM, Duff Papers, 6.
67 Ibid., 6.
68 Ibid., 1.
69 Ibid., 1-2.
70 "And now to this," said Martin. "The child of my brother, the child of Wilson Duff. I am going to give a name, as I don't consider us to be two men (rather, as one or related)." See "Potlatch Transcript," n.p.
71 Ibid., 2.
72 Ibid., 4.
73 Marjorie Halpin, "A Politics of Indian Art," keynote address to the Native American Art Studies Association Conference, Vancouver, August 1989, 6.
74 Nuytten, *The Totem Carvers,* 75-116.

Chapter 9: The Totem Pole Preservation Committee

1 "She'll Make the Team," *Native Voice,* January 1952, 7.
2 Valda Blundell, "Speaking the Art of Canada's Native Peoples: Anthropological Discourse and the Media," *Australian Canadian Studies* 7, 1 (1989): 28.
3 Walter Hardwick explains the provincial government's regulation of the forest industry during the 1950s as follows: "A series of Forest Management Licenses were issued through which the major companies agreed to administer their private land, timber licenses, and crown land in particular areas. In other areas the Provincial Forest Service administered Public Working Circles on a perpetual yield basis. The result of the sustained-yield programme,

insofar as size, numbers, and location of production sites is concerned, was that the large logging operations, whose cut was in excess of the annual increment in forest growth, had to decrease production which would ensure a sustained yield of timber. New sources were tapped in more peripheral regions extending to all sections of Vancouver Island, Queen Charlotte Islands and the northern mainland coast." See Walter Hardwick, *Geography of the Forest Industry of Coastal British Columbia* (Vancouver: Canadian Association of Geographers, Occasional Papers in Geography, 1963), 22.

4 John Bradbury, "British Columbia," in *A Geography of Canada: Heartland and Hinterland,* ed. L.D. McCann (Scarborough, ON: Prentice-Hall, 1982), 349-50.

5 Ibid.

6 Ibid.

7 Ibid., 351.

8 Hardwick, *Geography*, 2.

9 Wilson Duff, "Totem Pole Preservation in British Columbia," unpublished manuscript, RBCM, Duff Papers, 1.

10 Ibid.

11 Ibid., 12.

12 H.R. MacMillan to H.B. Hawthorn, 10 January 1952, UBC MOA Archives, Hawthorn Papers.

13 Ibid.

14 H.B. Hawthorn to H.R. MacMillan, 16 January 1952, UBC MOA Archives, Hawthorn Papers.

15 George F. MacDonald, *Haida Monumental Art: Villages of the Queen Charlotte Islands* (Vancouver/Seattle: UBC Press/University of Washington Press, 1983), 79-100.

16 BCPM, *Provincial Museum Annual Report for the Year 1956* (Victoria: Queen's Printer, 1957), 20.

17 Duff intervened when the bureau questioned whether or not the pole was worth the price, admonishing it as follows: "I think it would be unfair to compare a pole of such quality and significance with small poles carved for sale to tourists, and establish a price on that basis." See Wilson Duff to Victoria and Island Publicity Bureau, 14 August 1956, RBCM, Duff Papers.

18 BCPM, *Report, 1956,* D21.

19 Doris Shadbolt, *Bill Reid* (Vancouver: Douglas and McIntyre, 1987).

20 BCPM, *Report, 1956,* D21.

21 Copies of these posts replaced the Spence posts in the Thunderbird Arch erected in 1940. See BCPM, *Report, 1956,* D21.

22 Ibid., D21.

23 Ibid.

24 Ibid.

25 Ibid.

26 Charlie Clair to Wilson Duff, 28 February 1957, UBC MOA Archives, Hawthorn Papers, box 12, ser. 5, file 5-9.

27 H.R. MacMillan to H.B. Hawthorn, 10 September 1956, UBC MOA Archives, Hawthorn Papers, box 12, ser. 5, file 5-7.

28 Wilson Duff to Walter C. Koerner, 3 April 1957, UBC MOA Archives, Hawthorn Papers, box 12, ser. 5, file 5-9.

29 Audrey Hawthorn, *Kwakiutl Art* (Seattle: University of Washington Press, 1979).

30 BCPM, *Report, 1956,* D21.

31 W.B. McPhee to Wilson Duff, 1 May 1957, RBCM, Duff Files; *Native Voice* 11, 5 May 1957, 1-4.

32 H.R. MacMillan to H.B. Hawthorn, 10 September 1956, UBC MOA Archives, Hawthorn Papers, box 12, ser. 5, file 5-7.

33 Wilson Duff to Harry Hawthorn, 17 September 1957, UBC MOA Archives, Hawthorn Papers, box 12, ser. 5, file 5-9.

34 George MacDonald writes: "'People Think of This House Even When They Sleep Because the Master Feeds Everyone Who Calls' belonged to the Striped Town People. According to Duff and Kew, the remains of this house were 11.7 metres wide by 11.85 metres long (centre to centre of corner posts). The frontal pole was badly burned in the village fire of 1892, but the bottom figure of a beaver and one of the watchmen at the top survived." See

MacDonald, *Haida Monumental Art*, 107. The Striped Town People are one of the lineage groups of the Xa'gi Raven moiety. See Ibid., 11.

35 G.C. Andrew to H.B. Hawthorn, 29 July 1957, UBC MOA Archives, Hawthorn Papers, box 12, ser. 5, file 5-9.

36 Ibid.

37 P.P. Henson, Queen Charlotte Agency Superintendent, to W.S. Arneil, 4 December 1956, RBCM, Duff Files.

38 Molly Stewart to Indian Agent Anfield, 30 October 1956, RBCM, Duff Files.

39 Ibid.

40 Ibid.

41 Wilson Duff to W.S. Arneil, UBC MOA Archives, Hawthorn Papers, box 12, ser. 5, file 5-9.

42 Ibid.

43 J.L. Granatstein, "Culture and Scholarship: The First Ten Years of the Canada Council," *Canadian Historical Review* 65, 4 (1984): 449.

44 Ibid., 449-50; and University of British Columbia internal memorandum to Dean G.F. Curtis and Professor J. Deutsch, 9 December 1957, UBC Archives, Norman MacKenzie Papers, box 137, file 3.

45 Audrey Hawthorn, "H.R. MacMillan: An Appreciation," in *Northwest Coast Indian Artifacts from the H.R. MacMillan Collections in the Museum of Anthropology, UBC* (Vancouver: UBC Press, 1975); see also Karen Erica Duffek, "The Contemporary Northwest Coast Indian Market" (MA thesis, University of British Columbia, 1983), 27.

46 See, for example, Bill Reid, "The Art – An Appreciation," in *Arts of the Raven: Masterworks by the Northwest Coast Indian* (Vancouver: Vancouver Art Gallery, 1965), written only seven years after the implementation of the UBC Haida village project.

47 Shadbolt, *Bill Reid*, 40.

48 Shadbolt writes: "In the mid-sixties he did a series of black-and-white illustrations for Christie Harris's *Raven's Cry* ... a sentimental fictionalized account of the Edenshaw family's journey through acculturation ... In a revealing self-view at the time, Reid in the book's last illustration pictures himself in the lower foreground at work on a pole ... Lined up behind him loom the gigantic silent ghosts of his ancestors – 'Uncle Charlie' directly at his back." See Shadbolt, *Bill Reid*, 40.

49 Marcia Crosby, "Indian Art/Aboriginal Title" (MA thesis, UBC, Vancouver, 1994), 109.

50 Ibid., 114.

51 See, for example, Marjorie Halpin, "The Uses of Collections," in *Northwest Coast Indian Artifacts from the H.R. MacMillan Collections in the Museum of Anthropology, University of British Columbia*, ed. University of British Columbia Museum of Anthropology (Vancouver: UBC Press, 1975), 43.

52 "The Art Today," *Arts of the Raven*.

53 Doris Shadbolt, "Foreword," *Arts of the Raven*.

54 Ibid.

55 "Ceremony Marks Start of Totem Pole for Queen," *Native Voice*, April 1957, 7.

56 "Canada's Tallest Totem Pole Erected at Haddon Park," unidentified newspaper clipping, 16 October 1958, located in CVA.

57 "Totem Carver to See Queen," *Province*, 28 April 1958.

58 Wilson Duff, "Kitwancool," unpublished MS, 1952, 1, RBCM, Duff Papers.

59 Wilson Duff, "Digest of Recommendations," unpublished MS, 26 August 1952, RBCM, Duff Papers.

60 Wilson Duff, ed., *Histories, Territories, and Laws of the Kitwancool* (Victoria: British Columbia Provincial Museum, Anthropology in British Columbia Memoir No. 4, 1959), 12.

61 Ibid., 37.

62 Wilson Duff, 1952 field notes, UBC MOA Archives, Duff Papers, box 3, file 3-6.

63 Ibid.

64 Ibid.

65 Ibid.

66 Ibid.

67 Ibid.

68 Ibid.
69 Ibid.
70 Ibid.
71 Ibid.
72 Duff, "Kitwancool," n.p.
73 Ibid.
74 Duff, *Histories, Territories*, 12.
75 Marjorie Halpin, "Anthropology as Artifact," in *Consciousness and Inquiry: Ethnology and Canadian Realities*, ed. Frank Manning (Ottawa: National Museum of Man Mercury Series, CES Paper No. 89E, 1983), 262.
76 British Columbia Provincial Museum Press Release, n.d. (probably ca. 1959-60), contained in PABC B6045, file 64, TS1-W-002A.
77 Duff, *Histories, Territories*, 3.
78 BCPM Press Release, RBCM, Duff Papers.
79 Duff, *Histories, Territories*, 3.
80 Michael Kew to Peter Williams, 8 May 1959; Peter Williams to Michael Kew, 26 March 1959; Peter Williams to Wilson Duff, 2 May 1960 and 4 May 1960, PABC, Duff Papers.
81 To complicate matters even further, it was incorrectly identified in a photograph caption published in Duff, *Histories, Territories* (p. 22, plate 6).
82 Ibid., 23.
83 Peter Williams to Wilson Duff, 2 May 1960, PABC, Duff Papers.
84 Anonymous Department of Recreation and Conservation Memorandum, n.d. (after 1969), contained in RBCM, Duff Papers.
85 Cox was given a cash advance of $175 to cover expenses. Despite Cox's apparent understanding that she was to receive remuneration for her work, no wages were paid her. Michael Kew, writing on behalf of Duff, stated bluntly, "Our finances were not sufficient to pay more than the expenses of an interpreter." She received the $40.85 left over from the expense advance as "token payment" for her ten days' recording in 1958. See Michael Kew to Constance Cox, 1 December 1958, BCPA, Duff Papers.
86 Peter Williams to Wilson Duff, 19 November 1959, BCPA, Duff Papers. According to a 1976 letter from Duff to Peter Macnair, this pole "belonged to the house of Guno. At that time the chieftainship of this house was split: old Johnson Williams living at Kispiox had the name, while young Godfrey Good living at Kitwancool had the seat. I [Duff] arranged a straight purchase, and payments were accepted by both Johnson Williams and Godfrey Good." Quoted in Alan Hoover to Ronald W. Hawker, personal correspondence, 22 January 1998. The 1966 copy of this pole was made for the University of Victoria without the consent of either Williams or Good. In 1990 Godfrey Good, Chief Guno, approached the Royal British Columbia Museum and claimed that the museum had failed to follow through on an agreement to replicate the pole for re-erection in Gitanyow. The museum's position was that, although it had not agreed to this pole's replication as a condition for its removal, since a replica had been made for Victoria without the family's consent, the museum would fund the erection of a pole replica for Gitanyow as well. This pole was completed and raised in 1996.
87 Duff, *Histories, Territories*, 17.
88 Ibid., 13.
89 Ibid., 18.
90 Ibid.
91 Ibid.
92 Ibid., 13.
93 Ibid., 23.
94 Ibid., 22.
95 Ibid.
96 Ibid., 24.
97 Ibid.
98 See Duff, *Histories, Territories*.
99 Wilson Duff to Cyril S. Belshaw, 21 April 1960, RBCM, Duff Papers.

100 Crosby argues that this contradicted his textual stance, which tends to refute Aboriginal authority and legitimize that of the state cultural institutions. See Crosby, "Indian Art/ Aboriginal Title," 61-4. Others might argue that Duff's professional relationship with First Nations people evolved over his career to the point at which he was actively collaborating, as a representative of the museum, with First Nations groups. According to George Clutesi: "Wilson Duff encouraged all those who would listen by simply declaring that the Indian decline is over; that Indian leadership is indeed strengthening and that the present situation should not be used to judge either past Indian cultures or their capabilities for the future." See George Clutesi, "Wilson Duff: A Tribute," in *The World Is as Sharp as a Knife: An Anthology in Honour of Wilson Duff,* ed. Donald Abbott (Victoria: British Columbia Provincial Museum, 1981), 43. Peter Williams also eulogized Duff, stating, on behalf of the Gitanyow people, that "Professor Duff's honour and his faithful work will remain in our memory and go down in our history." See Peter Williams, "Tribute of The Kitwancool," in Abbott, *The World Is as Sharp as a Knife,* 47.

101 "Lecture Notes Anthropology 301, 1970," UBC MOA Archives, Duff Papers, box 8, file 8-24.

102 As Crosby points out, Canadian legislation coincided with the United Nations General Assembly's Declaration on the Granting of Independence to Colonial Countries and Peoples, which was aimed at ending colonialism internationally. Throughout her thesis, she further documents a range of social inequities that continued despite Diefenbaker's public assertions to the contrary. Seen in this context, Crosby suggests, "while the federal vote would ostensibly provide registered Indians with equal opportunity and access to democratic process, it also provided the Canadian government with an ideal (abstract) international profile in terms of law and policy that did not exist in fact." See Crosby, "Indian Art/ Aboriginal Title," 47.

Chapter 10: Tales of Ghosts That Hover in the World

1 Joan Vastokas, "Bill Reid and the Native Renaissance," in *Stone, Bones, and Skin: Ritual and Shamanic Art*, eds. Anne Trueblood Bordzky, Rose Danesewich, and Nick Johnson (Toronto: Society for Art Publications, 1977), 158.

2 Nicholas Thomas, *Colonialism's Culture: Anthropology, Travel and Government* (Princeton: Princeton University Press, 1994), 16.

3 Paul Connerton, *How Societies Remember* (Cambridge: Cambridge University Press, 1989), 1.

4 Thomas, *Colonialism's Culture*, 4-5.

5 Charles Stewart to Arthur Conan Doyle, 29 August 1924, from Indian Affairs, Black Series, reel C-10185, vol. 4086, file 507787.

6 Quoted in Douglas Cole, *Captured Heritage: The Scramble for Northwest Coast Artifacts* (Vancouver and Toronto: Douglas and McIntyre, 1985; rpt. UBC Press, 1995), 275.

7 Harlan I. Smith, "Restoration of Totem Poles in British Columbia," in *National Museum of Canada Annual Report for 1926* (Ottawa: King's Printer, 1928).

8 Diamond Jenness to Duncan Campbell Scott, 28 April 1926; Duncan Campbell Scott to Diamond Jenness, 26 April 1926 and 5 May 1926, Canadian Museum of Civilization, Sapir Correspondence, box 432, file 34.

9 George Raley, "Important Considerations Involved in the Treatise on 'Canadian Indian Art and Industries,'" n.d., PABC, Raley Papers.

10 Virginia Dominguez, "The Marketing of Heritage," *American Ethnologist* 13, 3 (1986): 548.

11 Aldona Jonaitis, "Traders of Tradition: The History of Haida Art," in *Robert Davidson: Eagle of the Dawn*, ed. Ian M. Thom (Seattle: University of Washington Press, 1993), 14.

12 George Manuel and Michael Postuns, *The Fourth World: An Indian Reality* (Don Mills, ON: Collier-Macmillan, 1974), 129.

13 H.B. Hawthorn, ed. *Report of Conference on Native Indian Affairs* (Victoria: BCIAWS, 1948), 16.

14 Ibid., 12.

15 Ibid., 14.

16 Duff, for example, reported 1963 population levels exceeding the 1885 census counts for the Haida, Tsimshian, Kwakwa̱ka̱'wakw, Nuxalk, Coast Salish, Interior Salish, and Athapaskan peoples. The total Aboriginal population for British Columbia had almost doubled from 22,605 in 1929 to 40,800 in 1963. See Wilson Duff, *The Indian History of British Columbia,*

vol. 1, *The Impact of the White Man* (Victoria: Provincial Museum of British Columbia Anthropology in British Columbia, Memoir No. 5, 1964), 39. Robert T. Boyd reports a total population increase on the Northwest Coast between 1928 and 1986 as close to 75,000. See Robert T. Boyd, "Demographic History, 1774-1874," in *Handbook of North American Indians*, vol. 7, *Northwest Coast*, ed. Wayne Suttles (Washington, DC: Smithsonian Institution, 1990), 136.

17 Marcia Crosby, "Indian Art/Aboriginal Title" (MA thesis, UBC, Vancouver, 1994), 113.

18 Thomas R. Berger, "Wilson Duff and Native Land Claims," in *The World Is as Sharp as a Knife: An Anthology in Honour of Wilson Duff*, ed. Donald Abbott (Victoria: British Columbia Provincial Museum, 1981), 49.

19 Gloria Cranmer Webster, "The Contemporary Potlatch," in *Chiefly Feasts: The Enduring Kwakiutl Potlatch*, ed. Aldona Jonaitis (New York: American Museum of Natural History, 1991), 227.

20 Wilson Duff to Cdr. J.W. McDowell, 14 June 1963, RBCM, Duff Papers.

21 Wilson Duff, 1952 field notes, UBC MOA Archives, Duff Papers, box 3, file 3-6.

22 Marjorie Halpin, "A Politics of Indian Art," keynote address to the Native American Art Studies Association Conference, Vancouver, August 1989, 5.

23 Helen Codere, *Fighting with Property: A Study of Kwakiutl Potlatching and Warfare, 1792-1930* (New York: J.J. Augustin, 1951).

Bibliography

Primary Sources

Canadian Museum of Civilization. Barbeau Northwest Coast Files. Centre for the Study of Canadian Folklore (Reference: B-F-159.4).

–. Jenness Correspondence. Box 432, file 34.

–. Sapir Correspondence. Box 429, files 57-58, 83.

City Archives of Vancouver. Vancouver Golden Jubilee Committee. VCA, AM 177, vols. 1-7.

–. Art, Historical and Scientific Association of Vancouver. VCA, AM 336.

British Columbia Archives. Raley Papers, HD R13 R13.3.

University of British Columbia Archives. Lewis Family Papers. Box 7.

–. Norman MacKenzie Papers. Box 194, file 3.

University of British Columbia Museum of Anthropology Archives. Hawthorn Papers. Box 12.

University of British Columbia Museum of Anthropology. Parallel Accession Files.

Secondary Sources

Abbott, Donald, ed. *The World Is as Sharp as a Knife: An Anthology in Honour of Wilson Duff.* Victoria: British Columbia Provincial Museum, 1981.

Ames, Michael M. *Cannibal Tours and Glass Boxes: The Anthropology of Museums.* Vancouver: UBC Press, 1992.

Anctil, Pierre, and Bruno Ramirez, eds. *If One Were to Write a History: Selected Writings by Robert F. Harney.* Toronto: Multicultural History Society of Ontario, 1991.

Appadurai, Arjun, ed. *The Social Life of Things: Commodities in Cultural Perspective.* Cambridge: Cambridge University Press, 1986.

Barbeau, C. Marius. *The Downfall of Temlaham.* Toronto: Macmillan, 1928.

–. *Totem Poles of the Gitksan, Upper Skeena River, British Columbia.* Bulletin No. 61. Anthropological Series 12. Ottawa: National Museum of Canada, 1929.

–. "The Indians of the Prairies and the Rockies: A Theme for Modern Painters." *The University of Toronto Quarterly* 1, 2 (1932).

–. "The Potlatch among the B.C. Indians and Section 149 of the Indian Act." Ottawa: Unpublished, 1934 (Canadian Museum of Civilization 11007.13, B12, F2, VII-X-46M).

–. "Backgrounds in Canadian Art." *Proceedings and Transactions of the Royal Society of Canada.* Third Series, 35 (1941).

–. "Frederick Alexie: A Primitive." *Canadian Review of Music and Art* 3, nos. 11 and 12 (1945).

–. "I was a Pioneer." *Oracle* 44 (1982).

–. *Totem Poles.* 2 vols. Rev. ed. Hull, QC: Canadian Museum of Civilization, 1990.

Berlo, Janet Catherine, ed. *The Early Years of Native American Art History: The Politics of Scholarship and Collecting.* Seattle/Vancouver: University of Washington Press/UBC Press, 1992.

Bhabha, Homi K. *The Location of Culture*. London and New York: Routledge, 1994.

Blackman, Margaret B. *During My Time: Florence Edenshaw Davidson, a Haida Woman*. Seattle: University of Washington Press, 1982.

Bliss, Michael. *Right Honourable Men: The Descent of Canadian Politics from Macdonald to Mulroney*. Toronto: HarperCollins, 1994.

Blundell, Valda. "Speaking the Art of Canada's Native Peoples: Anthropological Discourse and the Media." *Australian Canadian Studies* 7, 1 (1989).

Boas, Franz. *Contributions to the Ethnology of the Kwakiutl*. New York: Columbia University Press, 1925.

–. *Kwakiutl Culture as Reflected in Mythology*. New York: American Folklore Society, 1935.

–. *Primitive Art*. Cambridge, MA: Harvard University Press, 1927. Rpt. New York: Dover Publications, 1955.

–. *Kwakiutl Ethnography*, ed. Helen Codere. Chicago and London: University of Chicago Press, 1966.

Bothwell, Robert, Ian Drummond, and John English. *Canada 1900-1945*. Toronto: University of Toronto Press, 1987.

–. *Canada since 1945: Power, Politics, and Provincialism*. Rev. ed. Toronto: University of Toronto Press, 1989.

Bowman, Phylis. *Whistling through the Wind*. Prince Rupert: P. Bowman, 1980.

Braeman, John, Robert H. Bremner, and David Brody, eds. *The New Deal: The National Level*. Columbus: Ohio State University Press, 1975.

British Columbia Provincial Museum. *Report of the Provincial Museum of Natural History for the Years 1934-1960*. Victoria: Provincial Museum of Natural History, 1935-61.

Brody, J.J. *Indian Painters and White Patrons*. Albuquerque: University of New Mexico Press, 1971.

Canada. *Special Joint Committee of the Indian Act, Minutes of Proceedings and Evidence*. No. 1, 28-30 May 1946. Ottawa: King's Printer, 1950.

–. Department of Mines and Resources. *Report of Indian Affairs Branch for the Fiscal Year ended March 1950*. Ottawa: King's Printer, 1951.

Canadian Museum of Civilization. *In the Shadow of the Sun: Perspectives on Contemporary Native Art*. Ottawa: Canadian Ethnology Service, Mercury Series Paper 124, 1993.

Carr, Emily. *Hundreds and Thousands: The Journals of Emily Carr*. Toronto and Vancouver: Clarke, Irwin and Company, 1966.

Cassidy, Maureen. "The Skeena River Uprising of 1888." *British Columbia Historical News* 16, 3 (Spring 1983).

"Ceremony Marks Start of Totem Pole for Queen." *Native Voice*, April 1957.

Clever, Glenn, ed. *Duncan Campbell Scott: Selected Poetry*. Ottawa: Tecumseh Press, 1974.

Clifton, James A., ed. *The Invented Indian: Cultural Fictions and Government Policies*. New Brunswick, NJ: Transaction Publishers, 1990.

Clutesi, George. "The Urge to Create." *Native Voice*, June 1947.

–. "The Force of Propaganda." *Native Voice*, November 1947.

–. *Son of Raven, Son of Deer*. Sidney, BC: Gray's Publishing, 1967.

–. *Stand Tall, My Son*. Victoria: Newport Bay, 1990.

Cohodas, Marvin. *Basketweavers for the California Curio Trade: Elizabeth and Louise Hickox*. Tucson: University of Arizona Press, 1997.

Codere, Helen. *Fighting with Property: A Study of Kwakiutl Potlatching and Warfare, 1792-1930*. New York: J.J. Augustin, 1951.

Cole, Douglas. *Captured Heritage: The Scramble for Northwest Coast Artifacts*. Vancouver and Toronto: Douglas and McIntyre, 1985. Rpt. UBC Press, 1995.

Cole, Douglas, and Ira Chaikin. *An Iron Hand upon the People: The Law against the Potlatch on the Northwest Coast*. Vancouver/Seattle: Douglas and McIntyre/University of Washington Press, 1990.

Connerton, Paul. *How Societies Remember*. Cambridge: Cambridge University Press, 1989.

Coombes, Annie E. *Reinventing Africa: Museums, Material Culture and Popular Imagination in Late Victorian and Edwardian England*. New Haven and London: Yale University Press, 1994.

Crosby, Marcia. "Indian Art/Aboriginal Title." MA thesis, University of British Columbia, 1994.

Dawn, Leslie. *The Northwest Coast Native Print: A Contemporary Tradition Comes of Age.* Victoria: Art Gallery of Greater Victoria, 1984.

Dippie, Brian W. *The Vanishing American: White Attitudes and United States Indian Policy.* Middletown, CT: Wesleyan University Press, 1982.

Dominguez, Virginia, Frederic H. Douglas, and René d'Harnoncourt. *Indian Art of the United States.* New York: Museum of Modern Art, 1941.

–. "Invoking Culture: The Messy Side of 'Cultural Politics.'" *South Atlantic Quarterly* 91, 1 (Winter 1992).

Dragland, Stan. *Floating Voice: Duncan Campbell Scott and the Literature of Treaty 9.* Concord, ON: Anansi, 1994.

Drucker, Philip, and Robert F. Heizer. *To Make My Name Good: A Reexamination of the Southern Kwakiutl Potlatch.* Berkeley and Los Angeles: University of California Press, 1967.

Duff, Wilson. *The Indian History of British Columbia.* Vol. 1: *The Impact of the White Man.* Victoria: Provincial Museum of British Columbia Anthropology in British Columbia, Memoir No. 5, 1964.

–. *Images Stone B.C.: Thirty Centuries of Northwest Coast Indian Sculpture.* Toronto: Oxford University Press, 1975.

Duff, Wilson, ed. *Histories, Territories, and Laws of the Kitwancool.* Victoria: British Columbia Provincial Museum Anthropology in British Columbia Memoir No. 4, 1959.

Duffek, Karen Erica. "The Contemporary Northwest Coast Indian Market." MA thesis, University of British Columbia, 1983.

–. *Bill Reid: Beyond the Essential Form.* Vancouver: UBC Press, 1986.

Dyck, Noel, and James B. Waldram, eds. *Anthropology, Public Policy and Native Peoples in Canada.* Montreal and Kingston: McGill-Queen's University Press, 1993.

Ford, Clellan. *Smoke from Their Fires: The Life of a Kwakiutl Chief.* Archon Books, 1968.

Fraser, Nancy. *Unruly Practices: Power, Discourse, and Gender in Contemporary Social Theory.* Minneapolis: University of Minnesota Press, 1989.

Garfield, Viola. "Wood Carving and Painting." Unpublished manuscript, August-September 1934.

Garvey, Charlene. "Who Shall Remain Nameless? Makers and Collectors in the Museum of Anthropology's Nuu-chah-nulth Collection." MA thesis, University of British Columbia, 1994.

Gibbon, John Murray. *Canadian Mosaic: The Making of a Northern Nation.* Toronto: McClelland and Stewart, 1938.

Giddens, Anthony. *The Consequences of Modernity.* Stanford: Stanford University Press, 1990.

Goldman, Irving. *The Mouth of Heaven: An Introduction to Kwakiutl Religious Thought.* New York: John Wiley and Sons, 1975.

Goodfellow, John C. *The Totem Poles in Stanley Park, Vancouver.* Vancouver: Art, Historical and Scientific Association of Vancouver, n.d.

Graburn, Nelson H.H. *Eskimos without Igloos: Social and Economic Development in Sugluk.* Boston: Little, Brown, and Company, 1969.

Granatstein, J.L. "Culture and Scholarship: The First Ten Years of the Canada Council." *Canadian Historical Review* 65, 4 (1984).

Gunn, S.W.A. *A Complete Guide to the Totem Poles in Stanley Park, Vancouver, B.C.* Vancouver: W.E.G. MacDonald, 1965.

Gunther, Erna. *Indians of the Northwest Coast.* Seattle and Colorado Springs: Taylor Museum of the Colorado Springs Fine Arts Center and the Seattle Art Museum, 1950.

Hall, Edwin S., Margaret B. Blackman, and Vincent Rickard. *Northwest Coast Indian Graphics: An Introduction to Silk Screen Prints.* Vancouver: Douglas and McIntyre, 1981.

Halliday, W.M. *Potlatch and Totem and the Recollections of an Indian Agent.* London and Toronto: J.M. Dent, 1935.

Halpin, Marjorie M. *Totem Poles: An Illustrated Guide.* Vancouver: UBC Press, 1981.

–. *Jack Shadbolt and the Coastal Indian Image.* Vancouver: UBC Press, 1986.

–. "A Politics of Indian Art." Keynote address to the Native American Art Studies Association Conference, Vancouver, August 1989.

–. "A Critique of the Boasian Paradigm for Northwest Coast Art." *Culture* 14, 1 (1994).

Hardwick, Walter G. *Geography of the Forest Industry in Coastal British Columbia.* Vancouver: Canadian Association of Geographers Occasional Papers in Geography Number 5, 1963.

Hawker, Ronald W. "In the Way of the Whiteman's Totem Pole: Tsimshian Gravestones, 1879-1920." MA thesis, University of Victoria, 1988.

–. "The Johnson Street Gang: Early Native Art Dealers in Victoria." *British Columbia Historical News* 21, 1 (Winter 1989).

–. "Frederick Alexie: Euro-Canadian Discussions of a First Nations Artist." *Canadian Journal of Native Studies* 11, 2 (1991).

Hawthorn, Audrey. *Art of the Kwakiutl Indians and Other Northwest Coast Tribes.* Seattle: University of Washington Press, 1967.

–. *Kwakiutl Art.* Seattle: University of Washington Press, 1979.

–. *A Labour of Love: The Making of the Museum of Anthropology, UBC: The First Three Decades, 1947-1976.* Vancouver: University of British Columbia Museum of Anthropology Museum Note No. 33, 1993.

Hawthorn, H.B., ed. *Report of Conference on Native Indian Affairs.* Victoria: British Columbia Indian Arts and Welfare Society, 1948.

Hill, Tom, and Elizabeth McLuhan. *Norval Morrisseau and the Emergence of the Image Makers.* Toronto: Art Gallery of Ontario, 1985.

Hiller, Susan, ed. *The Myth of Primitivism: Perspectives on Art.* London and New York: Routledge, 1991.

Holm, Bill. *Northwest Coast Art: An Analysis of Form.* Seattle: University of Washington Press, 1965.

–. *Smoky-Top: The Art and Times of Willie Seaweed.* Vancouver and Toronto: Douglas and McIntyre, 1983.

Holm, Bill, and George Irving Quimby. *Edward S. Curtis in the Land of the War Canoes: A Pioneer Cinematographer in the Pacific Northwest.* Vancouver: Douglas and McIntyre, 1980.

Holm, Bill, and Bill Reid. *Form and Freedom: A Dialogue on Northwest Coast Indian Art.* Houston: Rice University Press, 1975.

Horn, Michiel. *The Great Depression of the 1930s in Canada.* Ottawa: Canadian Historical Association Historical Booklet No. 39, 1984.

–, ed. *The Dirty Thirties: Canadians in the Great Depression.* Toronto: Copp Clark, 1972.

Hull, Raymond, Gordon Soules, and Christine Soules. *Vancouver's Past.* Vancouver: Gordon Soules Economic and Marketing Research, 1974.

"Indian Girl's Paintings Have Been Purchased by the British Columbia Government." *Native Voice,* August 1949.

Jensen, Doreen, and Cheryl Brooks, eds. *In Celebration of Our Survival: The First Nations of British Columbia.* Vancouver: UBC Press, 1991.

Jensen, Doreen, and Polly Sargent. *Robes of Power: Totem Poles on Cloth.* Vancouver: University of British Columbia Museum of Anthropology Museum Note No. 17, 1986.

Johnson, F. Henry. *A History of Public Education in British Columbia.* Vancouver: UBC Press, 1964.

Jonaitis, Aldona. *From the Land of the Totem Poles: The Northwest Coast Indian Art Collection at the American Museum of Natural History.* New York/Seattle: American Museum of Natural History/University of Washington Press, 1991.

–, ed. *Chiefly Feasts: The Enduring Kwakiutl Potlatch.* New York/Vancouver: American Museum of Natural History/Douglas and McIntyre, 1991.

–, ed. *A Wealth of Thought: Franz Boas on Native American Art.* Seattle/Vancouver: University of Washington Press/Douglas and McIntyre, 1995.

Jules-Rosette, Bennetta. *The Messages of Tourist Art: An African Semiotic System in Comparative Perspective.* New York: Plenum Press, 1984.

Karp, Ivan, and Steven D. Lavine, eds. *Exhibiting Cultures: The Poetics and Politics of Museum Display.* Washington, DC: Smithsonian Institution Press, 1991.

Keithahn, Edward L. *Monuments in Cedar.* Ketchikan, AL: Roy Anderson, 1945.

Kew, J.E. Michael. *Sculpture and Engraving of the Central Coast Salish Indians.* Vancouver: University of British Columbia Museum of Anthropology Museum Note No. 9, 1980.

Knowles, Malcolm S. *A History of the Adult Education Movement in the United States.* Malabar, FL: Robert E. Krieger Publishing, 1977.

Knowles, Valerie. *Strangers at Our Gates: Canadian Immigration and Immigration Policy, 1540-1990.* Toronto: Dundurn Press, 1992.

'Ksan Association. *'Ksan, Hazelton, B.C.* Hazelton, BC: 'Ksan Association, 1970.

Lears, Jackson. *No Place of Grace: Antimodernism and the Transformation of American Culture, 1880-1920.* New York: Pantheon Books, 1981.

Leslie, John, and Ron Maguire, eds. *The Historical Development of the Indian Act.* Ottawa: Indian and Northern Affairs Canada, 1978.

Litt, Paul. *The Muses, the Masses, and the Massey Commission.* Toronto: University of Toronto Press, 1992.

Loo, Tina. "Dan Cranmer's Potlatch: Law as Coercion, Symbol and Rhetoric in British Columbia, 1884-1951." *Canadian Historical Review* 68, 2 (1992).

McCann, L.D., ed. *A Geography of Canada: Heartland and Hinterland.* Scarborough: Prentice-Hall, 1982.

MacDonald, George F. *Haida Monumental Art: Villages of the Queen Charlotte Islands.* Vancouver/Seattle: UBC Press/University of Washington Press, 1983.

McDonald, Robert A.J. *Making Vancouver: Class, Status, and Social Boundaries.* Vancouver: UBC Press, 1996.

McLaren, Angus. *Our Own Master Race: Eugenics in Canada, 1885-1945.* Toronto: McClelland and Stewart, 1990.

Macnair, Peter, Alan L. Hoover, and Kevin Neary. *The Legacy: Continuing Traditions of Canadian Northwest Coast Indian Art.* Victoria: British Columbia Provincial Museum, 1980.

Macnair, Peter, Robert Joseph, and Bruce Grenville. *Down from the Shimmering Sky: Masks of the Northwest Coast.* Vancouver and Toronto: Douglas and McIntyre, 1998.

Manning, Frank, ed. *Consciousness and Inquiry: Ethnology and Canadian Realities.* Ottawa: National Museum of Man Mercury Series, CES Paper No. 89E, 1983.

Manuel, George, and Michael Postuns. *The Fourth World: An Indian Reality.* Don Mills, ON: Collier-Macmillan Canada, 1974.

Marcus, George E., and Fred R. Myers, eds. *The Traffic in Culture: Refiguring Art and Anthropology.* Berkeley: University of California Press, 1995.

Matthews, J.S. *Conversations with Khahtsahlano, 1932-1954.* Vancouver: Vancouver City Archives, 1955.

Michaels, Walter Benn. "The Vanishing American." *American Literary History* 2, 2 (1990).

Miller, Jay, and Carol M. Eastman, eds. *The Tsimshian and Their Neighbors of the North Pacific Coast.* Seattle: University of Washington Press, 1984.

Miller, Polly. *Lost Heritage of Alaska: The Adventure and Art of the Alaskan Coastal Indians.* Cleveland and New York: World Publishing Company, 1967.

Morris, Rosalind C. *New Worlds from Fragments: Film, Ethnography and the Representation of Northwest Coast Cultures.* Boulder, CO: Westview Press, 1994.

Morrison, Ann. "Canadian Art and Cultural Appropriation: Emily Carr and the Exhibition of West Coast Art, Native and Modern." MA thesis, University of British Columbia, 1991.

Mortimore, G.E. "Indian Artist Makes Eloquent Plea." *Native Voice,* December 1949.

Murphy, Rae. *The Essentials of Canadian History: Canada since 1867, the Post-Confederate Nation.* Piscataway, NJ: Research and Education Association, 1993.

National Gallery of Canada. *Annual Report of the Board of Trustees for the Fiscal Year 1927-28.* Ottawa: National Gallery of Canada, 1928.

–. *Exhibition of Canadian West Coast Art, Native and Modern.* Toronto: Art Gallery of Toronto, 1928.

Neel, Ellen. "Ancient Art Being Preserved." *Native Voice,* September 1949.

Nemiroff, Diana, Robert Houle, and Charlotte Townsend-Galt. *Land Spirit Power: First Nations at the National Gallery of Canada.* Ottawa: National Gallery of Canada, 1992.

Newell, Dianne. *Tangled Webs of History: Indians and the Law in Canada's Pacific Coast Fisheries.* Toronto: University of Toronto Press, 1993.
"Nootka Basket Makers." *Native Voice*, October 1947.
Nuytten, Phil. *The Totem Carvers: Charlie James, Ellen Neel and Mungo Martin.* Vancouver: Panorama Publications, 1982.
O'Brian, John. *Capitalizing the Scenery: Landscape, Leisure and Tourism in British Columbia.* Vancouver: University of British Columbia, Morris and Helen Belkin Art Gallery, 1995.
O'Donnell, Jacqueline P. "The Native Brotherhood of British Columbia, 1931-1950: A New Phase in Native Political Organization." MA thesis, University of British Columbia, 1985.
Okanagan Society for the Revival of Indian Arts and Crafts. *Native Canadians: A Plan for the Rehabilitation of Indians.* Oliver, BC: unpublished, n.d.
Ormsby, Margaret. *British Columbia: A History.* Toronto: Macmillan, 1958.
Ortiz, Alfonso, ed. *Handbook of North American Indians.* Vol. 9: *Southwest.* Washington, DC: Smithsonian Institution, 1979.
–. *Handbook of North American Indians.* Vol. 10: *Southwest.* Washington, DC: Smithsonian Institution, 1983.
Paine, Robert, ed. *Indigenous Peoples and the Nation-State: Fourth World Politics in Canada, Australia, and Norway.* St. John's: Institute of Social and Economic Research, Memorial University of Newfoundland, 1985.
Palmer, Howard H. *Cultural Diversity and Canadian Education.* Ottawa: Carleton University, 1984.
Polk, James, ed. *Divisions on a Ground: Essays on Canadian Culture.* Toronto: Anansi, 1982.
Pollock, Griselda. *Vision and Difference: Femininity, Feminism and the Histories of Art.* London and New York: Routledge, 1988.
Ponting, J. Rick, and Roger Gibbons. *Out of Irrelevance: A Socio-political Introduction to Indian Affairs in Canada.* Toronto: Butterworths, 1980.
"Portland Art Museum Displays Young Native Art." *Native Voice*, October 1947.
Potlatch! A Strict Law Bids Us Dance, 16 mm, 53 min. Alert Bay: U'mista Cultural Society, 1975.
Raley, George H. "Canadian Indian Art and Industries: An Economic Problem of Today." *Journal of the Royal Society of Arts* 83 (September 1935).
–. *Our Totem Poles: A Souvenir of Vancouver.* Vancouver: Lumberman, 1937.
Ravenhill, Alice. *Native Tribes of British Columbia.* Victoria: C.R. Banfield, 1938.
–. "Address to the Royal Commission of Senators and Members of the House of Commons Appointed to Inquire into All Phases of the Affairs of Canadian Indians in May and October 1946." Victoria: unpublished.
–. *A Cornerstone of Canadian Culture: An Outline of the Arts and Crafts of the Indian Tribes of British Columbia.* Victoria: British Columbia Provincial Museum, Occasional Paper No. 5, 1944.
–. *Alice Ravenhill: The Memoirs of an Educational Pioneer.* Toronto and Vancouver: J.M. Dent and Sons, 1951.
"Recommendations of the B.C. Indian Arts and Welfare Society." *Native Voice*, June 1948.
Rosaldo, Renato. "Imperialist Nostalgia." *Representations* 26 (Spring 1989).
Roy, Patricia E. "British Columbia's Fear of Asians, 1900-1950," *Histoire Sociale/Social History* 13, 25.
Schafer, Paul D., and André Fortier. *Review of Federal Policies for the Arts in Canada, 1944-1988.* Ottawa: Canadian Conference of the Arts, 1989.
Schrader, Robert Fay. *The Indian Arts and Crafts Board: An Aspect of New Deal Indian Policy.* Albuquerque: University of New Mexico Press, 1983.
Seguin, Margaret, ed. *The Tsimshian: Images of the Past, Views for the Present.* Vancouver: UBC Press, 1984.
Selman, Gordon. "The Adult Educator: Change Agent or Program Technician?" *Canadian Journal of University Continuing Education* 9, 2 (1985).
Sewid-Smith, Daisy. *Persecution or Prosecution.* Cape Mudge, BC: Nu-Yum-Balees, 1979.
Shadbolt, Doris. *Bill Reid.* Vancouver and Toronto: Douglas and McIntyre, 1986.

"She'll Make the Team." *Native Voice*, January 1952.

Shea, Albert A., ed. *Culture in Canada: A Study of the Findings of the Royal Commission on National Development in the Arts, Letters, and Sciences, 1949-1951*. Toronto: Core, 1952.

Simmons, Deidre. "A History for Contemporary Canadian Indian Art." *European Review of Native American Studies* 5, 1 (1991).

Smith, Harlan I. "Restoration of Totem Poles in British Columbia." *National Museum of Canada Annual Report for 1926*. Ottawa: King's Printer, 1928.

Souster, Raymond, and Douglas Lochhead, eds. *Powassan's Drum: Poems of Duncan Campbell Scott*. Ottawa: Tecumseh Press, 1985.

Steele, Mike. *Stanley Park*. Surrey: Heritage House Publishing, 1993.

Suttles, Wayne. *Coast Salish Essays*. Vancouver/Seattle: Talonbooks/University of Washington Press, 1987.

Suttles, Wayne, ed. *Handbook of North American Indians*. Vol. 7, *Northwest Coast*. Washington, DC: Smithsonian Institution 1990.

Tale of the Nativity as Told by the Indian Children of Inkameep, The. Victoria: Society for the Furtherance of British Columbia Indian Arts and Welfare, 1945.

Taussig, Michael. *The Nervous System*. New York and London: Routledge, 1992.

"The Conference on Native Indian Affairs Successful." *Native Voice*, April 1948.

Tennant, Paul. *Aboriginal Peoples and Politics: The Indian Land Question, 1849-1989*. Vancouver: UBC Press, 1992.

Thom, Ian M., ed. *Robert Davidson: Eagle of the Dawn*. Seattle: University of Washington Press, 1995.

Thomas, Nicholas. *Entangled Objects: Exchange, Material Culture and Colonialism in the Pacific*. Cambridge, MA: Harvard University Press, 1991.

–. *Colonialism's Culture: Anthropology, Travel and Government*. Princeton: Princeton University Press, 1994.

Titley, Brian. *A Narrow Vision: Duncan Campbell Scott and the Administration of Indian Affairs*. Vancouver: UBC Press, 1986.

Torgovnick, Marianna. *Gone Primitive: Savage Intellects, Modern Lives*. Chicago and London: University of Chicago, 1990.

"Totem Carver to See Queen." *Province*, 28 April 1958.

"Totem Pole to Grace Rideau Hall Gardens: Ancient Relic to be Removed to Ottawa; Gift to Governor-General from Indians." *Victoria Daily Times*, 24 June 1929.

Trueblood Bordzky, Anne, Rose Danesewich, and Nick Johnson, eds. *Stone, Bones, and Skin: Ritual and Shamanic Art*. Toronto: Society for Art Publications, 1977.

University of British Columbia Museum of Anthropology. "First Nations of British Columbia." Vancouver: University of British Columbia Museum of Anthropology Map Project, 5 March 1996, n.p.

–. *Northwest Coast Indian Artifacts from the H.R. MacMillan Collections in the Museum of Anthropology, UBC*. Vancouver: UBC Press, 1975.

Vancouver Art Gallery. *Arts of the Raven: Masterworks of the Northwest Coast Indian*. Vancouver: Vancouver Art Gallery, 1965.

–. *Vancouver: Art and Artists, 1931-1983*. Vancouver: Vancouver Art Gallery, 1983.

Wa, Gisday, and Delgam Uukw. *The Spirit in the Land: The Opening Statement of the Gitksan and Wet'suwet'en Hereditary Chiefs in the Supreme Court of British Columbia*. Gabriola, BC: Reflections, 1989.

Whitaker, Reg. *Canadian Immigration Policy since Confederation*. Ottawa: Canadian Historical Association Canada's Ethnic Groups Booklet No. 15, 1991.

Woodcock, George. *Strange Bedfellows: The State and the Arts in Canada*. Vancouver and Toronto: Douglas and McIntyre, 1985.

Index

Note: (f) after a page reference indicates a figure

Printed and bound in Canada by Friesens

Set in Stone by Artegraphica Design Co. Ltd.

Copy editor: Joanne Richardson

Proofreader: Judith Walker

Indexer: Dolores Signori